SUN CHILD
MOON CHILD

JOHN ASTROP

with cartoons by the author

SUN CHILD
MOON CHILD

*How to make the most
of your relationship with your child*

PAN ORIGINAL
Pan Books London and Sydney

First published 1981 by Pan Books Ltd,
Cavaye Place, London SW10 9PG
© John Astrop 1981
ISBN 0 330 26283 1
Printed and bound in Great Britain by
Hazell Watson & Viney Ltd. Aylesbury, Bucks

to
Jackie, Sun Capricorn, Moon Capricorn
Jon, Sun Pisces, Moon Leo
Simon, Sun Virgo, Moon Aries
Ben, Sun Aries, Moon Libra

My thanks to
Dawn Pelling and Pauline Stone
for help, encouragement and criticism

CONTENTS

INTRODUCTION

After many years of study one discovers that astrology, like psychology, has different uses, approaches and views almost commensurate with the number of proponents. It is understandable that in the scattered bits and pieces that reach the public, this resolves itself into a question of belief or disbelief. The need to take a position on either side without evidence, has nothing to do with the validity of astrology, and everything to do with a 'blind faith' need to support the weaker aspects of our life understanding. Even prominent 'scientists' have made pronouncements based on no study of the subject whatever. A most unscientific approach in their terms. However, whether astrology is proved to be a science or an art, may take a long time – why it works, we may never know – but that it *does* work, every competent astrologer knows without any need for 'belief'.

Accepting the unlikely, but of course possible, premise that at a child's birth moment the cosmos reflects the nature of that event, astrologers have, for thousands of years, studied the meaning of planetary positions. Each age has produced and developed the particular kind of astrology to suit the needs of the time. During the last hundred years this has been directed to the complex problems of human relationships.

The current interest in sun sign astrology is the cause of much conflict and argument in serious astrological circles. The fact is that this 'tip of the iceberg' of astrological knowledge becoming, for many, all that astrology is, has contributed little to a general understanding of the depth of the subject.

There is no substitute for having a complete birth horoscope drawn, and discussed with a good astrologer. So why am I as a serious practising astrologer putting up yet another 'iceberg tip'? The need to get a little more self-understanding is often overlooked until a crisis point is reached, too late to avoid the pain and unhappiness this may cause oneself and others. If a little help can avert a few disasters, then so be it!

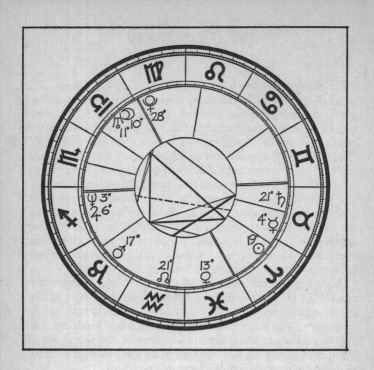

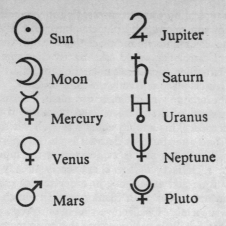

☉	Sun	♃	Jupiter
☽	Moon	♄	Saturn
☿	Mercury	♅	Uranus
♀	Venus	♆	Neptune
♂	Mars	♇	Pluto

♈	Aries	♎	Libra
♉	Taurus	♏	Scorpio
♊	Gemini	♐	Sagittarius
♋	Cancer	♑	Capricorn
♌	Leo	♒	Aquarius
♍	Virgo	♓	Pisces

On page x is a typical horoscope representing in symbolic form the positions of sun, moon, and planets above and below the horizon for the exact moment and place that a child was born. Any competent astrologer would cast exactly the same chart. It is unique. No other person can have the same chart unless born at the identical place at exactly the same time.

From this horoscope an astrologer can make a surprisingly accurate assessment of the character and potential of the individual concerned. This applies equally as well whether the chart is read soon after birth or decades later. The horoscope never changes. This, for me, is evidence that the moment a child is born, each facet of the character is already there, awaiting only time and experience in order to express itself. No child is an open book with blank pages on which we, as parents, can write a more idealized version of ourselves.

The idea that our little creations are the basic material on which we can project our hopes, reverse our failures, and make up for our deficiencies, may seem a thing of the past in this 'enlightened' age, but is it? How would we know? For a start, children are not only the most vulnerable members of society, being smaller, weaker and inexperienced, but they also have the least 'rights'. As adults, we can make publicly known any injustice, go before tribunals, demand fair wages, seek the protection of the law, and divorce difficult partners. If all that is necessary in order to negotiate successful adult/adult relationships how can we be so sure that all is well in a family partnership where the 'smallest' voice has no recourse to second opinion?

The truth is, regardless of natural love and affection we unthinkingly attempt to dominate, manipulate, cajole, and threaten our children into carbon copies of ourselves or the person we feel we should have been.

The degree to which we can accept and encourage development of the unique individuality of our children depends on how well we came through the experience with our own parents. The period when we are nearest to being and expressing our complete selves, is early childhood. This is also the time when our need for security and acceptance of what we are, is most powerful. Because of this need, the child will adapt and change the personality in order to maintain the love of the parent.

A mode of expression in the child may prove difficult to accept, but trying to eradicate this instead of sensitively teaching the child in what form you can find this real part of himself acceptable, is to undermine the confidence and truth of a human being. If one can only love conditionally, 'We don't want bad boys here, Mummy loves her *good* boy!' then the child in order to maintain this love, will either successfully meet the conditions and become a 'good' boy, or fail to meet them and believe in his 'badness'. Each way the child has been made to feel, unconsciously, that part of his real self is undesirable or inadequate.

These repressed parts of ourselves, like any other energies, do not disappear but move into the unconscious and carry on demanding action from there. As we are unaware of, or unable to control, these impulses they are passed on continuously to the detriment of our relationships until they are rediscovered and allowed positive conscious expression. For instance, the presence of a high degree of excess energy in a child may, with no suitable outlet, manifest as violent behaviour. With understanding, this can be guided into a creative project for positive expression, the reason for its existence anyway. Negatively, it is possible that by insensitively repressing the violence, the parent takes over and uses that same violence towards the child. How often do we say 'You made me cross' putting the responsibility for our own failure to assist firmly on Junior's shoulders.

Once we accept that none of our natural energies can be lost, only directed or misdirected, then we are on the road to deeper understanding of ourselves and our children.

Astrology may not provide all the answers but it can help in painting a picture of the energies we have and the potential for their positive or negative expression.

At this point I would like to make clear something of my own approach to astrology. These views are shared by many but they are by no means universal.

1 Lives are not shaped by the planets, but they reflect rather than direct our actions and feelings.

2 No one has a difficult chart or a bad aspect. The chart is us, and we are born with the potential flexibility and facility of dealing with our own natures.

3 We can predict events in the life through observing planetary transits and progressions around the horoscope. These show as the need to act, and the outcome is entirely in the hands of the person concerned.

4 Free will is related to our own complex characters and is not denied by prediction. Even our friends can make accurate assessments of what we may do under certain circumstances. A thrifty and cautious person can take a gamble but will rarely decide to do so. If such predictions are made on the basis of deep study of a horoscope they can be used positively and constructively in the life.

5 Astrology excuses none of our failures.

6 There are not just twelve different kinds of people but because of the ease of access to sun signs and, with this book, moon signs, we can get a little more insight into our relationships with others.

7 Sun-sign astrology is no substitute for a proper horoscope chart cast by a good astrologer, but the more we understand about ourselves, our basic energies and drives, the less we are in the hands of 'fate'. Sun-sign astrology is at least a start in the right direction.

HOW TO USE THE BOOK

If you've read this far without first dipping into your own sign I'd be very surprised. However, from whichever end of the book you have arrived at this point, stay with me to get the most out of the parent/child relationships described later. First of all, the keywords. These are a quick, easy to learn, simplification of the basic drives that manifest when sun or moon are in the signs. Like all simplifications, they are a guide but open to misinterpretation. In order to see the true meaning we may have to stand back from some of our own bias towards certain words. For instance the Leo's need to put on a show and enjoy the subsequent admiration is a basic drive that the modest Virgoan rarely has. Excessive bias can make Virgo see *admiration* as childish 'showing off' and Leo see *modesty* as 'holier than thou' prudishness. Yet ideally, these opposing views can make the closest of contact as 'scriptwriter and performer' 'planner and salesman' – each indispensable to the other. Use the keywords with an open mind and they won't become weapons.

The sun's positions define the creative spirit and the need to act, while the moon's positions indicate the emotional side of our natures, and the need to feel. Although I have pointed out the nature of possible clashes with each combination, nobody gets the wrong child! But we sometimes get the wrong ideas. To use the combinations is simple. For example: if the parent has sun in Libra, moon in Capricorn, and the child has sun in Cancer, moon in Virgo, first read Libra/Cancer sun then Capricorn/Virgo moon. Switching parent/child roles may be enlightening if not amusing, read how Junior would manage you if the boot were on the other foot. If you wish to expand further, read your child's signs with each of the other parents, representing the gamut of possibilities of aunts, uncles, teachers, etc.

For a birth in the UK turn to the British Summer Time tables on page xvii and subtract one or two hours if the birth date is between the dates of British Summer Time or Double

Summer Time. Look up the correct time in the moon tables (Page 1 onwards) to find the moon sign. For example: A birthday for 10 April 1964 at 10.30 p.m. Summer Time 1964 was from 22 March to 25 October so we subtract one hour. Now turn to the moon tables for 1964 and find the nearest date to 10 April.

DATE	TIME	SIGN
10	10.59 p.m.	♈

Our corrected time of 9.30 p.m. is one hour and twenty-nine minutes before the moon changed signs into Aries so for this birth time the moon was in the sign before, Pisces. Don't forget to subtract two hours for a birth during the period of Double Summer Time. Pages 204-5 give you an index of moon sign combinations.

There is a Zodiac sun sign table on page xviii. Many people have picked up the phrase 'being born on the cusp', ie born on the day that the sun changes signs, and are left in doubt as to which is their real sun sign. The popular idea that if you're born on the cusp, you are a little of each sign is a fallacy. Adjoining signs have such a different quality that it is relatively easy to fix on one or the other using the keywords as a guide. Pages 64-5 gives you the index for sun sign combinations.

BRITISH SUMMER TIME AND DOUBLE SUMMER TIME

1930	APR	13	– OCT	5	1954	APR	11 – OCT	3
1931	,,	19	– ,,	4	1955	,,	17 – ,,	2
1932	,,	17	– ,,	2	1956	,,	22 – ,,	7
1933	,,	9	– ,,	8	1957	,,	14 – ,,	6
1934	,,	22	– ,,	7	1958	,,	20 – ,,	5
1935	,,	14	– ,,	6	1959	,,	19 – ,,	4
1936	,,	19	– ,,	4	1960	,,	10 – ,,	2
1937	,,	18	– ,,	3	1961	MAR	26 – ,,	29
1938	,,	10	– ,,	2	1962	,,	25 – ,,	28
1939	,,	16	– NOV	19	1963	,,	31 – ,,	27
1940	FEB	25	– DEC	31	1964	,,	22 – ,,	25
1941	JAN	1	– DEC	31	1965	,,	21 – ,,	24
*DST	MAY	4	– AUG	10	1966	,,	20 – ,,	23
1942	JAN	1	– DEC	31	1967	,,	19 – ,,	29
*DST	APR	5	– AUG	9	1968	FEB	18 – DEC	31
1943	JAN	1	– DEC	31	1969	JAN	1 – ,,	31
*DST	APR	4	– AUG	15	1970	,,	1 – ,,	31
1944	JAN	1	– DEC	31	1971	,,	1 – OCT	27
*DST	APR	2	– SEP	17	1972	MAR	19 – ,,	29
1945	JAN	1	– DEC	31	1973	,,	18 – ,,	28
*DST	APR	2	– JUL	15	1974	,,	17 – ,,	27
1946	APR	14	– OCT	6	1975	,,	16 – ,,	26
1947	MAR	16	– NOV	2	1976	,,	21 – ,,	24
*DST	APR	13	– AUG	10	1977	,,	20 – ,,	23
1948	MAR	14	– OCT	31	1978	,,	19 – ,,	29
1949	APR	3	– OCT	30	1979	,,	18 – ,,	28
1950	,,	16	– ,,	22	1980	,,	16 – ,,	26
1951	,,	15	– ,,	21	1981	,,	22 – ,,	25
1952	,,	20	– ,,	26	1982	,,	21 – ,,	24
1953	,,	19	– ,,	4				

SUN SIGN TABLE

♈	ARIES	March 21–April 20
♉	TAURUS	April 21–May 21
♊	GEMINI	May 22–June 21
♋	CANCER	June 22–July 23
♌	LEO	July 24–August 23
♍	VIRGO	August 24–September 23
♎	LIBRA	September 24–October 23
♏	SCORPIO	October 24–November 22
♐	SAGITTARIUS	November 23–December 21
♑	CAPRICORN	December 22–January 20
♒	AQUARIUS	January 21–February 19
♓	PISCES	February 20–March 20

1930

JAN	TIME	FEB	TIME	MAR	TIME	APR	TIME	MAY	TIME	JUN	TIME
1 ♒	6 P 30	3 ♈	0 A 23	2 ♈	6 A 08	3 ♊	3 A 42	2 ♋	1 P 54	3 ♍	0 A 37
4 ♓	7 A 04	5 ♉	9 A 48	4 ♉	3 P 18	5 ♋	8 A 11	4 ♌	4 P 32	5 ♎	4 A 05
6 ♈	6 P 27	7 ♊	4 P 07	6 ♊	10 P 16	7 ♌	11 A 09	6 ♍	7 P 11	7 ♏	9 A 31
9 ♉	2 A 58	9 ♋	6 P 54	9 ♋	2 A 34	9 ♍	1 P 11	8 ♎	10 P 30	9 ♐	4 P 57
11 ♊	7 A 47	11 ♌	7 P 00	11 ♌	4 A 25	11 ♎	3 P 17	11 ♏	3 A 07	12 ♑	2 A 21
13 ♋	8 A 34	13 ♍	6 P 15	13 ♍	4 A 54	13 ♏	6 P 46	13 ♐	9 A 39	14 ♒	1 P 39
15 ♌	7 A 37	15 ♎	6 P 52	15 ♎	5 A 44	16 ♐	0 A 50	15 ♑	6 P 40	17 ♓	2 A 12
17 ♍	6 A 58	17 ♏	10 P 45	17 ♏	8 A 47	18 ♑	10 A 08	18 ♒	6 A 04	19 ♈	2 P 14
19 ♎	8 A 46	20 ♐	6 A 50	19 ♐	3 P 25	20 ♒	9 P 59	20 ♓	6 P 34	21 ♉	11 P 35
21 ♏	2 P 26	22 ♑	6 P 13	22 ♑	1 A 41	23 ♓	10 A 23	23 ♈	5 A 55	24 ♊	4 A 59
23 ♐	11 P 56	25 ♒	6 A 57	24 ♒	2 P 05	25 ♈	9 P 09	25 ♉	2 P 15	26 ♋	6 A 57
26 ♑	11 A 53	27 ♓	7 P 13	27 ♓	2 A 23	28 ♉	5 A 07	27 ♊	7 P 06	28 ♌	7 A 06
29 ♒	0 A 33			29 ♈	1 P 00	30 ♊	10 A 26	29 ♋	9 P 25	30 ♍	7 A 29
31 ♓	0 P 59			31 ♉	9 P 23			31 ♌	10 P 45		

JUL	TIME	AUG	TIME	SEPT	TIME	OCT	TIME	NOV	TIME	DEC	TIME
2 ♎	9 A 48	3 ♐	4 A 25	1 ♑	8 P 36	1 ♒	3 P 10	2 ♈	11 P 35	2 ♉	6 P 31
4 ♏	2 P 57	5 ♑	2 P 35	4 ♒	8 A 28	4 ♓	3 A 48	5 ♉	9 A 37	5 ♊	1 A 32
6 ♐	10 P 50	8 ♒	2 A 27	6 ♓	9 P 08	6 ♈	3 P 51	7 ♊	4 P 58	7 ♋	5 A 31
9 ♑	8 A 50	10 ♓	3 P 03	9 ♈	9 A 21	9 ♉	2 A 14	9 ♋	10 P 05	9 ♌	7 A 53
11 ♒	8 P 23	13 ♈	3 A 32	11 ♉	8 P 18	11 ♊	10 A 29	12 ♌	1 A 45	11 ♍	10 A 04
14 ♓	8 A 57	15 ♉	2 P 37	14 ♊	5 A 00	13 ♋	4 P 29	14 ♍	4 A 41	13 ♎	1 P 05
16 ♈	9 P 26	17 ♊	10 P 46	16 ♋	10 A 42	15 ♌	8 P 19	16 ♎	7 A 27	15 ♏	5 P 20
19 ♉	7 A 53	20 ♋	3 A 01	18 ♌	1 P 18	17 ♍	10 P 26	18 ♏	10 A 37	17 ♐	10 P 55
21 ♊	2 P 38	22 ♌	3 A 57	20 ♍	1 P 45	19 ♎	11 P 43	20 ♐	3 P 01	20 ♑	6 A 12
23 ♋	5 P 21	24 ♍	3 A 14	22 ♎	1 P 44	22 ♏	1 A 33	22 ♑	9 P 43	22 ♒	3 P 44
25 ♌	5 P 19	26 ♎	2 A 59	24 ♏	3 P 08	24 ♐	5 A 25	25 ♒	7 A 24	25 ♓	3 A 36
27 ♍	4 P 35	28 ♏	5 A 12	26 ♐	7 P 36	26 ♑	0 P 27	27 ♓	7 P 33	27 ♈	4 P 29
29 ♎	5 P 19	30 ♐	11 A 05	29 ♑	3 A 49	28 ♒	10 P 54	30 ♈	8 A 06	30 ♉	3 A 51
31 ♏	9 P 08					31 ♓	11 A 23				

1931

JAN		TIME	FEB		TIME	MAR		TIME	APR		TIME	MAY		TIME	JUN		TIME
1	♊	11 A 34	2	♌	3 A 24	1	♌	2 P 24	2	♎	0 A 49	1	♏	11 A 26	2	♑	3 A 08
3	♋	3 P 20	4	♍	2 A 57	3	♍	2 P 21	4	♏	0 A 51	3	♐	1 P 14	4	♒	10 A 24
5	♌	4 P 32	6	♎	2 A 55	5	♎	1 P 33	6	♐	2 A 53	5	♑	5 P 37	6	♓	9 P 01
7	♍	5 P 07	8	♏	5 A 06	7	♏	2 P 03	8	♑	8 A 22	8	♒	1 A 37	9	♈	9 A 44
9	♎	6 P 49	10	♐	10 A 22	9	♐	5 P 32	10	♒	5 P 43	10	♓	1 P 02	11	♉	9 P 54
11	♏	10 P 41	12	♑	6 P 40	12	♑	0 A 39	13	♓	5 A 49	13	♈	1 A 57	14	♊	7 A 21
14	♐	4 A 51	15	♒	5 A 15	14	♒	11 A 04	15	♈	6 P 48	15	♉	1 P 54	16	♋	1 P 38
16	♑	1 P 02	17	♓	5 P 24	16	♓	11 P 27	18	♉	6 A 50	17	♊	11 P 26	18	♌	5 P 36
18	♒	11 P 04	20	♈	6 A 21	19	♈	0 P 24	20	♊	4 P 55	20	♋	6 A 25	20	♍	8 P 32
21	♓	10 A 55	22	♉	6 P 53	22	♉	0 A 44	23	♋	0 A 42	22	♌	11 A 27	22	♎	11 P 23
23	♈	11 P 55	25	♊	5 A 12	24	♊	11 A 19	25	♌	6 A 03	24	♍	3 P 07	25	♏	2 A 35
26	♉	0 A 10	27	♋	11 A 47	26	♋	7 P 03	27	♍	9 A 09	26	♎	5 P 51	27	♐	6 A 27
28	♊	9 P 17				28	♌	11 P 29	29	♎	10 A 35	28	♏	8 P 08	29	♑	11 A 35
31	♋	2 A 09				31	♍	0 A 58				30	♐	10 P 48			

JUL		TIME	AUG		TIME	SEPT		TIME	OCT		TIME	NOV		TIME	DEC		TIME
1	♒	6 P 57	3	♈	1 A 10	1	♉	8 P 59	1	♊	3 P 03	2	♌	1 P 38	2	♍	0 A 17
4	♓	5 A 10	5	♉	2 P 05	4	♊	8 A 43	4	♋	0 A 37	4	♍	6 P 07	4	♎	3 A 44
6	♈	5 P 40	8	♊	1 A 01	6	♋	5 P 13	6	♌	6 A 48	6	♎	8 P 02	6	♏	5 A 43
9	♉	6 A 13	10	♋	8 A 09	8	♌	9 P 47	8	♍	9 A 34	8	♏	8 P 21	8	♐	7 A 04
11	♊	4 P 13	12	♌	11 A 31	10	♍	11 P 04	10	♎	9 A 50	10	♐	8 P 39	10	♑	9 A 18
13	♋	10 P 30	14	♍	0 P 25	12	♎	10 P 43	12	♏	9 A 19	12	♑	10 P 53	12	♒	2 P 11
15	♌	1 A 41	16	♎	0 P 45	14	♏	10 P 41	14	♐	9 A 52	15	♒	4 A 42	14	♓	10 P 51
18	♍	3 A 22	18	♏	2 P 11	17	♐	0 A 40	16	♑	1 P 19	17	♓	2 P 33	17	♈	10 A 50
20	♎	5 A 07	20	♐	5 P 48	19	♑	5 A 49	18	♒	8 P 40	20	♈	3 A 09	19	♉	11 P 45
22	♏	7 A 57	22	♑	11 P 58	21	♒	2 P 18	21	♓	7 A 33	22	♉	3 P 59	22	♊	10 A 59
24	♐	0 P 19	25	♒	8 A 38	24	♓	1 A 29	23	♈	8 P 21	25	♊	3 A 11	24	♋	7 P 21
26	♑	6 P 23	27	♓	7 P 28	26	♈	2 P 09	26	♉	9 A 12	27	♋	0 P 09	27	♌	1 A 16
29	♒	2 A 25	30	♈	7 A 57	29	♉	3 A 07	28	♊	8 P 47	29	♌	7 P 05	29	♍	5 A 40
31	♓	0 P 46							31	♋	6 A 26				31	♎	9 A 17

1932

JAN	TIME	FEB	TIME	MAR	TIME	APR	TIME	MAY	TIME	JUN	TIME
2 ♍	0 P 24	3 ♑	1 A 39	1 ♑	7 A 07	2 ♓	5 A 05	1 ♈	10 P 46	3 ♊	6 A 32
4 ♎	3 P 16	5 ♒	7 A 49	3 ♒	2 P 00	4 ♈	4 P 52	4 ♉	11 A 46	5 ♋	5 P 21
6 ♏	6 P 37	7 ♓	4 P 15	5 ♓	11 P 16	7 ♉	5 A 44	7 ♊	0 A 20	8 ♌	2 A 14
8 ♐	11 P 44	10 ♈	3 A 17	8 ♈	10 A 35	9 ♊	6 P 27	9 ♋	11 A 34	10 ♍	9 A 06
11 ♑	7 A 50	12 ♉	4 P 05	10 ♉	11 P 20	12 ♋	5 A 47	11 ♌	8 P 46	12 ♎	1 P 41
13 ♒	7 P 07	15 ♊	4 A 27	13 ♊	0 P 03	14 ♌	2 P 22	14 ♍	3 A 13	14 ♏	4 P 00
16 ♓	8 A 02	17 ♋	2 P 02	15 ♋	10 P 46	16 ♍	7 P 22	16 ♎	6 A 32	16 ♐	4 P 46
18 ♈	7 P 47	19 ♌	7 P 49	18 ♌	5 A 56	18 ♎	9 P 00	18 ♏	7 A 15	18 ♑	5 P 31
21 ♉	4 A 22	21 ♍	10 P 25	20 ♍	9 A 18	20 ♏	8 P 33	20 ♐	6 A 48	20 ♒	8 P 12
23 ♊	9 A 39	23 ♎	11 P 22	22 ♎	9 A 56	22 ♐	7 P 57	22 ♑	7 A 13	23 ♓	2 A 26
25 ♋	0 P 47	26 ♏	0 A 20	24 ♏	9 A 35	24 ♑	9 P 15	24 ♒	10 A 31	25 ♈	0 P 34
27 ♌	3 P 07	28 ♐	2 A 39	26 ♐	10 A 07	27 ♒	2 A 05	26 ♓	5 P 58	28 ♉	1 A 08
29 ♍	5 P 43			28 ♑	1 P 08	29 ♓	10 A 55	29 ♈	5 A 09	30 ♊	1 P 35
31 ♎	9 P 07			30 ♒	7 P 31			31 ♉	6 P 05		

JUL	TIME	AUG	TIME	SEPT	TIME	OCT	TIME	NOV	TIME	DEC	TIME
3 ♋	0 A 07	1 ♌	3 P 57	2 ♎	8 A 32	1 ♏	6 P 44	2 ♑	4 A 55	1 ♒	4 P 47
5 ♌	8 A 18	3 ♍	9 P 15	4 ♏	10 A 06	3 ♐	7 P 02	4 ♒	8 A 06	3 ♓	10 P 08
7 ♍	2 P 33	6 ♎	0 A 56	6 ♐	0 N 00	5 ♑	9 P 00	6 ♓	3 P 07	6 ♈	7 A 35
9 ♎	7 P 12	8 ♏	3 A 49	8 ♑	3 P 12	8 ♒	1 A 44	9 ♈	1 A 25	8 ♉	7 P 42
11 ♏	10 P 28	10 ♐	6 A 32	10 ♒	8 P 16	10 ♓	9 A 27	11 ♉	1 P 34	11 ♊	8 A 26
14 ♐	0 A 38	12 ♑	9 A 38	13 ♓	3 A 31	12 ♈	7 P 36	14 ♊	2 A 13	13 ♋	8 P 28
16 ♑	2 A 36	14 ♒	1 P 54	15 ♈	1 P 01	15 ♉	7 A 24	16 ♋	2 P 32	16 ♌	7 A 13
18 ♒	5 A 45	16 ♓	8 P 14	18 ♉	0 A 34	17 ♊	8 P 03	19 ♌	1 A 35	18 ♍	4 P 09
20 ♓	11 A 34	19 ♈	5 A 18	20 ♊	1 P 14	20 ♋	8 A 26	21 ♍	10 A 08	20 ♎	10 P 31
22 ♈	8 P 52	21 ♉	4 P 56	23 ♋	1 A 13	22 ♌	6 P 57	23 ♎	3 P 08	23 ♏	1 A 53
25 ♉	8 A 54	24 ♊	5 A 33	25 ♌	10 A 32	25 ♍	2 A 03	25 ♏	4 P 38	25 ♐	2 A 42
27 ♊	9 P 26	26 ♋	4 P 50	27 ♍	4 P 07	27 ♎	5 A 16	27 ♐	3 P 58	27 ♑	2 A 31
30 ♋	8 A 07	29 ♌	1 A 03	29 ♎	6 P 22	29 ♏	5 A 31	29 ♑	3 P 16	29 ♒	3 A 23
		31 ♍	5 A 58			31 ♐	4 A 40			31 ♓	7 A 17

1933

JAN		TIME	FEB		TIME	MAR		TIME	APR		TIME	MAY		TIME	JUN		TIME
2	♈	3 P 14	1	♉	10 A 40	3	♊	7 A 18	2	♋	3 A 50	1	♌	11 P 06	2	♎	11 P 14
5	♉	2 A 37	3	♊	11 P 05	5	♋	7 P 43	4	♌	3 P 16	4	♍	8 A 40	5	♏	2 A 24
7	♊	3 P 19	6	♋	11 A 13	8	♌	6 A 17	6	♍	11 P 33	6	♎	2 P 16	7	♐	2 A 32
10	♋	3 A 16	8	♌	9 P 16	10	♍	1 P 41	9	♎	3 A 59	8	♏	4 P 06	9	♑	1 A 33
12	♌	1 P 26	11	♍	4 A 42	12	♎	6 P 02	11	♏	5 A 32	10	♐	3 P 43	11	♒	1 A 42
14	♍	9 P 41	13	♎	9 A 59	14	♏	8 P 27	13	♐	5 A 52	12	♑	3 P 16	13	♓	4 A 51
17	♎	4 A 02	15	♏	1 P 46	16	♐	10 P 18	15	♑	6 A 54	14	♒	4 P 47	15	♈	11 A 51
19	♏	8 A 24	17	♐	4 P 23	19	♑	0 A 47	17	♒	10 A 03	16	♓	9 P 34	17	♉	10 P 12
21	♐	10 A 54	19	♑	7 P 23	21	♒	4 A 40	19	♓	3 P 55	19	♈	5 A 46	20	♊	10 A 06
23	♑	0 P 18	21	♒	10 P 29	23	♓	10 A 16	22	♈	0 A 14	21	♉	4 P 27	22	♋	11 P 07
25	♒	1 P 57	24	♓	2 A 57	25	♈	5 P 50	24	♉	10 A 31	24	♊	4 A 32	25	♌	11 A 17
27	♓	5 P 32	26	♈	9 A 43	28	♉	3 A 32	26	♊	10 P 18	26	♋	5 P 12	27	♍	10 P 01
30	♈	0 A 21	28	♉	7 P 21	30	♊	3 P 14	29	♋	10 A 58	29	♌	5 A 33	30	♎	6 A 10
												31	♍	4 P 05			

JUL		TIME	AUG		TIME	SEPT		TIME	OCT		TIME	NOV		TIME	DEC		TIME
2	♏	10 A 56	2	♑	9 P 40	1	♒	7 A 00	2	♈	10 P 51	1	♉	1 P 53	1	♊	6 A 45
4	♐	0 P 32	4	♒	10 P 22	3	♓	9 A 44	5	♉	6 A 19	4	♊	0 A 02	3	♋	6 P 53
6	♑	0 P 15	7	♓	0 A 11	5	♈	2 P 15	7	♊	4 P 19	6	♋	0 P 05	6	♌	7 A 49
8	♒	0 P 05	9	♈	4 A 42	7	♉	9 P 36	10	♋	4 A 29	9	♌	0 A 58	8	♍	7 P 59
10	♓	2 P 02	11	♉	0 P 45	10	♊	8 A 01	12	♌	5 P 01	11	♍	0 P 24	11	♎	5 A 17
12	♈	7 P 32	13	♊	11 P 57	12	♋	8 P 25	15	♍	3 A 24	13	♎	8 P 11	13	♏	10 A 26
15	♉	4 A 50	16	♋	0 P 32	15	♌	8 A 30	17	♎	10 A 07	15	♏	11 P 52	15	♐	11 A 49
17	♊	4 P 44	19	♌	0 A 23	17	♍	6 P 12	19	♏	1 P 27	18	♐	0 A 35	17	♑	11 A 08
20	♋	5 A 24	21	♍	10 A 07	20	♎	0 A 51	21	♐	2 P 54	20	♑	0 A 24	19	♒	10 A 38
22	♌	5 P 18	23	♎	5 P 29	22	♏	4 A 59	23	♑	4 P 14	22	♒	1 A 21	21	♓	10 P 34
25	♍	3 A 35	25	♏	10 P 44	24	♐	7 A 49	25	♒	4 P 49	24	♓	4 A 51	23	♈	5 P 17
27	♎	11 A 44	28	♐	2 A 21	26	♑	10 A 23	27	♓	11 P 17	26	♈	11 A 13	26	♉	1 A 43
29	♏	5 P 20	30	♑	4 A 52	28	♒	1 P 27	30	♈	5 A 41	28	♉	8 P 04	28	♊	0 P 43
31	♐	8 P 26				30	♓	5 P 27							31	♋	1 A 07

JAN	TIME	FEB	TIME	MAR	TIME	APR	TIME	MAY	TIME	JUN	TIME
2 ♌	1P56	1 ♍	8A01	3 ♎	0A02	1 ♏	1P35	1 ♐	1A02	1 ♒	11A55
5 ♍	2A08	3 ♎	6P00	5 ♏	6A59	3 ♐	5P37	3 ♑	2A53	3 ♓	2P07
7 ♎	0P20	6 ♏	1A30	7 ♐	11A58	5 ♑	8P45	5 ♒	5A06	5 ♈	6P32
9 ♏	7P11	8 ♐	6A14	9 ♑	3P22	7 ♒	11P43	7 ♓	8A26	8 ♉	1A17
11 ♐	10P17	10 ♑	8A23	11 ♒	5P36	10 ♓	2A52	9 ♈	1P09	10 ♊	10A14
13 ♑	10P37	12 ♒	8A57	13 ♓	7P25	12 ♈	6A40	11 ♉	7P24	12 ♋	9P14
15 ♒	9P56	14 ♓	9A39	15 ♈	10P00	14 ♉	11A56	14 ♊	3A38	15 ♌	9A53
17 ♓	10P17	16 ♈	11A39	18 ♉	2A46	16 ♊	7P41	16 ♋	2P17	17 ♍	10P51
20 ♈	1A28	18 ♉	5P04	20 ♊	10A52	19 ♋	6A26	19 ♌	2A54	20 ♎	9A59
22 ♉	8A26	21 ♊	2A17	22 ♋	10P13	21 ♌	7P10	21 ♍	3P35	22 ♏	5P25
24 ♊	6P54	23 ♋	2P23	25 ♌	11A03	24 ♍	7A20	24 ♎	1A43	24 ♐	8P49
27 ♋	7A24	26 ♌	3A13	27 ♍	10P44	26 ♎	4P32	26 ♏	7A52	26 ♑	9P24
29 ♌	8P11	28 ♍	2P46	30 ♎	7A37	28 ♏	10P07	28 ♐	10A28	28 ♒	9P02
								30 ♑	11A12	30 ♓	9P28

JUL	TIME	AUG	TIME	SEPT	TIME	OCT	TIME	NOV	TIME	DEC	TIME
3 ♈	0A39	1 ♉	1P25	2 ♋	3P40	2 ♌	11A44	1 ♍	8A36	1 ♎	4A39
5 ♉	6A47	3 ♊	9P49	5 ♌	4A32	5 ♍	0A31	3 ♎	7P41	3 ♏	1P05
7 ♊	3P55	6 ♋	9A13	7 ♍	5P16	7 ♎	11A20	6 ♏	3A32	5 ♐	5P53
10 ♋	3A20	8 ♌	10P08	10 ♎	4A23	9 ♏	7P31	8 ♐	8A33	7 ♑	8P09
12 ♌	4P07	11 ♍	10A59	12 ♏	1P19	12 ♐	1A32	10 ♑	11A56	9 ♒	9P34
15 ♍	5A07	13 ♎	10P32	14 ♐	8P03	14 ♑	6A04	12 ♒	2P52	11 ♓	11P31
17 ♎	4P47	16 ♏	7A51	17 ♑	0A35	16 ♒	9A32	14 ♓	5P56	14 ♈	2A52
20 ♏	1A31	18 ♐	2P11	19 ♒	3A07	18 ♓	0P10	16 ♈	9P26	16 ♉	7A56
22 ♐	6A28	20 ♑	5P27	21 ♓	4A14	20 ♈	2P28	19 ♉	1A47	18 ♊	2P58
24 ♑	8A04	22 ♒	6P18	23 ♈	5A13	22 ♉	5P34	21 ♊	7A47	21 ♋	0A11
26 ♒	7A43	24 ♓	6P08	25 ♉	7A47	24 ♊	10P58	23 ♋	4P25	23 ♌	11A37
28 ♓	7A20	26 ♈	6P44	27 ♊	1P34	27 ♋	7A46	26 ♌	3A54	26 ♍	0A32
30 ♈	8A46	28 ♉	9P55	29 ♋	11P14	29 ♌	7P43	28 ♍	4P52	28 ♎	0P59
		31 ♊	4A56							30 ♏	10P41

1935

JAN	TIME	FEB	TIME	MAR	TIME	APR	TIME	MAY	TIME	JUN	TIME
2 ♐	4 A 27	2 ♒	6 P 26	2 ♒	5 A 16	2 ♈	3 P 31	2 ♉	2 A 09	2 ♋	8 P 44
4 ♑	6 A 44	4 ♓	5 P 46	4 ♓	5 A 13	4 ♉	4 P 18	4 ♊	5 A 26	5 ♌	6 A 19
6 ♒	7 A 04	6 ♈	5 P 49	6 ♈	4 A 41	6 ♊	7 P 36	6 ♋	11 A 50	7 ♍	6 P 26
8 ♓	7 A 17	8 ♉	8 P 22	8 ♉	5 A 43	9 ♋	2 A 49	8 ♌	9 P 55	10 ♎	6 A 59
10 ♈	9 A 03	11 ♊	2 A 35	10 ♊	10 A 12	11 ♌	1 P 52	11 ♍	10 A 26	12 ♏	5 P 35
12 ♉	1 P 25	13 ♋	0 P 24	12 ♋	6 P 52	14 ♍	2 A 47	13 ♎	10 P 48	15 ♐	0 A 57
14 ♊	8 P 43	16 ♌	0 A 35	15 ♌	6 A 48	16 ♎	3 P 01	16 ♏	8 A 53	17 ♑	5 A 21
17 ♋	6 A 37	18 ♍	1 P 33	17 ♍	7 P 51	19 ♏	1 A 09	18 ♐	4 P 12	19 ♒	7 A 56
19 ♌	6 P 27	21 ♎	2 A 02	20 ♎	8 A 08	21 ♐	9 A 06	20 ♑	9 P 20	21 ♓	9 A 57
22 ♍	7 A 20	23 ♏	1 P 04	22 ♏	6 P 46	23 ♑	3 P 13	23 ♒	1 A 08	23 ♈	0 P 21
24 ♎	7 P 59	25 ♐	9 P 40	25 ♐	3 A 23	25 ♒	7 P 43	25 ♓	4 A 13	25 ♉	3 P 54
27 ♏	6 A 46	28 ♑	3 A 04	27 ♑	9 A 48	27 ♓	10 P 39	27 ♈	6 A 59	27 ♊	9 P 06
29 ♐	2 P 10			29 ♒	1 P 41	30 ♈	0 A 26	29 ♉	9 A 58	30 ♋	4 A 27
31 ♑	5 P 48			31 ♓	3 P 14			31 ♊	2 P 11		

JUL	TIME	AUG	TIME	SEPT	TIME	OCT	TIME	NOV	TIME	DEC	TIME
2 ♌	0 P 13	1 ♍	9 A 06	2 ♏	4 P 22	2 ♐	8 A 40	3 ♒	4 A 38	2 ♓	2 P 02
5 ♍	2 A 08	3 ♎	9 P 54	5 ♐	2 A 48	4 ♑	5 P 02	5 ♓	8 A 20	4 ♈	4 P 52
7 ♎	2 P 52	6 ♏	9 A 57	7 ♑	10 A 08	6 ♒	10 P 20	7 ♈	9 A 54	6 ♉	7 P 02
10 ♏	2 A 14	8 ♐	7 P 24	9 ♒	1 P 44	9 ♓	0 A 26	9 ♉	10 A 29	8 ♊	9 P 37
12 ♐	10 A 27	11 ♑	1 A 10	11 ♓	2 P 15	11 ♈	0 A 20	11 ♊	11 A 52	11 ♋	1 A 54
14 ♑	3 P 03	13 ♒	3 A 21	13 ♈	1 P 21	12 ♉	11 P 53	13 ♋	3 P 56	13 ♌	9 A 07
16 ♒	4 P 53	15 ♓	3 A 18	15 ♉	1 P 10	15 ♊	1 A 14	15 ♌	11 P 51	15 ♍	7 P 33
18 ♓	5 P 31	17 ♈	2 A 55	17 ♊	3 P 48	17 ♋	6 A 21	18 ♍	11 A 51	18 ♎	7 A 58
20 ♈	6 P 34	19 ♉	4 A 08	19 ♋	10 P 27	19 ♌	3 P 36	20 ♎	11 P 52	20 ♏	8 P 00
22 ♉	9 P 21	21 ♊	8 A 25	22 ♌	8 A 50	22 ♍	3 A 44	23 ♏	11 A 36	23 ♐	5 A 44
25 ♊	2 A 42	23 ♋	4 P 17	24 ♍	9 P 18	24 ♎	4 P 31	25 ♐	9 P 10	25 ♑	0 P 27
27 ♋	10 A 43	26 ♌	3 A 00	27 ♎	10 A 06	27 ♏	4 A 14	28 ♑	4 A 28	27 ♒	4 P 46
29 ♌	9 P 04	28 ♍	3 P 20	29 ♏	10 P 06	29 ♐	2 P 17	30 ♒	10 A 00	29 ♓	7 P 42
		31 ♎	4 A 08			31 ♑	10 P 31			31 ♈	10 P 16

1936

JAN
		TIME
3	♉	1 A 11
5	♊	5 A 04
7	♋	10 A 29
9	♌	6 P 02
12	♍	4 A 05
14	♎	4 P 10
17	♏	4 A 38
19	♐	3 P 12
21	♑	10 P 18
24	♒	2 A 02
26	♓	3 A 35
28	♈	4 A 36
30	♉	6 A 37

FEB
		TIME
1	♊	10 A 38
3	♋	4 P 58
6	♌	1 A 26
8	♍	11 A 48
10	♎	11 P 46
13	♏	0 P 24
15	♐	11 P 56
18	♑	8 A 21
20	♒	0 P 46
22	♓	1 P 55
24	♈	1 P 35
26	♉	1 P 51
28	♊	4 P 30

MAR
		TIME
1	♋	10 P 26
4	♌	7 A 20
6	♍	6 P 18
9	♎	6 A 27
11	♏	7 P 03
14	♐	7 A 06
16	♑	4 P 51
18	♒	10 P 52
21	♓	0 A 59
23	♈	0 A 31
24	♉	11 P 37
27	♊	0 A 31
29	♋	4 A 52
31	♌	1 P 04

APR
		TIME
3	♍	0 A 07
5	♎	0 P 31
8	♏	1 A 05
10	♐	1 P 03
12	♑	11 P 23
15	♒	6 A 49
17	♓	10 A 37
19	♈	11 A 20
21	♉	10 A 37
23	♊	10 A 38
25	♋	1 P 23
27	♌	8 P 03
30	♍	6 A 22

MAY
		TIME
2	♎	6 P 43
5	♏	7 A 16
7	♐	6 P 54
10	♑	4 A 56
12	♒	0 P 47
14	♓	5 P 53
16	♈	8 P 14
18	♉	8 P 47
20	♊	9 P 12
22	♋	11 P 19
25	♌	4 A 42
27	♍	1 P 48
30	♎	1 A 38

JUN
		TIME
1	♏	2 P 13
4	♐	1 A 37
6	♑	11 A 02
8	♒	6 P 17
11	♓	11 P 26
13	♈	2 A 47
15	♉	4 A 48
17	♊	6 A 30
19	♋	9 A 09
21	♌	2 P 06
23	♍	10 P 15
26	♎	9 A 24
28	♏	9 P 52

JUL
		TIME
1	♐	9 A 27
3	♑	6 P 34
6	♒	0 A 56
8	♓	5 A 10
10	♈	8 A 10
12	♉	10 A 46
14	♊	1 P 38
16	♋	5 P 28
18	♌	10 P 58
21	♍	6 A 54
23	♎	5 P 31
26	♏	5 A 54
28	♐	5 P 36
31	♑	3 A 23

AUG
		TIME
2	♒	9 A 25
4	♓	0 P 36
6	♈	2 P 21
8	♉	4 P 12
10	♊	7 P 12
12	♋	11 P 52
15	♌	6 A 20
17	♍	2 P 45
20	♎	1 A 17
22	♏	1 P 36
25	♐	2 A 09
27	♑	0 P 16
29	♒	7 P 12
31	♓	10 P 05

SEPT
		TIME
2	♈	9 A 43
4	♉	11 P 04
7	♊	0 A 55
9	♋	5 A 16
11	♌	0 P 13
13	♍	9 P 20
16	♎	8 A 12
18	♏	8 P 32
21	♐	9 A 24
23	♑	8 P 52
26	♒	4 A 53
28	♓	8 A 38
30	♈	9 A 10

OCT
		TIME
2	♉	8 A 25
4	♊	8 A 37
6	♋	11 A 28
8	♌	5 P 45
11	♍	3 A 01
13	♎	2 P 19
16	♏	2 A 47
18	♐	3 P 38
21	♑	3 A 37
23	♒	1 P 00
25	♓	6 P 28
27	♈	8 P 09
29	♉	7 P 34
31	♊	6 P 49

NOV
		TIME
2	♋	8 P 00
5	♌	0 A 37
7	♍	9 A 00
9	♎	8 P 15
12	♏	8 A 52
14	♐	9 P 34
17	♑	9 A 20
19	♒	7 P 11
22	♓	2 A 04
24	♈	5 A 37
26	♉	6 A 29
28	♊	6 A 11
30	♋	6 A 40

DEC
		TIME
2	♌	9 A 43
4	♍	4 P 31
7	♎	2 A 55
9	♏	3 P 28
12	♐	4 A 07
14	♑	3 P 25
17	♒	0 A 42
19	♓	7 A 43
21	♈	0 P 26
23	♉	3 P 05
25	♊	4 P 24
27	♋	5 P 20
29	♌	8 P 14

1937

JAN	TIME	FEB	TIME	MAR	TIME	APR	TIME	MAY	TIME	JUN	TIME
1 ♍	1 A 50	2 ♏	7 A 11	1 ♏	3 P 23	3 ♑	0 A 13	2 ♒	6 P 05	1 ♓	8 A 56
3 ♎	10 A 56	4 ♐	7 P 58	4 ♐	4 A 08	5 ♒	10 A 38	5 ♓	1 A 51	3 ♈	2 P 20
5 ♏	10 P 59	7 ♑	7 A 32	6 ♑	4 P 20	7 ♓	4 P 45	7 ♈	5 A 43	5 ♉	4 P 34
8 ♐	11 A 42	9 ♒	3 P 57	9 ♒	1 A 29	9 ♈	7 P 25	9 ♉	6 A 29	7 ♊	4 P 46
10 ♑	10 P 50	11 ♓	9 P 07	11 ♓	6 A 48	11 ♉	7 P 39	11 ♊	5 A 57	9 ♋	4 P 33
13 ♒	7 A 23	14 ♈	0 A 11	13 ♈	8 A 59	13 ♊	7 P 36	13 ♋	6 A 03	11 ♌	5 P 48
15 ♓	1 P 28	16 ♉	2 A 35	15 ♉	9 A 55	15 ♋	9 P 07	15 ♌	8 A 30	13 ♍	10 P 07
17 ♈	5 P 48	18 ♊	5 A 23	17 ♊	11 A 19	18 ♌	1 A 16	17 ♍	2 P 21	16 ♎	6 A 11
19 ♉	9 P 07	20 ♋	9 A 05	19 ♋	2 P 27	20 ♍	8 A 18	19 ♎	11 P 38	18 ♏	5 P 32
21 ♊	11 P 53	22 ♌	1 P 51	21 ♌	7 P 38	22 ♎	5 P 53	22 ♏	11 A 18	21 ♐	6 A 24
24 ♋	2 A 39	24 ♍	8 P 07	24 ♍	2 A 46	25 ♏	5 A 21	25 ♐	0 A 10	23 ♑	6 P 56
26 ♌	6 A 10	27 ♎	4 A 30	26 ♎	11 A 46	27 ♐	6 P 05	27 ♑	0 P 54	26 ♒	5 A 52
28 ♍	11 A 31			28 ♏	10 P 53	30 ♑	6 A 56	30 ♒	0 A 10	28 ♓	2 P 36
30 ♎	7 P 53			31 ♐	11 A 31					30 ♈	8 P 46

JUL	TIME	AUG	TIME	SEPT	TIME	OCT	TIME	NOV	TIME	DEC	TIME
3 ♉	0 A 31	1 ♊	9 A 28	1 ♌	9 P 23	1 ♍	8 A 30	2 ♏	7 A 49	2 ♐	2 A 06
5 ♊	2 A 13	3 ♋	11 A 33	4 ♍	1 A 37	3 ♎	3 P 33	4 ♐	7 P 48	4 ♑	3 P 07
7 ♋	2 A 54	5 ♌	1 P 36	6 ♎	7 A 50	6 ♏	0 A 58	7 ♑	8 A 50	7 ♒	3 A 38
9 ♌	4 A 02	7 ♍	4 P 56	8 ♏	5 P 00	8 ♐	0 P 45	9 ♒	9 P 16	9 ♓	2 P 20
11 ♍	7 A 19	9 ♎	11 P 03	11 ♐	5 A 00	11 ♑	1 A 45	12 ♓	7 A 03	11 ♈	9 P 50
13 ♎	2 P 06	12 ♏	8 A 38	13 ♑	5 P 49	13 ♒	1 P 36	14 ♈	0 P 58	14 ♉	1 A 43
16 ♏	0 A 39	14 ♐	8 P 59	16 ♒	4 A 47	15 ♓	9 P 57	16 ♉	3 P 10	16 ♊	2 A 40
18 ♐	1 P 09	17 ♑	9 A 36	18 ♓	0 P 19	18 ♈	2 A 28	18 ♊	3 P 10	18 ♋	2 A 03
21 ♑	1 A 48	19 ♒	8 P 02	20 ♈	4 P 29	20 ♉	4 A 08	20 ♋	2 P 48	20 ♌	1 A 53
23 ♒	0 P 19	22 ♓	3 A 25	22 ♉	6 P 49	22 ♊	4 A 40	22 ♌	3 P 57	22 ♍	4 A 02
25 ♓	8 P 18	24 ♈	8 A 22	24 ♊	8 P 48	24 ♋	5 A 49	24 ♍	8 P 01	24 ♎	9 A 55
28 ♈	2 A 13	26 ♉	11 A 56	26 ♋	11 P 26	26 ♌	8 A 44	27 ♎	3 A 26	26 ♏	7 P 47
30 ♉	6 A 29	28 ♊	3 P 02	29 ♌	3 A 16	28 ♍	2 P 03	29 ♏	1 P 46	29 ♐	8 A 12
		30 ♋	6 P 03			30 ♎	9 P 50			31 ♑	9 P 16

1938

JAN
Day	Sign	Time
3	♒	9 A 30
5	♓	8 P 04
8	♈	4 A 48
10	♉	10 A 04
12	♊	0 P 49
14	♋	1 P 21
16	♌	1 P 09
18	♍	2 P 14
20	♎	6 P 32
23	♏	3 A 00
25	♐	2 P 51
28	♑	3 A 57
30	♒	3 P 59

FEB
Day	Sign	Time
2	♓	1 A 56
4	♈	9 A 53
6	♉	3 P 56
8	♊	8 P 05
10	♋	10 P 23
12	♌	11 P 34
15	♍	1 A 00
17	♎	4 A 32
19	♏	11 A 37
21	♐	10 P 36
24	♑	11 A 27
26	♒	11 P 32

MAR
Day	Sign	Time
1	♓	9 A 12
3	♈	4 P 14
5	♉	9 P 28
8	♊	1 A 32
10	♋	4 A 45
12	♌	7 A 22
14	♍	10 A 06
16	♎	2 P 06
18	♏	8 P 58
21	♐	7 A 03
23	♑	7 P 31
26	♒	7 A 55
28	♓	5 P 48
31	♈	0 A 29

APR
Day	Sign	Time
2	♉	4 A 41
4	♊	7 A 33
6	♋	10 A 07
8	♌	10 P 51
10	♍	4 P 53
12	♎	10 P 05
15	♏	5 A 24
17	♐	3 P 21
20	♑	3 A 32
22	♒	4 P 09
25	♓	2 A 49
27	♈	10 A 06
29	♉	2 P 00

MAY
Day	Sign	Time
1	♊	3 P 44
3	♋	4 P 52
5	♌	6 P 44
7	♍	10 P 21
10	♎	4 A 08
12	♏	0 P 17
14	♐	10 A 51
17	♑	11 P 36
19	♒	11 A 07
22	♓	7 P 31
24	♈	0 A 12
27	♉	1 A 49
29	♊	1 A 52
31	♋	

JUN
Day	Sign	Time
2	♌	2 A 11
4	♍	4 A 25
6	♎	9 A 37
8	♏	6 P 04
11	♐	4 A 58
13	♑	5 P 20
16	♒	6 A 06
18	♓	6 P 01
21	♈	3 A 35
23	♉	9 A 48
25	♊	4 P 02
27	♋	0 P 27
29	♌	11 A 46

JUL
Day	Sign	Time
1	♍	3 P 57
3	♎	4 P 12
5	♏	11 P 53
8	♐	10 A 46
10	♑	11 P 21
13	♒	0 P 06
15	♓	11 P 53
18	♈	10 A 01
20	♉	5 P 28
22	♊	9 P 42
24	♋	10 A 54
26	♌	10 P 25
28	♍	10 P 18
31	♎	0 A 42

AUG
Day	Sign	Time
2	♏	6 A 53
4	♐	5 P 04
7	♑	5 A 34
9	♒	6 P 15
12	♓	5 A 43
14	♈	3 P 33
16	♉	11 P 22
19	♊	4 A 47
21	♋	7 A 37
23	♌	8 A 26
25	♍	8 A 43
27	♎	10 A 28
29	♏	3 P 29

SEPT
Day	Sign	Time
1	♐	0 A 32
3	♑	0 P 30
6	♒	1 A 09
8	♓	0 P 29
10	♈	9 P 38
13	♉	4 A 51
15	♊	10 A 23
17	♋	2 P 08
19	♌	4 P 25
21	♍	6 P 02
23	♎	8 P 22
26	♏	1 A 02
28	♐	9 A 04
30	♑	8 P 21

OCT
Day	Sign	Time
3	♒	8 A 56
5	♓	8 P 24
8	♈	5 A 20
10	♉	11 A 42
12	♊	4 P 09
14	♋	7 P 30
16	♌	10 P 19
19	♍	1 A 10
21	♎	4 A 46
23	♏	10 A 01
25	♐	5 P 58
28	♑	4 A 40
30	♒	5 P 07

NOV
Day	Sign	Time
2	♓	5 A 05
4	♈	2 P 33
6	♉	8 P 37
9	♊	0 A 01
11	♋	1 A 59
13	♌	3 A 51
15	♍	6 A 40
17	♎	11 A 03
19	♏	5 P 28
22	♐	2 A 00
24	♑	0 P 38
27	♒	0 A 59
29	♓	1 P 29

DEC
Day	Sign	Time
1	♈	11 P 57
4	♉	6 A 57
6	♊	10 A 18
8	♋	11 A 07
10	♌	11 A 18
12	♍	0 P 37
14	♎	4 P 30
16	♏	11 P 16
19	♐	8 A 33
21	♑	7 P 39
24	♒	7 A 59
26	♓	8 P 40
29	♈	6 A 15
31	♉	4 P 43

1939

JAN		TIME	FEB		TIME	MAR		TIME
2	♊	9 P 14	1	♋	8 A 57	2	♌	7 P 28
4	♋	10 P 17	3	♌	9 A 05	4	♍	7 P 20
6	♌	9 P 32	5	♍	7 A 35	6	♎	7 P 35
8	♍	9 P 28	7	♎	8 A 33	8	♏	10 P 05
10	♎	11 P 16	9	♏	0 P 22	11	♐	4 A 28
13	♏	4 A 58	11	♐	8 P 28	13	♑	2 P 36
15	♐	2 P 10	14	♑	7 A 42	16	♒	3 A 01
18	♑	1 A 44	16	♒	8 P 22	18	♓	3 P 31
20	♒	2 A 16	19	♓	8 A 52	21	♈	2 A 38
23	♓	2 A 50	21	♈	8 P 21	23	♉	0 P 02
25	♈	2 P 40	24	♉	6 A 17	25	♊	7 P 12
28	♉	0 A 24	26	♊	1 A 47	28	♋	0 A 16
30	♊	6 A 46	28	♋	6 P 03	30	♌	3 A 12

APR		TIME	MAY		TIME	JUN		TIME
1	♍	4 A 38	2	♏	5 P 39	1	♐	7 A 17
3	♎	5 A 51	4	♐	11 P 15	4	♑	3 P 52
5	♏	8 A 24	7	♑	7 A 36	6	♒	2 A 42
7	♐	1 P 48	9	♒	6 P 42	8	♓	3 P 04
9	♑	10 P 51	12	♓	7 A 08	11	♈	2 A 58
12	♒	10 A 34	14	♈	6 P 43	13	♉	0 P 42
14	♓	11 P 03	17	♉	3 A 24	15	♊	6 P 29
17	♈	10 A 13	19	♊	11 A 04	17	♋	9 P 04
19	♉	6 P 54	21	♋	0 P 24	19	♌	9 P 58
22	♊	1 A 13	23	♌	3 P 14	21	♍	10 P 57
24	♋	5 A 41	25	♍	4 P 52	24	♎	1 A 34
26	♌	8 A 54	27	♎	8 P 09	26	♏	6 A 54
28	♍	6 A 37	30	♏	0 A 46	28	♐	1 P 40
30	♎	2 P 03				30	♑	10 P 56

JUL		TIME	AUG		TIME	SEPT		TIME
3	♒	9 A 55	2	♓	4 A 41	3	♉	10 A 47
5	♓	10 P 18	4	♈	5 P 21	5	♊	7 P 58
8	♈	10 A 50	7	♉	4 A 04	8	♋	1 A 47
10	♉	9 P 22	9	♊	1 P 04	10	♌	4 A 07
13	♊	4 A 14	11	♋	5 P 18	12	♍	4 A 08
15	♋	6 A 47	13	♌	6 P 07	14	♎	3 A 41
17	♌	7 A 29	15	♍	5 P 20	16	♏	4 A 48
19	♍	7 A 08	17	♎	5 P 05	18	♐	9 A 05
21	♎	8 A 14	19	♏	7 P 25	20	♑	5 P 13
23	♏	0 P 04	22	♐	1 A 18	23	♒	4 A 25
25	♐	7 P 13	24	♑	10 A 35	25	♓	4 P 59
28	♑	4 A 53	26	♒	6 P 10	28	♈	5 A 20
30	♒	4 P 15	29	♓	10 A 43	30	♉	4 P 28
			31	♈	11 P 14			

OCT		TIME	NOV		TIME	DEC		TIME
3	♊	10 A 34	1	♋	1 P 47	3	♍	2 A 23
5	♋	8 A 16	3	♌	7 P 00	5	♎	5 A 23
7	♌	0 P 20	5	♍	8 P 55	7	♏	8 A 57
9	♍	1 P 45	7	♎	11 P 03	9	♐	1 P 33
11	♎	2 P 16	10	♏	1 A 16	11	♑	7 P 55
13	♏	3 P 44	12	♐	4 A 44	14	♒	4 A 45
15	♐	6 P 39	14	♑	10 A 43	16	♓	4 P 19
18	♑	1 A 27	16	♒	8 P 03	19	♈	5 A 01
20	♒	11 A 40	19	♓	10 A 00	21	♉	4 P 28
23	♓	0 A 05	21	♈	8 P 33	24	♊	0 A 32
25	♈	0 P 28	24	♉	7 A 21	26	♋	5 A 00
27	♉	11 P 05	26	♊	3 P 07	28	♌	7 A 07
30	♊	7 A 30	28	♋	8 P 09	30	♍	8 A 31
			30	♌	11 P 33			

1940

JAN	TIME	FEB	TIME	MAR	TIME	APR	TIME	MAY	TIME	JUN	TIME
1 ♎	10 A 44	2 ♐	1 A 39	2 ♑	2 P 46	1 ♒	7 A 16	1 ♓	1 A 58	2 ♉	10 A 42
3 ♏	2 P 37	4 ♑	9 A 27	5 ♒	1 P 09	3 ♓	7 P 12	3 ♈	2 P 50	4 ♊	8 P 45
5 ♐	8 P 14	6 ♒	7 P 24	7 ♓	1 P 07	6 ♈	8 A 10	6 ♉	3 A 10	7 ♋	3 A 59
7 ♑	3 A 32	9 ♓	6 A 59	10 ♈	2 A 00	8 ♉	8 P 37	8 ♊	1 P 33	9 ♌	9 A 00
10 ♒	0 P 43	11 ♈	7 P 49	12 ♉	2 A 44	11 ♊	7 A 31	10 ♋	9 P 31	11 ♍	0 P 41
13 ♓	0 A 05	14 ♉	8 A 35	15 ♊	1 A 48	13 ♋	4 P 01	13 ♌	3 A 19	13 ♎	3 P 44
15 ♈	0 P 55	16 ♊	7 P 05	17 ♋	9 A 56	15 ♌	9 P 39	15 ♍	7 A 16	15 ♏	6 P 32
17 ♉	1 A 11	19 ♋	1 A 40	19 ♌	2 P 13	18 ♍	0 A 31	17 ♎	9 A 40	17 ♐	9 P 35
20 ♊	10 A 30	21 ♌	4 A 15	21 ♍	3 P 19	20 ♎	1 A 21	19 ♏	11 A 12	20 ♑	1 A 48
22 ♋	3 P 32	23 ♍	4 A 10	23 ♎	2 P 48	22 ♏	1 A 34	21 ♐	1 P 01	22 ♒	8 A 18
24 ♌	5 P 09	25 ♎	3 A 31	25 ♏	2 P 35	24 ♐	2 A 52	23 ♑	4 P 38	24 ♓	5 P 57
26 ♍	5 P 12	27 ♏	4 A 18	27 ♐	4 P 34	26 ♑	6 A 54	25 ♒	11 P 23	27 ♈	6 A 13
28 ♎	5 P 46	29 ♐	7 A 57	29 ♑	10 P 05	28 ♒	2 P 41	28 ♓	9 A 39	29 ♉	6 P 50
30 ♏	8 P 22							30 ♈	10 P 17		

JUL	TIME	AUG	TIME	SEPT	TIME	OCT	TIME	NOV	TIME	DEC	TIME
2 ♊	5 A 12	3 ♌	1 A 16	1 ♍	0 P 56	2 ♏	11 P 15	1 ♐	10 A 22	3 ♒	3 A 18
4 ♋	0 P 11	5 ♍	2 A 49	3 ♎	0 P 54	4 ♐	11 P 59	3 ♑	0 P 23	5 ♓	11 A 35
6 ♌	4 P 11	7 ♎	3 A 51	5 ♏	1 P 18	7 ♑	3 A 34	5 ♒	6 P 07	7 ♈	11 P 28
8 ♍	6 P 44	9 ♏	5 A 48	7 ♐	3 P 39	9 ♒	10 A 45	8 ♓	3 A 49	10 ♉	0 P 26
10 ♎	9 P 08	11 ♐	9 A 30	9 ♑	8 P 50	11 ♓	9 P 19	10 ♈	4 P 13	13 ♊	0 A 05
13 ♏	0 A 08	13 ♑	3 P 17	12 ♒	4 A 55	14 ♈	9 A 50	13 ♉	5 A 11	15 ♋	9 A 18
15 ♐	4 A 06	15 ♒	11 P 11	14 ♓	3 P 25	16 ♉	10 P 48	15 ♊	4 P 59	17 ♌	4 P 15
17 ♑	9 A 19	18 ♓	9 A 11	17 ♈	3 A 44	19 ♊	10 A 58	18 ♋	2 A 50	19 ♍	9 P 33
19 ♒	4 P 24	20 ♈	9 P 16	19 ♉	4 P 44	21 ♋	9 P 14	20 ♌	10 A 37	22 ♎	1 A 35
22 ♓	2 A 02	23 ♉	10 A 16	22 ♊	5 A 03	24 ♌	4 A 46	22 ♍	4 P 08	24 ♏	4 A 29
24 ♈	2 P 02	25 ♊	10 P 08	24 ♋	2 P 56	26 ♍	9 A 07	24 ♎	7 P 22	26 ♐	6 A 37
27 ♉	2 A 53	28 ♋	6 A 49	26 ♌	9 P 03	28 ♎	10 A 35	26 ♏	8 P 44	28 ♑	8 A 59
29 ♊	2 P 03	30 ♌	11 A 31	28 ♍	9 P 36	30 ♏	10 A 25	28 ♐	9 P 20	30 ♒	1 P 09
31 ♋	9 P 27			30 ♎	11 P 45			30 ♑	10 P 55		

1941

JAN	TIME	FEB	TIME	MAR	TIME	APR	TIME	MAY	TIME	JUN	TIME
1 ♓	8 P 40	3 ♉	4 P 41	2 ♉	0 P 22	1 ♊	8 A 05	1 ♋	1 A 53	2 ♍	0 A 34
4 ♈	7 A 36	5 ♊	5 P 07	5 ♊	1 A 09	3 ♋	7 P 40	3 ♌	11 A 33	4 ♎	5 A 13
6 ♉	8 P 27	8 ♋	2 A 53	7 ♋	0 P 04	6 ♌	4 A 21	5 ♍	6 P 01	6 ♏	7 A 12
9 ♊	8 A 25	10 ♌	9 A 05	9 ♌	7 P 14	8 ♍	9 A 18	7 ♎	9 P 06	8 ♐	7 A 24
11 ♋	5 P 31	12 ♍	0 P 22	11 ♍	10 P 47	10 ♎	10 A 53	9 ♏	9 P 31	10 ♑	7 A 33
13 ♌	5 P 36	14 ♎	2 P 07	13 ♎	11 P 50	12 ♏	10 A 32	11 ♐	8 P 52	12 ♒	9 A 44
16 ♍	3 A 45	16 ♏	3 P 36	16 ♏	0 A 04	14 ♐	10 A 08	13 ♑	9 P 09	14 ♓	3 P 37
18 ♎	7 A 00	18 ♐	6 P 39	18 ♐	1 A 12	16 ♑	11 A 38	16 ♒	0 A 21	17 ♈	1 A 33
20 ♏	10 A 04	20 ♑	10 P 56	20 ♑	4 A 29	18 ♒	4 P 34	18 ♓	7 A 37	19 ♉	2 P 02
22 ♐	1 P 17	23 ♒	5 A 04	22 ♒	10 A 36	21 ♓	1 A 11	20 ♈	6 P 35	22 ♊	2 A 42
24 ♑	5 P 02	25 ♓	1 P 19	24 ♓	7 P 33	23 ♈	0 P 34	23 ♉	7 A 25	24 ♋	1 P 50
26 ♒	10 P 09	27 ♈	11 P 56	27 ♈	6 A 41	26 ♉	1 A 22	25 ♊	8 P 09	26 ♌	10 P 52
29 ♓	5 A 37			29 ♉	7 P 13	28 ♊	2 P 11	28 ♋	7 A 35	29 ♍	6 A 01
31 ♈	4 P 03							30 ♌	5 P 14		

JUL	TIME	AUG	TIME	SEPT	TIME	OCT	TIME	NOV	TIME	DEC	TIME
1 ♎	11 A 16	1 ♐	10 P 49	2 ♒	11 A 39	2 ♓	0 A 30	3 ♉	3 A 20	2 ♊	10 P 00
3 ♏	2 P 32	4 ♑	2 A 27	4 ♓	5 P 54	4 ♈	9 A 39	5 ♊	3 P 53	5 ♋	10 A 22
5 ♐	4 P 12	6 ♒	4 A 35	7 ♈	2 A 31	6 ♉	8 P 53	8 ♋	4 A 24	7 ♌	9 P 41
7 ♑	5 P 22	8 ♓	9 A 52	9 ♉	1 P 32	9 ♊	9 A 22	10 ♌	3 P 47	10 ♍	7 A 10
9 ♒	7 P 40	10 ♈	6 P 15	12 ♊	2 A 05	11 ♋	9 P 50	13 ♍	0 A 23	12 ♎	1 P 44
12 ♓	0 A 47	13 ♉	5 A 33	14 ♋	2 P 09	14 ♌	8 A 27	15 ♎	5 A 16	14 ♏	4 P 48
14 ♈	9 A 37	15 ♊	6 P 08	16 ♌	11 P 30	16 ♍	3 P 34	17 ♏	6 A 37	16 ♐	5 P 09
16 ♉	9 P 31	18 ♋	5 A 34	19 ♍	5 A 25	18 ♎	6 P 50	19 ♐	5 A 53	18 ♑	4 P 27
19 ♊	10 A 09	20 ♌	2 P 14	21 ♎	8 A 15	20 ♏	7 P 25	21 ♑	5 A 14	20 ♒	4 P 57
21 ♋	9 P 12	22 ♍	7 P 50	23 ♏	9 A 24	22 ♐	7 P 02	23 ♒	6 A 50	22 ♓	8 P 38
24 ♌	5 A 46	24 ♎	11 P 19	25 ♐	11 A 25	24 ♑	7 P 44	25 ♓	0 P 09	25 ♈	4 A 27
26 ♍	0 P 04	27 ♏	1 A 48	27 ♑	0 P 45	26 ♒	11 P 08	27 ♈	9 P 30	27 ♉	3 P 44
28 ♎	4 P 40	29 ♐	4 A 14	29 ♒	5 P 19	29 ♓	5 A 53	30 ♉	9 A 19	30 ♊	4 A 26
30 ♏	8 P 07	31 ♑	7 A 19			31 ♈	3 P 39				

1942

JAN
Day	Sign	TIME
1	♋	4 P 41
4	♌	3 A 30
6	♍	0 P 41
8	♎	7 P 45
11	♏	0 A 20
13	♐	2 A 29
15	♑	3 A 07
17	♒	3 A 55
19	♓	6 A 46
21	♈	1 P 09
23	♉	11 P 21
26	♊	11 A 44
29	♋	0 A 01
31	♌	10 A 37

FEB
Day	Sign	TIME
2	♍	6 P 55
5	♎	1 A 15
7	♏	5 A 54
9	♐	9 A 05
11	♑	11 A 18
13	♒	1 P 28
15	♓	4 P 53
17	♈	10 P 50
20	♉	7 A 59
22	♊	7 P 49
25	♋	8 A 43
27	♌	7 P 02

MAR
Day	Sign	TIME
2	♍	3 A 02
4	♎	8 A 21
6	♏	11 A 50
8	♐	2 P 28
10	♑	5 P 09
12	♒	8 P 33
15	♓	1 A 11
17	♈	7 A 43
19	♉	4 P 41
22	♊	4 A 01
24	♋	4 P 32
27	♌	4 A 01
29	♍	0 P 36
31	♎	4 P 09

APR
Day	Sign	TIME
2	♏	7 P 52
4	♐	9 P 05
6	♑	10 P 45
9	♒	2 A 00
11	♓	7 A 22
13	♈	2 P 51
16	♉	0 A 20
18	♊	11 A 36
21	♋	0 A 09
23	♌	0 P 22
25	♍	9 P 58
28	♎	3 A 45
30	♏	5 A 56

MAY
Day	Sign	TIME
2	♐	6 A 02
4	♑	6 A 05
6	♒	7 A 58
8	♓	0 P 44
10	♈	8 P 55
13	♉	6 A 39
15	♊	6 P 16
18	♋	6 A 50
20	♌	6 A 05
23	♍	7 P 19
25	♎	6 A 05
27	♏	1 P 20
29	♐	5 P 11
31	♑	4 P 38
		3 P 45

JUN
Day	Sign	TIME
2	♒	4 P 02
4	♓	7 P 18
7	♈	2 A 15
9	♉	0 P 16
12	♊	0 A 13
14	♋	0 P 51
17	♌	1 A 18
19	♍	0 P 33
21	♎	8 P 59
24	♏	1 A 45
26	♐	3 A 05
28	♑	2 A 30
30	♒	2 A 05

JUL
Day	Sign	TIME
2	♓	3 A 51
4	♈	9 A 12
6	♉	6 P 26
9	♊	6 A 11
11	♋	6 P 51
14	♌	7 A 06
16	♍	6 P 06
19	♎	2 A 58
21	♏	9 A 00
23	♐	11 A 58
25	♑	0 P 38
27	♒	0 P 37
29	♓	1 P 51
31	♈	5 P 59

AUG
Day	Sign	TIME
2	♉	5 A 26
5	♊	0 P 55
8	♋	1 A 29
10	♌	1 P 39
13	♍	0 A 06
15	♎	8 A 29
17	♏	2 P 36
19	♐	6 P 33
21	♑	8 P 45
23	♒	10 P 07
25	♓	11 P 58
28	♈	3 A 43
30	♉	10 A 30

SEPT
Day	Sign	TIME
1	♊	8 P 43
4	♋	9 A 00
6	♌	9 P 12
9	♍	7 A 29
11	♎	3 P 03
13	♏	8 P 16
15	♐	11 P 57
18	♑	2 A 48
20	♒	5 A 28
22	♓	8 A 34
24	♈	0 P 57
26	♉	7 P 37
29	♊	5 A 07

OCT
Day	Sign	TIME
1	♋	5 P 03
4	♌	5 A 33
6	♍	4 P 11
8	♎	11 P 28
11	♏	3 A 43
13	♐	6 A 09
15	♑	8 A 14
17	♒	11 A 02
19	♓	3 P 05
21	♈	8 P 39
24	♉	3 A 55
26	♊	1 P 19
29	♋	1 A 02
31	♌	1 P 48

NOV
Day	Sign	TIME
3	♍	1 A 15
5	♎	9 A 19
7	♏	1 P 26
9	♐	2 P 46
11	♑	3 P 19
13	♒	4 P 51
15	♓	8 P 31
18	♈	2 A 33
20	♉	10 A 39
22	♊	8 P 37
25	♋	8 A 17
27	♌	9 P 08
30	♍	9 A 28

DEC
Day	Sign	TIME
2	♎	6 P 50
4	♏	0 M 00
7	♐	1 A 30
9	♑	1 A 07
11	♒	2 A 38
13	♓	3 A 01
15	♈	8 A 07
17	♉	4 P 18
20	♊	2 A 48
22	♋	2 P 46
25	♌	3 A 35
27	♍	4 P 08
30	♎	2 A 40

1943

JAN	TIME	FEB	TIME	MAR	TIME	APR	TIME	MAY	TIME	JUN	TIME
1 ♏	9 A 37	1 ♑	11 P 11	1 ♑	7 A 17	1 ♓	6 P 27	1 ♈	4 A 41	2 ♊	0 A 32
3 ♐	0 P 34	3 ♒	11 P 10	3 ♒	8 A 56	3 ♈	9 P 20	3 ♉	9 A 58	4 ♋	10 A 45
5 ♑	0 P 35	5 ♓	11 P 11	5 ♓	9 A 54	6 ♉	8 A 43	5 ♊	5 P 19	6 ♌	11 P 04
7 ♒	11 A 41	8 ♈	1 A 06	7 ♈	11 A 42	8 ♊	7 P 06	8 ♋	3 A 19	9 ♍	0 P 04
9 ♓	0 P 03	10 ♉	6 A 21	9 ♉	3 P 56	10 ♋	7 A 40	10 ♌	3 P 39	11 ♎	11 P 17
11 ♈	3 P 23	12 ♊	3 P 27	11 ♊	11 P 44	13 ♌	7 P 56	13 ♍	4 A 19	14 ♏	6 A 54
13 ♉	10 P 26	15 ♋	3 A 26	14 ♋	10 A 52	15 ♍	7 A 37	15 ♎	2 P 42	16 ♐	10 A 36
16 ♊	8 A 40	17 ♌	4 P 18	16 ♌	11 P 40	18 ♎	0 P 04	17 ♏	9 P 14	18 ♑	11 A 29
18 ♋	8 P 55	20 ♍	4 A 17	19 ♍	11 A 42	20 ♏	0 P 04	20 ♐	0 A 29	20 ♒	11 A 33
21 ♌	9 A 44	22 ♎	2 P 29	21 ♎	9 P 17	22 ♐	3 P 56	22 ♑	2 A 02	22 ♓	0 P 37
23 ♍	10 P 01	24 ♏	11 P 13	24 ♏	4 A 20	24 ♑	6 P 40	24 ♒	2 A 25	24 ♈	3 P 55
26 ♎	8 A 45	27 ♐	3 A 56	26 ♐	9 A 22	26 ♒	9 P 26	26 ♓	6 A 00	26 ♉	9 P 55
28 ♏	4 P 48			28 ♑	1 P 06	29 ♓	0 A 37	28 ♈	10 A 18	29 ♊	6 A 28
30 ♐	9 P 29			30 ♒	3 P 57			30 ♉	4 P 26		

JUL	TIME	AUG	TIME	SEPT	TIME	OCT	TIME	NOV	TIME	DEC	TIME
1 ♋	5 P 15	3 ♍	0 A 44	1 ♎	6 P 31	1 ♏	9 A 04	2 ♑	3 A 34	1 ♒	1 P 01
4 ♌	5 A 40	5 ♎	0 P 51	4 ♏	4 A 18	3 ♐	5 P 01	4 ♒	7 A 09	3 ♓	3 P 36
6 ♍	6 P 43	7 ♏	10 P 35	6 ♐	11 A 38	5 ♑	10 P 08	6 ♓	10 A 16	5 ♈	7 P 01
9 ♎	6 A 15	10 ♐	5 A 03	8 ♑	4 P 11	8 ♒	1 A 43	8 ♈	1 P 10	7 ♉	11 P 32
11 ♏	3 P 37	12 ♑	8 A 06	10 ♒	6 P 46	10 ♓	3 A 43	10 ♉	4 P 33	10 ♊	5 A 34
13 ♐	8 P 31	14 ♒	8 A 36	12 ♓	7 P 11	12 ♈	5 A 12	12 ♊	9 P 35	12 ♋	1 P 46
15 ♑	10 P 03	16 ♓	8 A 07	14 ♈	7 P 11	14 ♉	7 A 29	15 ♋	5 A 26	15 ♌	0 A 39
17 ♒	9 P 46	18 ♈	8 A 34	16 ♉	9 P 19	16 ♊	0 P 07	17 ♌	4 P 29	17 ♍	1 P 21
19 ♓	9 P 34	20 ♉	11 A 39	19 ♊	2 A 48	18 ♋	8 P 32	20 ♍	5 A 20	20 ♎	1 A 52
21 ♈	11 P 13	22 ♊	6 P 39	21 ♋	0 P 10	21 ♌	8 A 14	22 ♎	5 P 16	22 ♏	11 A 45
24 ♉	3 A 57	25 ♋	5 A 10	24 ♌	0 A 34	23 ♍	9 P 09	25 ♏	2 A 04	24 ♐	5 P 40
26 ♊	0 P 05	27 ♌	5 P 49	26 ♍	1 P 30	26 ♎	8 A 35	27 ♐	7 A 33	26 ♑	8 P 21
28 ♋	11 P 05	30 ♍	6 A 46	29 ♎	0 A 53	28 ♏	5 P 12	29 ♑	10 A 42	28 ♒	9 P 21
31 ♌	11 A 43					30 ♐	11 P 11			30 ♓	10 P 19

1944

Table of Moon sign ingresses with dates and times (A = a.m., P = p.m.).

JAN

Date	Sign	Time
2	♈	0 A 37
4	♉	4 A 08
6	♊	11 A 45
8	♋	8 P 50
11	♌	7 A 59
13	♍	8 P 39
16	♎	9 A 29
18	♏	8 P 23
21	♐	3 A 47
23	♑	7 A 23
25	♒	8 A 08
27	♓	7 A 48
29	♈	8 A 16
31	♉	11 A 08

FEB

Date	Sign	Time
2	♊	5 P 22
5	♋	2 A 43
7	♌	2 P 19
10	♍	3 A 08
12	♎	3 P 53
15	♏	3 A 21
17	♐	0 P 15
19	♑	5 P 29
21	♒	7 P 08
23	♓	7 P 33
25	♈	6 P 33
27	♉	7 P 41

MAR

Date	Sign	Time
1	♊	0 A 12
3	♋	8 A 40
5	♌	8 P 20
8	♍	9 A 17
10	♎	9 P 54
13	♏	9 A 12
15	♐	6 P 27
18	♑	1 A 08
20	♒	4 A 50
22	♓	5 A 56
24	♈	5 A 42
26	♉	6 A 04
28	♊	9 A 01
30	♋	4 P 02

APR

Date	Sign	Time
2	♌	2 A 56
4	♍	3 P 48
7	♎	4 A 20
9	♏	3 P 10
11	♐	11 P 58
14	♑	6 A 53
16	♒	11 A 46
18	♓	2 P 27
20	♈	3 P 43
22	♉	4 P 30
24	♊	7 P 03
27	♋	0 A 54
29	♌	10 A 37

MAY

Date	Sign	Time
1	♍	11 P 04
4	♎	11 A 40
6	♏	10 P 15
9	♐	6 A 25
11	♑	0 P 33
13	♒	5 P 09
15	♓	8 P 33
17	♈	11 P 02
20	♉	1 A 17
22	♊	4 A 30
24	♋	10 A 05
26	♌	7 P 08
29	♍	6 A 59
31	♎	7 P 35

JUN

Date	Sign	Time
3	♏	6 A 28
5	♐	2 P 26
7	♑	7 P 38
9	♒	11 P 11
12	♓	1 A 58
14	♈	4 A 41
16	♉	7 A 53
18	♊	0 P 11
20	♋	6 P 31
23	♌	3 A 28
25	♍	2 P 58
28	♎	3 A 39
30	♏	3 P 08

JUL

Date	Sign	Time
2	♐	11 P 33
5	♑	4 A 38
7	♒	7 A 12
9	♓	8 A 40
11	♈	10 A 18
13	♉	1 P 17
15	♊	6 P 14
18	♋	1 A 24
20	♌	10 A 52
22	♍	10 P 26
25	♎	11 A 07
27	♏	11 P 14
30	♐	8 A 48

AUG

Date	Sign	Time
1	♑	2 P 39
3	♒	5 P 09
5	♓	3 P 02
7	♈	3 P 45
9	♉	5 P 45
11	♊	7 P 23
14	♋	11 P 43
16	♌	7 A 06
19	♍	5 P 09
21	♎	5 A 01
24	♏	5 P 44
26	♐	6 A 12
29	♑	4 P 49
31	♒	0 A 06

SEPT

Date	Sign	Time
2	♓	4 A 12
4	♈	3 A 28
6	♉	3 A 33
8	♊	6 A 18
10	♋	0 P 47
12	♌	10 P 54
15	♍	11 A 02
17	♎	10 P 52
20	♏	0 P 12
22	♐	11 P 14
25	♑	7 A 52
27	♒	1 P 09
29	♓	2 P 56

OCT

Date	Sign	Time
1	♈	2 P 29
3	♉	1 P 46
5	♊	3 P 02
7	♋	8 P 02
10	♌	5 A 06
12	♍	5 P 04
15	♎	5 A 54
17	♏	6 P 02
20	♐	4 A 48
22	♑	1 P 47
24	♒	8 P 15
26	♓	11 P 48
29	♈	0 A 52
31	♉	0 A 47

NOV

Date	Sign	Time
2	♊	1 A 33
4	♋	5 A 09
6	♌	0 P 45
9	♍	0 A 01
11	♎	0 P 44
14	♏	0 A 45
16	♐	0 A 00
18	♑	7 P 18
21	♒	1 A 44
23	♓	6 A 16
25	♈	8 A 56
27	♉	10 A 22
29	♊	11 A 55

DEC

Date	Sign	Time
1	♋	3 P 19
3	♌	9 P 58
6	♍	8 A 05
8	♎	8 P 28
11	♏	8 A 41
13	♐	6 P 47
16	♑	2 A 19
18	♒	7 A 43
20	♓	11 A 39
22	♈	2 P 42
24	♉	5 P 25
26	♊	8 P 28
29	♋	0 A 47
31	♌	7 A 22

1945

JAN	TIME	FEB	TIME	MAR	TIME	APR	TIME	MAY	TIME	JUN	TIME
2 ♍	4 P 52	1 ♎	0 P 46	3 ♏	8 A 32	2 ♐	3 A 05	1 ♑	7 P 37	2 ♓	3 P 23
5 ♎	4 A 45	4 ♏	1 A 21	5 ♐	8 P 41	4 ♑	1 P 50	4 ♒	4 A 02	4 ♈	6 P 48
7 ♏	5 P 11	6 ♐	0 P 58	8 ♑	6 A 34	6 ♒	9 P 22	6 ♓	9 A 18	6 ♉	8 P 22
10 ♐	3 A 52	8 ♑	9 P 24	10 ♒	0 P 39	9 ♓	1 A 04	8 ♈	11 A 24	8 ♊	9 P 16
12 ♑	11 A 27	11 ♒	2 A 07	12 ♓	2 P 49	11 ♈	1 A 35	10 ♉	11 A 24	10 ♋	11 P 07
14 ♒	3 P 55	13 ♓	3 A 50	14 ♈	2 P 32	13 ♉	0 A 41	12 ♊	11 A 12	13 ♌	3 A 24
16 ♓	6 P 26	15 ♈	4 A 13	16 ♉	1 P 56	15 ♊	0 A 36	14 ♋	0 P 52	15 ♍	11 A 07
18 ♈	8 P 22	17 ♉	5 A 08	18 ♊	3 P 06	17 ♋	3 A 20	16 ♌	6 P 01	17 ♎	10 P 08
20 ♉	10 P 50	19 ♊	8 A 03	20 ♋	7 P 36	19 ♌	9 A 53	19 ♍	3 A 00	20 ♏	10 A 35
23 ♊	2 A 37	21 ♋	1 P 44	23 ♌	3 A 36	21 ♍	8 P 05	21 ♎	2 P 44	22 ♐	10 P 25
25 ♋	8 A 07	23 ♌	10 P 01	25 ♍	2 P 11	24 ♎	8 A 14	24 ♏	3 A 20	25 ♑	8 A 12
27 ♌	3 P 34	26 ♍	8 A 15	28 ♎	2 A 16	26 ♏	8 P 52	26 ♐	3 P 10	27 ♒	3 P 35
30 ♍	1 A 11	28 ♎	7 P 57	30 ♏	2 P 50	29 ♐	8 A 55	29 ♑	1 A 22	29 ♓	8 P 49
								31 ♒	9 A 34		

JUL	TIME	AUG	TIME	SEPT	TIME	OCT	TIME	NOV	TIME	DEC	TIME
2 ♈	0 A 27	2 ♊	11 A 22	3 ♌	3 A 23	2 ♍	5 P 35	1 ♎	10 A 09	1 ♏	4 A 44
4 ♉	3 A 04	4 ♋	3 P 23	5 ♍	11 A 37	5 ♎	4 A 18	3 ♏	10 P 30	3 ♐	5 P 28
6 ♊	5 A 20	6 ♌	8 P 54	7 ♎	9 P 51	7 ♏	4 P 25	6 ♐	11 A 18	6 ♑	5 A 22
8 ♋	8 A 11	9 ♍	4 A 26	10 ♏	9 A 49	10 ♐	5 A 18	8 ♑	11 P 33	8 ♒	3 P 32
10 ♌	0 P 43	11 ♎	2 P 23	12 ♐	10 P 28	12 ♑	5 P 30	11 ♒	9 A 57	11 ♓	11 P 16
12 ♍	8 P 01	14 ♏	2 A 26	15 ♑	10 A 11	15 ♒	3 A 00	13 ♓	5 P 00	13 ♈	4 A 11
15 ♎	6 A 14	16 ♐	2 P 55	17 ♒	6 P 15	17 ♓	8 A 30	15 ♈	8 P 19	15 ♉	6 A 27
17 ♏	6 P 28	19 ♑	1 A 25	19 ♓	10 P 14	19 ♈	10 A 08	17 ♉	8 P 46	17 ♊	7 A 02
20 ♐	6 A 35	21 ♒	8 A 29	21 ♈	11 P 08	21 ♉	9 A 29	19 ♊	8 P 04	19 ♋	7 A 29
22 ♑	4 P 26	23 ♓	0 P 05	23 ♉	11 P 55	23 ♊	8 A 47	21 ♋	8 P 19	21 ♌	9 A 33
24 ♒	11 P 12	25 ♈	1 P 30	25 ♊	11 P 36	25 ♋	10 A 13	23 ♌	11 P 18	23 ♍	2 P 46
27 ♓	3 A 25	27 ♉	2 P 34	28 ♋	2 A 42	27 ♌	2 P 57	26 ♍	6 A 03	25 ♎	11 P 49
29 ♈	6 A 07	29 ♊	4 P 48	30 ♌	8 A 49	29 ♍	11 P 15	28 ♎	4 P 20	28 ♏	11 A 42
31 ♉	8 A 30	31 ♋	9 P 03							31 ♐	0 A 30

1946

JAN	TIME
2 ♑	0P10
4 ♒	9P32
7 ♓	4A42
9 ♈	9A52
11 ♉	1P23
13 ♊	3P43
15 ♋	5P34
17 ♌	8P11
20 ♍	0A50
22 ♎	8A38
24 ♏	7P43
27 ♐	8A25
29 ♑	8P11

FEB	TIME
1 ♒	5A16
3 ♓	11A30
5 ♈	3P36
7 ♉	6P48
9 ♊	9P47
12 ♋	1A01
14 ♌	4A55
16 ♍	10A07
18 ♎	5P44
21 ♏	4A11
23 ♐	4P42
26 ♑	4A54
28 ♒	2P29

MAR	TIME
2 ♓	8P17
4 ♈	11P20
7 ♉	1A10
9 ♊	3A16
11 ♋	6A34
13 ♌	11A18
15 ♍	5P38
18 ♎	1A47
20 ♏	0P08
23 ♐	0A31
25 ♑	1P15
27 ♒	11P40
30 ♓	6A17

APR	TIME
1 ♈	9A10
3 ♉	10A57
5 ♊	10A29
7 ♋	0P26
9 ♌	4P44
11 ♍	11P28
14 ♎	8A17
16 ♏	7P07
19 ♐	7A30
21 ♑	8P26
24 ♒	7A51
26 ♓	3P45
28 ♈	7P35
30 ♉	8P27

MAY	TIME
2 ♊	8P07
4 ♋	8P31
6 ♌	11P15
9 ♍	5A04
11 ♎	1P57
14 ♏	1A12
16 ♐	1P48
19 ♑	2A40
21 ♒	2P27
23 ♓	11P30
26 ♈	4A55
28 ♉	6A58
30 ♊	6A54

JUN	TIME
1 ♋	7A12
3 ♌	7A48
5 ♍	0P02
7 ♎	8P05
10 ♏	7A08
12 ♐	7P51
15 ♑	8A38
17 ♒	8P11
20 ♓	5A36
22 ♈	0P16
24 ♉	3P49
26 ♊	5P04
28 ♋	5P12
30 ♌	5P55

JUL	TIME
2 ♍	8P56
5 ♎	3A31
7 ♏	1P46
10 ♐	2A21
12 ♑	3P03
15 ♒	2A12
17 ♓	11A11
19 ♈	5P54
21 ♉	10P25
24 ♊	1A15
26 ♋	2A43
28 ♌	4A01
30 ♍	6A41

AUG	TIME
1 ♎	0P09
3 ♏	9P30
6 ♐	9A38
8 ♑	10P19
11 ♒	9A19
13 ♓	5P36
15 ♈	11P33
18 ♉	3A56
20 ♊	7A20
22 ♋	10A07
24 ♌	0P30
26 ♍	4P00
28 ♎	9P25
31 ♏	5A57

SEPT	TIME
2 ♐	6P19
5 ♑	6A21
7 ♒	5P35
10 ♓	1A37
12 ♈	6A41
14 ♉	10A03
16 ♊	0P47
18 ♋	3P44
20 ♌	7P16
23 ♍	0A36
25 ♎	5A47
27 ♏	2P16
30 ♐	1A32

OCT	TIME
2 ♑	2P28
5 ♒	2A19
7 ♓	11A03
9 ♈	3P58
11 ♉	6P18
13 ♊	7P39
15 ♋	9P29
18 ♌	0A42
20 ♍	5A42
22 ♎	0P36
24 ♏	9P47
27 ♐	9A05
29 ♑	9P59

NOV	TIME
1 ♒	10A32
3 ♓	8P22
6 ♈	2A18
8 ♉	4A42
10 ♊	5A07
12 ♋	5A20
14 ♌	7A01
16 ♍	11A10
18 ♎	6P18
21 ♏	4A03
23 ♐	3P46
26 ♑	4A40
28 ♒	5P26

DEC	TIME
1 ♓	4A22
3 ♈	11A44
5 ♉	3P41
7 ♊	4P26
9 ♋	3P48
11 ♌	3P54
13 ♍	6P20
16 ♎	0A18
18 ♏	9A47
20 ♐	9P51
23 ♑	10A51
25 ♒	11P27
28 ♓	10A40
30 ♈	7P23

1947

JAN
Date		TIME
2	♉	1 A 02
4	♊	3 A 22
6	♋	3 A 27
8	♌	2 A 56
10	♍	3 A 50
12	♎	7 A 59
14	♏	4 P 19
17	♐	4 A 06
19	♑	5 P 11
22	♒	5 A 37
24	♓	4 P 23
27	♈	1 A 08
29	♉	7 A 44
31	♊	11 A 53

FEB
Date		TIME
2	♋	1 P 39
4	♌	2 P 02
6	♍	2 P 45
8	♎	5 P 44
11	♏	0 A 35
13	♐	11 A 16
16	♑	0 A 12
18	♒	0 P 39
20	♓	10 P 54
23	♈	6 A 56
25	♉	1 P 07
27	♊	5 P 47

MAR
Date		TIME
1	♋	5 P 36
3	♌	11 P 00
6	♍	0 A 49
8	♎	3 A 55
10	♏	9 A 53
12	♐	7 P 37
15	♑	8 A 02
17	♒	8 P 33
20	♓	6 A 56
22	♈	3 P 17
24	♉	8 P 21
26	♊	11 P 15
29	♋	2 A 26
31	♌	5 A 23

APR
Date		TIME
2	♍	8 A 31
4	♎	0 P 41
6	♏	3 P 46
9	♐	4 A 16
11	♑	4 P 09
14	♒	4 A 50
16	♓	2 P 22
18	♈	11 P 21
21	♉	3 A 53
23	♊	6 A 28
25	♋	8 A 24
27	♌	10 A 46
29	♍	2 P 17

MAY
Date		TIME
1	♎	7 P 27
4	♏	2 A 39
6	♐	0 P 10
8	♑	11 P 53
11	♒	0 P 42
14	♓	0 A 18
16	♈	8 A 55
18	♉	1 P 52
20	♊	3 P 49
22	♋	4 P 29
24	♌	5 P 21
26	♍	7 P 54
29	♎	0 A 58
31	♏	8 A 45

JUN
Date		TIME
2	♐	6 P 57
5	♑	6 A 52
7	♒	7 P 37
10	♓	7 A 46
12	♈	5 P 30
14	♉	11 P 40
17	♊	2 A 19
19	♋	2 A 32
21	♌	2 A 09
23	♍	3 A 07
25	♎	6 A 31
27	♏	2 P 18
30	♐	0 A 49

JUL
Date		TIME
2	♑	1 P 03
5	♒	1 A 49
7	♓	2 P 03
10	♈	0 A 32
12	♉	8 A 10
14	♊	0 P 17
16	♋	1 P 14
18	♌	0 P 35
20	♍	0 P 20
22	♎	2 P 36
24	♏	8 P 46
27	♐	6 A 44
29	♑	7 P 02

AUG
Date		TIME
1	♒	7 P 50
3	♓	7 P 48
6	♈	6 A 19
8	♉	3 P 37
10	♊	8 P 14
12	♋	10 P 45
14	♌	11 P 06
16	♍	10 P 53
19	♎	0 A 10
21	♏	4 A 40
23	♐	1 P 36
26	♑	1 A 32
28	♒	2 P 19
31	♓	2 A 02

SEPT
Date		TIME
2	♈	0 P 04
4	♉	8 P 08
7	♊	2 A 15
9	♋	6 A 10
11	♌	8 A 10
13	♍	8 A 52
15	♎	10 A 18
17	♏	2 P 14
19	♐	9 P 55
22	♑	9 A 00
24	♒	9 P 37
27	♓	9 A 24
29	♈	6 P 57

OCT
Date		TIME
2	♉	2 A 13
4	♊	7 A 43
6	♋	11 A 48
8	♌	2 P 41
10	♍	4 P 58
12	♎	8 P 26
14	♏	11 P 50
17	♐	6 A 57
19	♑	5 P 16
22	♒	5 A 40
24	♓	5 P 44
27	♈	3 A 28
29	♉	10 A 16
31	♊	2 P 36

NOV
Date		TIME
2	♋	5 P 32
4	♌	8 P 04
6	♍	10 P 58
9	♎	2 A 45
11	♏	8 A 06
13	♐	3 P 35
16	♑	1 A 41
18	♒	1 P 45
21	♓	2 A 15
23	♈	0 P 53
25	♉	8 P 02
27	♊	11 P 35
30	♋	1 A 31

DEC
Date		TIME
2	♌	2 A 32
4	♍	4 A 26
6	♎	8 A 17
8	♏	2 P 27
10	♐	10 P 53
13	♑	9 A 16
15	♒	9 P 17
18	♓	9 A 59
20	♈	9 P 34
23	♉	6 A 08
25	♊	10 A 46
27	♋	0 P 03
29	♌	11 A 43
31	♍	11 A 47

1948

JAN	TIME	FEB	TIME	MAR	TIME	APR	TIME	MAY	TIME	JUN	TIME
2 ♎	3 P 12	1 ♏	2 A 33	1 ♐	5 P 45	2 ♒	11 P 20	2 ♓	7 P 43	1 ♈	3 P 53
4 ♏	7 P 54	3 ♐	10 A 26	4 ♑	3 A 53	5 ♓	11 A 56	5 ♈	7 A 26	4 ♉	1 A 39
7 ♐	4 A 44	5 ♑	9 P 31	6 ♒	4 P 15	7 ♈	11 P 10	7 ♉	4 P 45	6 ♊	8 A 04
9 ♑	3 P 42	8 ♒	9 A 59	9 ♓	4 A 52	10 ♉	8 A 57	9 ♊	11 P 16	8 ♋	11 A 28
12 ♒	3 A 54	10 ♓	10 P 36	11 ♈	4 P 32	12 ♊	4 P 18	12 ♋	3 A 36	10 ♌	1 P 11
14 ♓	4 P 39	13 ♈	10 A 36	14 ♉	2 A 39	14 ♋	9 P 39	14 ♌	6 A 38	12 ♍	2 P 49
17 ♈	4 A 41	15 ♉	9 P 05	16 ♊	10 A 44	17 ♌	1 A 14	16 ♍	9 A 15	14 ♎	5 P 35
19 ♉	2 P 53	18 ♊	4 A 52	18 ♋	3 P 54	19 ♍	3 A 29	18 ♎	0 P 07	16 ♏	10 P 07
21 ♊	8 P 55	20 ♋	9 A 06	20 ♌	6 P 55	21 ♎	5 A 17	20 ♏	3 P 57	19 ♐	4 A 31
23 ♋	11 P 18	22 ♌	10 A 06	22 ♍	7 P 41	23 ♏	7 A 51	22 ♐	3 P 46	21 ♑	0 P 52
25 ♌	10 P 58	24 ♍	9 A 21	24 ♎	8 P 04	25 ♐	0 P 31	25 ♑	5 A 10	23 ♒	11 P 17
27 ♍	10 P 00	26 ♎	9 A 07	26 ♏	9 P 55	27 ♑	8 P 26	27 ♒	3 P 31	26 ♓	11 A 24
29 ♎	10 P 35	28 ♏	11 A 24	29 ♐	2 A 50	30 ♒	7 A 17	30 ♓	3 A 45	28 ♈	11 P 54
				31 ♑	11 A 33						

JUL	TIME	AUG	TIME	SEPT	TIME	OCT	TIME	NOV	TIME	DEC	TIME
1 ♉	10 A 39	2 ♋	10 A 17	2 ♍	6 P 20	2 ♎	4 A 31	2 ♐	6 P 50	2 ♑	9 A 17
3 ♊	5 P 44	4 ♌	8 A 11	4 ♎	5 P 38	4 ♏	5 A 51	4 ♑	11 P 45	4 ♒	5 P 35
5 ♋	9 P 02	6 ♍	7 A 26	6 ♏	6 P 38	6 ♐	7 A 58	7 ♒	7 A 10	7 ♓	4 A 48
7 ♌	9 P 52	8 ♎	7 A 33	8 ♐	10 P 57	8 ♑	2 P 32	9 ♓	8 P 34	9 ♈	5 P 29
9 ♍	10 P 06	10 ♏	9 A 58	11 ♑	6 A 59	11 ♒	0 A 45	12 ♈	9 A 11	12 ♉	5 A 06
11 ♎	11 P 35	12 ♐	3 P 52	13 ♒	5 P 59	13 ♓	1 P 03	14 ♉	8 P 21	14 ♊	1 P 43
14 ♏	3 A 32	15 ♑	0 A 54	16 ♓	6 A 26	16 ♈	0 A 34	17 ♊	4 A 59	16 ♋	6 P 57
16 ♐	10 A 12	17 ♒	0 P 02	18 ♈	7 P 01	18 ♉	0 P 54	19 ♋	11 A 10	18 ♌	10 P 02
18 ♑	7 P 15	20 ♓	0 A 23	21 ♉	6 A 44	20 ♊	10 P 12	21 ♌	3 P 31	21 ♍	0 A 03
21 ♒	6 A 03	22 ♈	1 P 04	23 ♊	4 P 37	23 ♋	6 A 13	23 ♍	6 P 47	23 ♎	3 A 00
23 ♓	6 P 14	25 ♉	1 A 00	25 ♋	11 P 40	25 ♌	10 A 09	25 ♎	9 P 32	25 ♏	6 A 40
26 ♈	6 A 57	27 ♊	11 A 39	28 ♌	3 A 30	27 ♍	0 P 53	28 ♏	0 A 03	27 ♐	11 A 28
28 ♉	6 P 30	29 ♋	4 P 30	30 ♍	4 A 38	29 ♎	0 P 51	30 ♐	3 A 55	29 ♑	5 P 49
31 ♊	2 A 56	31 ♌	6 P 11			31 ♏	3 P 33				

1949

JAN.		TIME	FEB		TIME	MAR		TIME	APR		TIME	MAY		TIME	JUN		TIME
1	≈	2 A 10	2	♈	9 A 05	1	♈	3 P 36	2	♊	10 P 00	2	♋	0 P 42	1	♌	0 A 34
3	♓	0 P 58	4	♉	9 P 55	4	♉	4 A 31	5	♋	7 A 07	4	♌	7 P 08	3	♍	4 A 52
6	♈	1 A 39	7	♊	8 A 37	6	♊	4 P 02	7	♌	0 P 58	6	♍	11 P 07	5	♎	7 A 58
8	♉	2 P 01	9	♋	3 P 19	9	♋	0 A 15	9	♍	3 P 30	9	♎	1 A 05	7	♏	10 A 14
10	♊	11 P 25	11	♌	5 P 06	11	♌	4 A 28	11	♎	3 P 55	11	♏	1 A 53	9	♐	0 P 24
13	♋	4 A 52	13	♍	6 P 06	13	♍	5 A 21	13	♏	3 P 29	13	♐	3 A 00	11	♑	3 P 42
15	♌	4 A 06	15	♎	5 P 46	15	♎	4 A 40	15	♐	4 P 27	15	♑	6 A 00	13	≈	9 P 31
17	♍	7 A 52	17	♏	6 P 57	17	♏	4 A 29	17	♑	7 P 46	17	≈	0 P 19	16	♓	6 A 42
19	♎	9 A 04	19	♐	10 P 54	19	♐	6 A 35	20	≈	4 A 04	19	♓	10 P 29	18	♈	6 P 45
21	♏	0 N 00	22	♑	5 A 53	21	♑	0 P 37	22	♓	3 P 08	22	♈	11 A 01	21	♉	7 A 28
23	♐	5 P 10	24	≈	3 P 26	23	≈	9 P 14	25	♈	4 A 00	24	♉	11 P 39	23	♊	6 P 16
26	♑	0 A 24	27	♓	2 A 55	26	♓	8 A 51	27	♉	4 P 39	27	♊	10 A 25	26	♋	1 A 58
28	≈	9 A 28				28	♈	9 P 42	30	♊	3 A 45	29	♋	6 P 36	28	♌	6 A 59
30	♓	8 P 28				31	♉	10 A 29							30	♍	10 A 26

JUL		TIME	AUG		TIME	SEPT		TIME	OCT		TIME	NOV		TIME	DEC		TIME
2	♎	1 P 22	3	♐	1 A 26	1	♑	0 P 06	1	♓	1 A 18	2	♉	5 A 34	2	♉	1 A 20
4	♏	4 P 23	5	♑	6 A 37	3	≈	7 P 39	3	♈	11 A 21	4	♊	6 P 36	4	♊	1 P 28
6	♐	7 P 46	7	≈	1 P 34	6	♓	5 A 29	5	♉	11 P 29	7	♋	6 A 53	6	♋	11 P 29
9	♑	0 A 04	9	♓	10 P 49	8	♈	5 P 13	8	♊	0 P 26	9	♌	5 P 33	9	♌	7 A 26
11	≈	6 A 11	12	♈	10 A 20	11	♉	6 A 11	11	♋	1 A 00	12	♍	1 A 56	11	♍	1 P 30
13	♓	3 P 02	14	♉	11 P 18	13	♊	6 P 44	13	♌	11 A 50	14	♎	7 A 40	13	♎	5 P 42
16	♈	2 A 45	17	♊	11 A 22	16	♋	4 A 47	15	♍	7 P 30	16	♏	10 A 35	15	♏	8 P 12
18	♉	3 P 35	19	♋	8 P 09	18	♌	11 A 03	17	♎	11 P 37	18	♐	11 A 18	17	♐	9 P 32
21	♊	2 A 53	22	♌	1 A 02	20	♍	1 P 32	20	♏	0 A 44	20	♑	11 A 15	19	♑	11 P 03
23	♋	10 A 51	24	♍	2 A 54	22	♎	1 P 41	22	♐	0 A 19	22	≈	0 P 20	22	≈	2 A 30
25	♌	3 P 18	26	♎	3 A 25	24	♏	1 P 21	24	♑	0 A 11	24	♓	4 P 28	24	♓	9 A 22
27	♍	5 P 35	28	♏	4 A 21	26	♐	2 P 22	26	≈	2 A 16	27	♈	0 A 40	26	♈	8 P 07
29	♎	7 P 21	30	♐	7 A 03	28	♑	6 P 11	28	♓	7 A 54	29	♉	0 P 18	29	♉	8 A 59
31	♏	9 P 46							30	♈	5 P 23				31	♊	9 P 13

1950

JAN	TIME	FEB	TIME	MAR	TIME	APR	TIME	MAY	TIME	JUN	TIME
3 ♋	6 A 54	1 ♌	10 P 30	1 ♌	8 A 27	2 ♎	0 A 37	1 ♏	11 A 38	1 ♑	9 P 30
5 ♌	1 P 56	4 ♍	2 A 34	3 ♍	0 P 23	4 ♏	0 A 35	3 ♐	10 A 51	3 ♒	11 P 25
7 ♍	7 P 05	6 ♎	5 A 18	5 ♎	1 P 59	6 ♐	0 A 40	5 ♑	11 A 08	6 ♓	5 A 02
9 ♎	11 P 07	8 ♏	7 A 50	7 ♏	1 P 17	8 ♑	2 A 34	7 ♒	2 P 24	8 ♈	2 P 46
12 ♏	2 A 26	10 ♐	10 A 52	9 ♐	4 P 39	10 ♒	7 A 28	9 ♓	9 P 39	11 ♉	3 A 13
14 ♐	5 A 16	12 ♑	2 P 45	11 ♑	8 P 11	12 ♓	3 P 39	12 ♈	8 A 47	13 ♊	4 P 03
16 ♑	8 A 07	14 ♒	7 P 59	14 ♒	1 A 55	15 ♈	2 A 33	14 ♉	8 P 59	16 ♋	3 A 43
18 ♒	0 P 07	17 ♓	3 A 14	16 ♓	10 A 01	17 ♉	2 P 59	17 ♊	9 A 52	18 ♌	1 P 36
20 ♓	6 P 45	19 ♈	1 P 02	18 ♈	8 P 23	20 ♊	3 A 54	19 ♋	9 P 48	20 ♍	9 P 28
23 ♈	4 A 41	22 ♉	1 A 12	21 ♉	8 A 32	22 ♋	3 P 59	22 ♌	8 A 04	22 ♎	3 P 06
25 ♉	5 P 07	24 ♊	2 P 02	23 ♊	9 P 26	25 ♌	1 A 52	24 ♍	3 P 47	25 ♏	6 A 16
28 ♊	5 A 40	27 ♋	0 A 58	26 ♋	9 A 15	27 ♍	8 A 27	26 ♎	8 P 21	27 ♐	7 A 25
30 ♋	3 P 47			28 ♌	6 P 00	29 ♎	11 A 25	28 ♏	8 P 21	29 ♑	7 A 45
				30 ♍	10 P 55			30 ♐	9 P 43		

JUL	TIME	AUG	TIME	SEPT	TIME	OCT	TIME	NOV	TIME	DEC	TIME
1 ♒	9 A 21	2 ♈	7 A 05	1 ♉	2 A 21	3 ♋	10 A 58	2 ♌	5 A 34	1 ♍	9 P 35
3 ♓	1 P 52	4 ♉	6 P 07	3 ♊	2 P 47	5 ♌	9 P 36	4 ♍	2 P 19	4 ♎	4 A 36
5 ♈	10 P 28	7 ♊	6 A 43	6 ♋	2 A 51	8 ♍	4 A 49	6 ♎	7 P 05	6 ♏	7 A 29
8 ♉	10 A 13	9 ♋	4 P 28	8 ♌	0 P 33	10 ♎	8 A 26	8 ♏	8 P 26	8 ♐	7 A 15
10 ♊	11 P 01	12 ♌	3 A 33	10 ♍	6 P 51	12 ♏	9 A 44	10 ♐	7 P 52	10 ♑	6 A 38
13 ♋	10 A 34	14 ♍	10 A 02	12 ♎	10 P 25	14 ♐	9 A 45	12 ♑	7 P 29	12 ♒	6 A 12
15 ♌	7 P 50	16 ♎	2 P 30	15 ♏	0 A 26	16 ♑	10 A 55	14 ♒	9 P 20	14 ♓	10 A 12
18 ♍	3 A 03	18 ♏	5 P 48	17 ♐	2 A 13	18 ♒	2 P 28	17 ♓	2 A 44	16 ♈	6 P 02
20 ♎	8 A 32	20 ♐	8 P 35	19 ♑	4 A 50	20 ♓	8 P 56	19 ♈	11 A 39	19 ♉	5 A 11
22 ♏	0 P 27	22 ♑	11 P 25	21 ♒	9 A 01	23 ♈	6 A 00	21 ♉	11 P 09	21 ♊	5 P 48
24 ♐	2 P 54	25 ♒	2 A 55	23 ♓	3 P 11	25 ♉	5 P 04	24 ♊	11 A 38	24 ♋	6 A 17
26 ♑	4 P 39	27 ♓	8 A 04	25 ♈	11 P 34	28 ♊	5 A 22	27 ♋	0 A 12	26 ♌	5 P 44
28 ♒	6 P 58	29 ♈	3 P 47	28 ♉	10 A 09	30 ♋	6 P 02	29 ♌	0 P 02	29 ♍	3 A 38
30 ♓	11 P 24			30 ♊	10 P 27					31 ♎	11 A 20

1951

JAN	TIME	FEB	TIME	MAR	TIME	APR	TIME	MAY	TIME	JUN	TIME
2 ♏	4 P 00	1 ♐	1 A 13	2 ♑	9 A 30	2 ♓	10 P 47	2 ♈	11 A 27	1 ♉	2 A 35
4 ♐	5 P 36	3 ♑	5 A 13	4 ♒	0 P 10	5 ♈	5 A 18	4 ♉	8 P 48	3 ♊	2 P 03
6 ♑	5 P 32	5 ♒	4 A 05	6 ♓	3 P 46	7 ♉	1 P 53	7 ♊	7 A 51	6 ♋	2 P 31
8 ♒	5 P 38	7 ♓	6 A 32	8 ♈	9 P 20	10 ♊	0 A 43	9 ♋	7 P 02	8 ♌	3 P 11
10 ♓	8 P 02	9 ♈	11 A 42	11 ♉	5 A 35	12 ♋	1 P 05	12 ♌	8 A 49	11 ♍	2 A 43
13 ♈	1 A 24	11 ♉	8 P 36	13 ♊	4 P 37	15 ♌	1 A 14	14 ♍	7 P 40	13 ♎	11 A 30
15 ♉	0 P 10	14 ♊	8 A 19	16 ♋	5 A 05	17 ♍	11 A 07	17 ♎	2 A 59	15 ♏	4 P 13
18 ♊	0 A 36	16 ♋	8 P 49	18 ♌	4 P 43	19 ♎	5 P 09	19 ♏	6 A 19	17 ♐	5 P 24
20 ♋	1 P 06	19 ♌	7 A 59	21 ♍	1 A 34	21 ♏	7 P 52	21 ♐	6 A 42	19 ♑	5 P 38
23 ♌	3 A 17	21 ♍	4 P 41	23 ♎	7 A 18	23 ♐	8 P 40	23 ♑	6 A 08	21 ♒	4 P 07
25 ♍	9 A 25	23 ♎	10 P 54	25 ♏	10 A 35	25 ♑	9 P 22	25 ♒	6 A 45	23 ♓	5 P 53
27 ♎	4 P 45	26 ♏	3 A 29	27 ♐	0 P 40	27 ♒	11 P 36	27 ♓	10 A 06	25 ♈	11 P 17
29 ♏	10 P 47	28 ♐	6 A 49	29 ♑	2 P 51	30 ♓	4 A 16	29 ♈	4 P 55	28 ♉	8 A 19
				31 ♒	6 P 04					30 ♊	7 P 53

JUL	TIME	AUG	TIME	SEPT	TIME	OCT	TIME	NOV	TIME	DEC	TIME
3 ♋	8 A 27	2 ♌	3 A 06	3 ♏	5 A 29	2 ♐	6 P 21	1 ♑	5 A 18	2 ♒	3 P 46
5 ♌	9 P 00	4 ♍	2 P 17	5 ♐	11 A 49	4 ♑	9 P 47	3 ♒	6 A 40	4 ♓	6 P 21
8 ♍	8 A 35	6 ♎	11 P 30	7 ♑	4 P 10	7 ♒	0 A 30	5 ♓	8 A 45	6 ♈	11 P 22
10 ♎	6 P 01	9 ♏	6 A 21	9 ♒	7 P 05	9 ♓	3 A 20	7 ♈	0 P 23	9 ♉	7 A 05
13 ♏	12 A 12	11 ♐	10 A 29	11 ♓	9 P 12	11 ♈	6 A 47	9 ♉	5 P 54	11 ♊	4 P 55
15 ♐	2 A 59	13 ♑	12 P 18	13 ♈	11 P 24	13 ♉	11 A 19	12 ♊	1 A 09	14 ♋	4 A 23
17 ♑	3 A 13	15 ♒	0 P 54	16 ♉	2 A 50	15 ♊	5 P 40	14 ♋	10 A 16	16 ♌	5 P 05
19 ♒	2 A 43	17 ♓	2 P 20	18 ♊	8 A 44	18 ♋	2 A 26	16 ♌	9 P 30	19 ♍	5 A 50
21 ♓	3 A 33	19 ♈	5 P 01	20 ♋	5 P 50	20 ♌	1 P 43	19 ♍	10 A 12	21 ♎	4 P 37
23 ♈	7 A 24	21 ♉	11 P 31	23 ♌	5 A 50	23 ♍	2 A 23	21 ♎	10 P 32	23 ♏	11 P 31
25 ♉	3 P 08	24 ♊	9 A 28	25 ♍	6 P 05	25 ♎	1 P 59	24 ♏	8 A 06	26 ♐	2 A 22
28 ♊	2 A 09	26 ♋	9 P 44	28 ♎	5 A 01	27 ♏	10 P 20	26 ♐	1 P 31	28 ♑	2 A 22
30 ♋	2 P 42	29 ♌	10 A 10	30 ♏	1 P 08	30 ♐	3 A 06	28 ♑	3 P 18	30 ♒	1 A 38
		31 ♍	8 P 58					30 ♒	3 P 23		

1952

JAN

Day		TIME
1	♓	2 A 26
3	♈	5 A 47
5	♉	0 P 57
7	♊	11 P 13
10	♋	11 A 00
12	♌	11 P 42
15	♍	0 P 12
17	♎	11 P 14
20	♏	7 A 28
22	♐	0 P 20
24	♑	1 P 38
26	♒	1 P 07
28	♓	0 P 59
30	♈	2 P 45

FEB

Day		TIME
1	♉	8 P 06
4	♊	5 A 19
6	♋	5 P 18
9	♌	6 A 13
11	♍	6 P 10
14	♎	4 A 59
16	♏	1 P 59
18	♐	7 P 52
20	♑	10 P 57
22	♒	11 P 49
24	♓	11 P 51
27	♈	1 A 05
29	♉	4 A 54

MAR

Day		TIME
2	♊	0 P 36
5	♋	0 A 06
7	♌	1 P 57
10	♍	1 A 02
12	♎	11 A 27
14	♏	7 P 25
17	♐	1 A 30
19	♑	5 A 32
21	♒	8 A 20
23	♓	9 A 37
25	♈	11 A 21
27	♉	2 P 43
29	♊	9 P 22

APR

Day		TIME
1	♋	7 A 48
3	♌	8 P 45
6	♍	8 A 50
8	♎	6 P 53
11	♏	2 A 12
13	♐	7 A 16
15	♑	11 A 29
17	♒	2 P 21
19	♓	4 P 53
21	♈	8 P 12
24	♉	0 A 21
26	♊	6 A 49
28	♋	4 P 23

MAY

Day		TIME
1	♌	4 A 24
3	♍	5 P 07
6	♎	3 A 27
8	♏	10 A 32
10	♐	2 P 45
12	♑	5 P 24
14	♒	7 P 44
16	♓	10 P 26
19	♈	2 A 20
21	♉	7 A 33
23	♊	2 P 51
26	♋	0 A 29
28	♌	0 P 12
31	♍	1 A 02

JUN

Day		TIME
2	♎	0 P 34
4	♏	8 P 15
7	♐	0 A 20
9	♑	1 A 53
11	♒	2 A 58
13	♓	4 A 17
15	♈	7 A 48
17	♉	1 P 18
19	♊	9 P 31
22	♋	7 A 41
24	♌	7 P 30
27	♍	8 A 09
29	♎	8 P 21

JUL

Day		TIME
2	♏	5 A 18
4	♐	10 A 38
6	♑	0 P 20
8	♒	0 P 10
10	♓	0 N 00
12	♈	2 P 05
14	♉	8 P 37
17	♊	3 A 03
19	♋	1 A 37
22	♌	2 P 26
24	♍	2 A 36
27	♎	1 P 08
29	♏	0 A 48
31	♐	7 P 57

AUG

Day		TIME
2	♑	10 P 52
4	♒	11 P 26
6	♓	10 P 42
8	♈	11 P 08
11	♉	2 A 01
13	♊	8 A 36
15	♋	7 P 24
18	♌	7 A 23
20	♍	8 P 04
23	♎	8 A 01
25	♏	6 P 21
28	♐	2 A 45
30	♑	7 A 41

SEPT

Day		TIME
1	♒	9 A 25
3	♓	9 A 10
5	♈	9 A 10
7	♉	11 A 10
10	♊	4 P 27
12	♋	1 A 42
15	♌	2 P 15
17	♍	2 A 44
19	♎	2 P 11
22	♏	0 A 28
24	♐	8 A 28
26	♑	2 P 15
28	♒	5 P 48
30	♓	6 P 49

OCT

Day		TIME
2	♈	7 P 45
4	♉	9 P 30
7	♊	1 A 42
9	♋	9 A 34
11	♌	9 P 10
14	♍	10 A 00
16	♎	9 P 52
19	♏	7 A 02
21	♐	2 P 20
23	♑	7 P 41
26	♒	0 A 17
28	♓	2 A 12
30	♈	4 A 27

NOV

Day		TIME
1	♉	7 A 14
3	♊	11 A 39
5	♋	6 P 28
8	♌	5 A 24
10	♍	3 P 42
13	♎	3 A 53
15	♏	1 P 37
17	♐	9 P 53
20	♑	1 A 55
22	♒	5 A 15
24	♓	4 A 57
26	♈	10 A 48
28	♉	2 P 49
30	♊	8 P 13

DEC

Day		TIME
3	♋	3 A 30
5	♌	1 P 35
8	♍	2 A 02
10	♎	2 P 36
13	♏	0 A 56
15	♐	7 A 30
17	♑	10 A 41
19	♒	0 P 20
21	♓	2 P 00
23	♈	4 P 21
25	♉	8 P 53
28	♊	2 A 58
30	♋	11 A 15

1953

JAN	TIME
1 ♌	9 P 34
4 ♍	9 A 36
6 ♎	10 P 30
9 ♏	9 A 53
11 ♐	5 P 29
13 ♑	9 P 11
15 ♒	10 P 10
17 ♓	10 P 19
19 ♈	10 P 17
22 ♉	2 A 27
24 ♊	8 A 32
26 ♋	5 P 25
29 ♌	4 A 28
31 ♍	4 P 27

FEB	TIME
3 ♎	5 A 24
5 ♏	9 P 19
8 ♐	2 A 35
10 ♑	7 A 23
12 ♒	9 A 08
14 ♓	8 A 53
16 ♈	8 A 32
18 ♉	9 A 52
20 ♊	2 P 47
22 ♋	11 P 09
25 ♌	11 A 37
27 ♍	10 P 59

MAR	TIME
2 ♎	11 A 24
4 ♏	11 P 31
7 ♐	9 A 53
9 ♑	4 P 12
11 ♒	7 P 38
13 ♓	7 P 54
15 ♈	7 P 14
17 ♉	7 P 44
19 ♊	10 P 51
22 ♋	5 A 42
24 ♌	4 P 50
27 ♍	5 A 18
29 ♎	5 P 51

APR	TIME
1 ♏	5 A 27
3 ♐	3 P 33
5 ♑	10 P 56
8 ♒	3 A 46
10 ♓	5 A 38
12 ♈	6 A 00
14 ♉	6 A 33
16 ♊	8 A 47
18 ♋	2 P 04
20 ♌	11 P 53
23 ♍	0 P 12
26 ♎	1 A 00
28 ♏	0 P 12
30 ♐	9 P 09

MAY	TIME
3 ♒	4 A 11
5 ♒	9 A 30
7 ♓	0 P 51
9 ♈	2 P 48
11 ♉	4 P 18
13 ♊	6 P 44
15 ♋	11 P 36
18 ♌	7 A 57
20 ♍	7 P 36
23 ♎	8 A 12
25 ♏	7 P 36
28 ♐	4 A 26
30 ♑	10 A 32

JUN	TIME
1 ♒	2 P 45
3 ♓	6 P 25
5 ♈	8 P 58
7 ♉	10 P 43
10 ♊	2 A 22
12 ♋	7 A 30
14 ♌	3 P 30
17 ♍	3 A 32
19 ♎	4 P 06
22 ♏	4 A 15
24 ♐	1 P 17
26 ♑	6 P 37
28 ♒	10 P 03

JUL	TIME
1 ♓	0 A 12
3 ♈	2 A 14
5 ♉	5 A 29
7 ♊	10 A 04
9 ♋	4 P 25
12 ♌	0 A 52
14 ♍	11 A 14
16 ♎	11 P 48
19 ♏	0 P 12
21 ♐	10 P 19
24 ♑	4 A 28
26 ♒	7 A 13
28 ♓	8 A 15
30 ♈	9 A 07

AUG	TIME
1 ♉	10 A 50
3 ♊	3 P 26
5 ♋	10 P 14
8 ♌	7 A 23
10 ♍	6 P 19
13 ♎	6 A 45
15 ♏	7 P 33
18 ♐	6 A 38
20 ♑	2 P 16
22 ♒	5 P 21
24 ♓	6 P 22
26 ♈	5 P 53
28 ♉	6 P 28
30 ♊	9 P 30

SEPT	TIME
2 ♋	3 A 38
4 ♌	1 P 11
7 ♍	1 A 00
9 ♎	1 P 00
12 ♏	1 A 44
14 ♐	1 P 22
16 ♑	10 P 33
19 ♒	3 A 10
21 ♓	4 A 57
23 ♈	8 A 31
25 ♉	4 A 41
27 ♊	5 A 35
29 ♋	10 A 13

OCT	TIME
1 ♌	7 P 02
4 ♍	6 A 39
6 ♎	7 P 20
9 ♏	7 A 48
11 ♐	7 P 24
14 ♑	4 A 41
16 ♒	11 A 18
18 ♓	2 P 39
20 ♈	3 P 27
22 ♉	3 P 04
24 ♊	3 P 52
26 ♋	6 P 55
29 ♌	2 A 14
31 ♍	1 P 01

NOV	TIME
3 ♎	2 A 02
5 ♏	2 P 22
8 ♐	1 A 15
10 ♑	10 A 29
12 ♒	5 P 23
14 ♓	7 P 53
17 ♈	0 A 19
19 ♉	1 A 25
21 ♊	2 A 18
23 ♋	4 A 59
25 ♌	10 A 53
27 ♍	8 P 48
30 ♎	9 A 22

DEC	TIME
2 ♏	9 P 53
5 ♐	8 A 33
7 ♑	5 P 06
9 ♒	11 P 01
12 ♓	3 A 36
14 ♈	6 A 54
16 ♉	9 A 25
18 ♊	11 A 40
20 ♋	3 P 00
22 ♌	8 P 37
25 ♍	5 A 15
27 ♎	5 P 18
30 ♏	6 A 07

1954

Top half (January – June)

JAN	TIME	FEB	TIME	MAR	TIME	APR	TIME	MAY	TIME	JUN	TIME
1 ♐	5 P 18	1 ♒	3 P 26	2 ♒	1 A 44	2 ♈	3 P 13	2 ♉	1 A 35	2 ♋	0 P 51
4 ♑	1 A 06	4 ♓	5 P 59	4 ♓	4 A 01	4 ♉	2 P 51	4 ♊	1 A 15	4 ♌	4 P 31
6 ♒	6 A 01	6 ♈	7 P 25	6 ♈	4 A 26	6 ♊	2 P 59	6 ♋	2 A 43	6 ♍	11 P 55
8 ♓	9 A 59	8 ♉	9 P 11	8 ♉	4 A 50	8 ♋	5 P 52	8 ♌	7 A 28	9 ♎	11 A 00
10 ♈	0 P 31	11 ♊	0 A 21	10 ♊	6 A 30	11 ♌	0 A 22	10 ♍	4 P 11	12 ♏	0 A 06
12 ♉	3 P 15	13 ♋	5 A 36	12 ♋	11 A 08	13 ♍	10 A 14	13 ♎	4 A 20	14 ♐	0 N 00
14 ♊	6 P 40	15 ♌	0 P 30	14 ♌	6 P 25	15 ♎	10 P 23	15 ♏	5 P 12	16 ♑	10 P 19
16 ♋	11 P 22	17 ♍	9 P 50	17 ♍	4 A 31	18 ♏	10 P 59	18 ♐	5 A 12	19 ♒	6 A 28
19 ♌	5 A 20	20 ♎	9 A 11	19 ♎	4 P 02	20 ♐	11 P 18	20 ♑	4 P 03	21 ♓	0 P 43
21 ♍	1 P 57	22 ♏	9 P 34	22 ♏	4 A 29	23 ♑	10 A 38	23 ♒	0 A 55	23 ♈	4 P 50
24 ♎	1 A 30	25 ♐	9 A 00	24 ♐	5 P 09	25 ♒	7 P 14	25 ♓	7 A 12	25 ♉	7 P 46
26 ♏	2 P 03	27 ♑	7 P 49	27 ♑	4 A 01	28 ♓	0 A 21	27 ♈	10 A 31	27 ♊	9 P 17
29 ♐	1 A 50			29 ♒	11 A 18	30 ♈	1 A 53	29 ♉	0 N 00	29 ♋	11 P 10
31 ♑	10 A 33			31 ♓	2 P 50			31 ♊	11 A 50		

Bottom half (July – December)

JUL	TIME	AUG	TIME	SEPT	TIME	OCT	TIME	NOV	TIME	DEC	TIME
2 ♌	2 A 20	3 ♎	2 A 57	1 ♏	10 P 41	1 ♐	6 P 31	3 ♒	0 M 00	2 ♓	2 P 21
4 ♍	8 A 32	5 ♏	3 P 01	4 ♐	11 A 23	4 ♑	6 A 53	5 ♓	7 A 24	4 ♈	7 P 25
6 ♎	6 P 45	8 ♐	3 A 52	6 ♑	11 P 08	6 ♒	4 P 25	7 ♈	10 A 58	6 ♉	9 P 32
9 ♏	7 A 23	10 ♑	2 P 27	9 ♒	7 A 28	8 ♓	10 P 08	9 ♉	11 A 04	8 ♊	9 P 29
11 ♐	7 P 39	12 ♒	9 P 44	11 ♓	0 N 00	11 ♈	0 A 01	11 ♊	10 A 36	10 ♋	9 P 28
14 ♑	5 A 54	15 ♓	2 A 10	13 ♈	1 P 27	13 ♉	0 A 17	13 ♋	10 A 36	12 ♌	11 P 20
16 ♒	1 P 15	17 ♈	4 A 34	15 ♉	2 P 17	15 ♊	11 P 51	15 ♌	1 P 45	15 ♍	4 A 07
18 ♓	6 P 16	19 ♉	6 A 33	17 ♊	3 P 21	17 ♋	1 A 21	17 ♍	7 P 50	17 ♎	1 P 11
21 ♈	0 A 13	21 ♊	9 A 13	19 ♋	6 P 25	19 ♌	5 A 44	20 ♎	6 A 13	20 ♏	1 A 20
23 ♉	4 A 53	23 ♋	1 P 04	22 ♌	0 A 05	21 ♍	1 P 55	22 ♏	6 P 40	22 ♐	1 P 48
25 ♊	7 A 36	25 ♌	6 P 31	24 ♍	8 A 12	24 ♎	0 A 13	25 ♐	7 A 23	25 ♑	1 A 46
27 ♋	10 A 48	28 ♍	1 A 41	26 ♎	6 P 07	26 ♏	0 P 24	27 ♑	7 P 04	27 ♒	11 A 49
29 ♌	3 P 10	30 ♎	11 A 03	29 ♏	5 A 57	29 ♐	0 A 55	30 ♒	6 A 00	29 ♓	7 P 56
31 ♍	8 P 09					31 ♑	1 P 12				

1955

JAN	TIME	FEB	TIME	MAR	TIME	APR	TIME	MAY	TIME	JUN	TIME
1 ♈	1 A 46	1 ♊	2 P 09	2 ♋	10 P 47	1 ♌	8 A 29	3 ♎	4 A 39	1 ♏	9 P 24
3 ♉	5 A 29	3 ♋	4 P 34	5 ♌	2 A 43	3 ♍	2 P 37	5 ♏	3 P 21	4 ♐	9 A 49
5 ♊	6 A 59	5 ♌	7 P 20	7 ♍	8 A 02	5 ♎	10 P 47	8 ♐	3 A 36	6 ♑	10 P 18
7 ♋	8 A 06	7 ♍	11 P 31	9 ♎	3 P 13	8 ♏	9 A 04	10 ♑	4 P 17	9 ♒	10 A 13
9 ♌	9 A 43	10 ♎	6 A 14	12 ♏	1 A 17	10 ♐	8 P 57	13 ♒	4 A 24	11 ♓	8 P 35
11 ♍	1 P 49	12 ♏	4 P 48	14 ♐	1 P 02	13 ♑	9 A 59	15 ♓	2 P 11	14 ♈	3 A 35
13 ♎	9 P 12	15 ♐	5 A 35	17 ♑	2 A 00	15 ♒	9 P 30	17 ♈	7 P 16	16 ♉	7 A 18
16 ♏	8 A 48	17 ♑	5 P 43	19 ♒	0 P 34	18 ♓	5 A 19	19 ♉	9 P 15	18 ♊	7 A 43
18 ♐	9 P 24	20 ♒	3 A 23	21 ♓	7 P 30	20 ♈	9 A 25	21 ♊	8 P 59	20 ♋	7 A 25
21 ♑	9 A 25	22 ♓	10 A 00	23 ♈	10 P 48	22 ♉	10 A 23	23 ♋	8 P 40	22 ♌	7 A 38
23 ♒	6 P 41	24 ♈	2 P 04	26 ♉	0 A 39	24 ♊	10 A 43	25 ♌	9 P 53	24 ♍	10 A 29
26 ♓	1 A 53	26 ♉	5 P 05	28 ♊	2 A 04	26 ♋	11 A 22	28 ♍	2 A 11	26 ♎	4 P 56
28 ♈	7 A 32	28 ♊	7 P 52	30 ♋	4 A 18	28 ♌	2 P 08	30 ♎	10 A 07	29 ♏	3 A 32
30 ♉	11 A 20					30 ♍	8 P 03				

JUL	TIME	AUG	TIME	SEPT	TIME	OCT	TIME	NOV	TIME	DEC	TIME
1 ♐	3 P 51	2 ♒	10 P 19	1 ♓	3 P 09	1 ♈	5 A 53	1 ♊	7 P 53	1 ♋	6 A 10
4 ♑	4 A 24	5 ♓	7 A 33	3 ♈	9 P 23	3 ♉	9 A 18	3 ♋	8 P 39	3 ♌	6 A 26
6 ♒	3 P 49	7 ♈	3 P 03	6 ♉	1 A 49	5 ♊	11 A 21	5 ♌	10 P 21	5 ♍	9 A 05
9 ♓	1 A 55	9 ♉	8 P 04	8 ♊	5 A 12	7 ♋	1 P 21	8 ♍	2 A 39	7 ♎	3 P 02
11 ♈	9 A 49	11 ♊	11 P 51	10 ♋	7 A 50	9 ♌	4 P 23	10 ♎	9 A 27	10 ♏	0 A 24
13 ♉	2 P 53	14 ♋	1 A 50	12 ♌	10 A 50	11 ♍	9 P 04	12 ♏	6 P 28	12 ♐	0 N 00
15 ♊	5 P 05	16 ♌	3 A 44	14 ♍	2 P 38	14 ♎	3 A 26	15 ♐	5 A 37	15 ♑	0 A 19
17 ♋	5 P 43	18 ♍	6 A 11	16 ♎	7 P 49	16 ♏	11 A 49	17 ♑	5 P 48	17 ♒	1 P 00
19 ♌	6 P 06	20 ♎	10 A 32	19 ♏	3 A 33	18 ♐	10 P 07	20 ♒	6 A 21	20 ♓	0 A 47
21 ♍	8 P 11	22 ♏	6 P 38	21 ♐	2 P 01	21 ♑	10 A 36	22 ♓	5 P 54	22 ♈	10 A 08
24 ♎	1 A 18	25 ♐	6 A 19	24 ♑	3 A 22	23 ♒	11 P 18	25 ♈	1 A 47	24 ♉	3 P 26
26 ♏	10 A 28	27 ♑	6 P 55	26 ♒	3 P 08	26 ♓	9 A 42	27 ♉	5 A 35	26 ♊	5 P 27
28 ♐	10 P 41	30 ♒	6 A 23	29 ♓	0 A 16	28 ♈	4 P 07	29 ♊	6 A 26	28 ♋	5 P 11
31 ♑	11 A 36					30 ♉	6 P 50			30 ♌	4 P 41

1956

JAN	TIME	FEB	TIME	MAR	TIME	APR	TIME	MAY	TIME	JUN	TIME
1 ♍	6 P 00	2 ♏	2 P 06	3 ♐	8 A 37	2 ♑	4 A 44	2 ♒	1 A 19	3 ♈	7 A 37
3 ♎	10 P 11	5 ♐	0 A 49	5 ♑	8 P 49	4 ♒	5 P 48	4 ♓	1 P 33	5 ♉	1 P 33
6 ♏	6 A 38	7 ♑	1 P 38	8 ♒	9 A 36	7 ♓	4 A 59	6 ♈	10 P 14	7 ♊	4 P 21
8 ♐	6 P 16	10 ♒	2 A 00	10 ♓	8 P 23	9 ♈	0 P 55	9 ♉	3 A 24	9 ♋	4 P 38
11 ♑	6 A 55	12 ♓	1 P 09	13 ♈	4 A 48	11 ♉	6 P 28	11 ♊	6 A 01	11 ♌	4 P 34
13 ♒	7 P 33	14 ♈	9 P 57	15 ♉	10 A 57	13 ♊	9 P 42	13 ♋	7 A 12	13 ♍	6 P 13
16 ♓	6 A 53	17 ♉	5 A 12	17 ♊	3 P 37	16 ♋	0 A 31	15 ♌	8 A 38	15 ♎	10 P 24
18 ♈	4 P 19	19 ♊	9 A 45	19 ♋	6 P 39	18 ♌	3 A 03	17 ♍	11 A 39	18 ♏	5 A 27
20 ♉	11 P 17	21 ♋	0 P 47	21 ♌	9 P 21	20 ♍	6 A 28	19 ♎	4 P 45	20 ♐	3 P 33
23 ♊	2 A 50	23 ♌	1 P 38	23 ♍	11 P 51	22 ♎	11 A 08	21 ♏	0 M 00	23 ♑	2 A 50
25 ♋	3 A 58	25 ♍	2 P 50	26 ♎	3 A 08	24 ♏	5 P 24	24 ♐	9 A 16	25 ♒	3 P 16
27 ♌	3 A 58	27 ♎	5 P 32	28 ♏	8 A 42	27 ♐	1 A 44	26 ♑	8 P 17	28 ♓	4 A 12
29 ♍	4 A 20	29 ♏	11 P 11	30 ♐	5 P 04	29 ♑	1 P 00	29 ♒	8 A 46	30 ♈	3 P 15
31 ♎	7 A 14							31 ♓	9 P 15		

JUL	TIME	AUG	TIME	SEPT	TIME	OCT	TIME	NOV	TIME	DEC	TIME
2 ♉	10 P 39	1 ♊	11 A 29	1 ♌	11 P 18	1 ♍	8 A 41	1 ♏	10 P 56	1 ♐	1 P 08
5 ♊	2 A 24	3 ♋	1 P 27	3 ♍	11 P 41	3 ♎	10 A 41	4 ♐	5 A 14	3 ♑	10 P 44
7 ♋	3 A 25	5 ♌	1 P 25	6 ♎	0 A 38	5 ♏	1 P 46	6 ♑	2 P 33	6 ♒	10 A 00
9 ♌	2 A 45	7 ♍	1 P 08	8 ♏	4 A 01	7 ♐	8 P 00	9 ♒	2 A 08	8 ♓	10 P 53
11 ♍	2 A 41	9 ♎	2 P 13	10 ♐	10 A 43	10 ♑	5 A 46	11 ♓	3 P 11	11 ♈	11 A 00
13 ♎	5 A 10	11 ♏	6 P 45	12 ♑	9 P 48	12 ♒	6 P 16	14 ♈	2 A 06	13 ♉	7 P 27
15 ♏	11 A 16	14 ♐	2 A 54	15 ♒	10 A 50	15 ♓	6 A 55	16 ♉	9 A 50	16 ♊	0 A 06
17 ♐	8 P 57	16 ♑	2 P 51	17 ♓	10 P 44	17 ♈	5 P 14	18 ♊	2 P 02	18 ♋	1 A 58
20 ♑	8 A 48	19 ♒	3 A 44	20 ♈	9 A 17	20 ♉	0 A 26	20 ♋	4 P 36	20 ♌	2 A 21
22 ♒	9 P 29	21 ♓	3 P 55	22 ♉	5 P 19	22 ♊	5 A 31	22 ♌	6 P 11	22 ♍	3 A 27
25 ♓	9 A 49	24 ♈	2 A 38	24 ♊	11 P 27	24 ♋	9 A 31	24 ♍	8 P 51	24 ♎	6 A 16
27 ♈	9 P 12	26 ♉	11 A 38	27 ♋	3 A 46	26 ♌	0 P 21	27 ♎	0 A 33	26 ♏	11 A 29
30 ♉	6 A 09	28 ♊	6 P 08	29 ♌	6 A 50	28 ♍	3 P 14	29 ♏	5 A 56	28 ♐	7 P 38
		30 ♋	9 P 51			30 ♎	6 P 26			31 ♑	5 A 43

1957

JAN	TIME	FEB	TIME	MAR	TIME	APR	TIME	MAY	TIME	JUN	TIME
2 ♒	5 P 18	1 ♓	0 P 25	3 ♈	6 A 51	1 ♉	11 P 24	1 ♊	1 P 37	2 ♌	4 A 37
5 ♓	5 A 57	4 ♈	0 A 49	5 ♉	5 P 44	4 ♊	7 A 44	3 ♋	7 P 00	4 ♍	7 A 17
7 ♈	6 P 01	6 ♉	11 A 37	8 ♊	2 A 06	6 ♋	1 P 35	5 ♌	10 P 52	6 ♎	10 A 10
10 ♉	4 A 23	8 ♊	7 P 25	10 ♋	7 A 31	8 ♌	5 P 26	8 ♍	1 A 45	8 ♏	2 P 08
12 ♊	10 A 27	10 ♋	10 P 59	12 ♌	10 A 02	10 ♍	7 P 14	10 ♎	4 A 11	10 ♐	7 P 18
14 ♋	0 P 58	12 ♌	11 P 58	14 ♍	9 A 55	12 ♎	8 P 17	12 ♏	7 A 17	13 ♑	2 A 42
16 ♌	0 P 48	14 ♍	11 P 27	16 ♎	10 A 05	14 ♏	10 P 00	14 ♐	11 A 08	15 ♒	0 P 24
18 ♍	0 P 29	16 ♎	11 P 20	18 ♏	11 A 31	17 ♐	1 A 52	16 ♑	6 P 05	18 ♓	0 A 19
20 ♎	1 P 22	19 ♏	1 A 45	20 ♐	4 P 04	19 ♑	9 A 00	19 ♒	4 A 03	20 ♈	1 P 23
22 ♏	5 P 44	21 ♐	7 A 45	23 ♑	0 A 47	21 ♒	8 P 24	21 ♓	4 P 39	22 ♉	0 M 00
25 ♐	1 A 20	23 ♑	5 P 48	25 ♒	0 P 49	24 ♓	8 A 59	24 ♈	5 A 08	25 ♊	7 A 24
27 ♑	11 A 37	26 ♒	6 A 16	28 ♓	1 A 30	26 ♈	8 P 59	26 ♉	2 P 56	27 ♋	10 A 41
29 ♒	11 P 48	28 ♓	6 P 43	30 ♈	1 P 22	29 ♉	6 A 42	28 ♊	9 P 47	29 ♌	0 P 30
								31 ♋	1 A 44		

JUL	TIME	AUG	TIME	SEPT	TIME	OCT	TIME	NOV	TIME	DEC	TIME
1 ♍	1 P 28	2 ♏	1 A 02	2 ♑	8 P 51	2 ♒	2 P 01	1 ♈	9 A 45	1 ♈	6 A 25
3 ♎	3 P 35	4 ♐	6 A 44	5 ♒	7 A 59	5 ♓	2 A 44	3 ♉	10 P 30	3 ♉	6 P 00
5 ♏	7 P 25	6 ♑	3 P 08	7 ♓	8 P 28	7 ♈	3 P 14	6 ♊	9 A 44	6 ♊	3 A 06
8 ♐	1 A 29	9 ♒	2 A 10	10 ♈	8 A 46	10 ♉	2 A 45	8 ♋	7 P 05	8 ♋	9 A 12
10 ♑	9 A 23	11 ♓	2 P 02	12 ♉	8 P 57	12 ♊	0 P 56	11 ♌	2 A 23	10 ♌	1 P 44
12 ♒	7 P 53	14 ♈	2 A 46	15 ♊	7 A 22	14 ♋	8 P 37	13 ♍	7 A 39	12 ♍	5 P 05
15 ♓	7 A 46	16 ♉	3 P 08	17 ♋	2 P 40	17 ♌	1 A 55	15 ♎	11 A 40	14 ♎	7 P 32
17 ♈	8 P 28	19 ♊	0 A 50	19 ♌	6 P 40	19 ♍	4 A 34	17 ♏	1 P 31	16 ♏	10 P 48
20 ♉	8 A 14	21 ♋	6 A 45	21 ♍	7 P 22	21 ♎	5 A 31	19 ♐	3 P 31	19 ♐	2 A 37
22 ♊	4 P 50	23 ♌	8 A 52	23 ♎	7 P 05	23 ♏	5 A 56	21 ♑	6 P 11	21 ♑	7 A 42
24 ♋	8 P 58	25 ♍	8 A 51	25 ♏	7 P 14	25 ♐	7 A 50	23 ♒	10 P 29	23 ♒	3 P 07
26 ♌	10 P 24	27 ♎	8 A 15	27 ♐	9 P 48	27 ♑	0 P 34	26 ♓	6 A 08	26 ♓	1 A 53
28 ♍	10 P 24	29 ♏	9 A 24	30 ♑	3 A 56	29 ♒	9 P 31	28 ♈	5 P 30	28 ♈	2 P 27
30 ♎	10 P 54	31 ♐	1 P 06							31 ♉	2 A 38

1958

JAN	TIME	FEB	TIME	MAR	TIME	APR	TIME	MAY	TIME	JUN	TIME
2 ♊	0 P 33	1 ♋	4 A 21	2 ♌	6 P 03	1 ♍	5 A 49	2 ♏	3 P 53	1 ♐	3 A 01
4 ♋	6 P 16	3 ♌	7 A 29	4 ♍	7 P 14	3 ♎	5 A 56	4 ♐	4 P 34	3 ♑	5 A 19
6 ♌	9 P 37	5 ♍	8 A 32	6 ♎	6 P 43	5 ♏	5 A 20	6 ♑	7 P 14	5 ♒	10 A 33
8 ♍	11 P 35	7 ♎	9 A 17	8 ♏	6 P 55	7 ♐	6 A 20	9 ♒	1 A 29	7 ♓	7 P 43
11 ♎	1 A 36	9 ♏	10 A 31	10 ♐	9 P 19	9 ♑	9 A 55	11 ♓	0 N 00	10 ♈	7 A 46
13 ♏	4 A 28	11 ♐	2 P 41	13 ♑	2 A 51	11 ♒	6 P 05	14 ♈	0 A 37	12 ♉	8 P 28
15 ♐	8 A 56	13 ♑	9 P 17	15 ♒	11 A 49	14 ♓	5 P 27	16 ♉	1 P 00	15 ♊	7 A 33
17 ♑	3 P 10	16 ♒	6 A 05	17 ♓	11 P 18	16 ♈	6 P 04	18 ♊	11 P 55	17 ♋	3 P 44
19 ♒	11 P 18	18 ♓	4 P 57	20 ♈	11 A 48	19 ♉	6 A 33	21 ♋	9 A 11	19 ♌	10 P 02
22 ♓	9 A 39	21 ♈	5 A 09	23 ♉	0 A 06	21 ♊	5 P 54	23 ♌	4 P 10	22 ♍	2 A 41
24 ♈	10 P 05	23 ♉	5 P 54	25 ♊	0 P 12	24 ♋	3 A 49	25 ♍	9 P 20	24 ♎	6 A 11
27 ♉	10 A 59	26 ♊	5 A 43	27 ♋	9 P 38	26 ♌	11 A 05	28 ♎	0 A 26	26 ♏	8 A 27
29 ♊	9 P 27	28 ♋	2 P 08	30 ♌	3 A 40	28 ♍	3 P 00	30 ♏	1 A 33	28 ♐	11 A 31
						30 ♎	4 P 24			30 ♑	2 P 47

JUL	TIME	AUG	TIME	SEPT	TIME	OCT	TIME	NOV	TIME	DEC	TIME
2 ♒	7 P 54	1 ♓	0 P 24	2 ♉	7 P 11	2 ♏	2 P 36	1 ♋	7 A 43	3 ♍	5 A 30
5 ♓	4 A 08	3 ♈	11 P 24	5 ♊	7 A 51	5 ♐	1 A 50	3 ♌	5 P 19	5 ♎	9 A 41
7 ♈	3 P 39	6 ♉	11 A 48	7 ♋	6 P 22	7 ♑	10 A 10	5 ♍	10 P 47	7 ♏	11 A 22
10 ♉	4 A 25	9 ♊	0 A 07	10 ♌	0 A 57	9 ♒	2 P 09	8 ♎	1 A 33	9 ♐	0 N 00
12 ♊	3 P 53	11 ♋	9 A 45	12 ♍	3 A 47	11 ♓	3 P 18	10 ♏	1 A 39	11 ♑	1 P 00
15 ♋	0 A 11	13 ♌	2 P 45	14 ♎	4 A 14	13 ♈	2 P 40	12 ♐	1 A 22	13 ♒	4 P 04
17 ♌	5 A 37	15 ♍	5 P 27	16 ♏	4 A 04	15 ♉	2 P 37	14 ♑	2 A 16	15 ♓	10 P 35
19 ♍	8 A 56	17 ♎	6 P 41	18 ♐	5 A 21	17 ♊	4 P 31	16 ♒	6 A 18	18 ♈	9 A 02
21 ♎	11 A 21	19 ♏	7 P 44	20 ♑	9 A 04	19 ♋	10 P 08	18 ♓	1 P 57	20 ♉	9 P 53
23 ♏	1 P 45	21 ♐	10 P 34	22 ♒	3 P 59	22 ♌	7 A 22	21 ♈	1 A 49	23 ♊	10 A 12
25 ♐	5 P 22	24 ♑	3 A 30	25 ♓	1 A 57	24 ♍	7 P 30	23 ♉	2 P 27	25 ♋	8 P 35
27 ♑	10 P 02	26 ♒	10 A 32	27 ♈	1 P 13	27 ♎	8 A 09	26 ♊	2 A 53	28 ♌	4 A 47
30 ♒	4 A 15	28 ♓	7 P 50	30 ♉	1 A 44	29 ♏	8 P 20	28 ♋	1 P 44	30 ♍	10 A 57
		31 ♈	6 A 51					30 ♌	10 P 53		

1959

JAN – JUN

JAN	TIME	FEB	TIME	MAR	TIME	APR	TIME	MAY	TIME	JUN	TIME
1 ♎	3 P 39	2 ♐	3 A 10	1 ♐	8 A 40	1 ♒	11 P 11	1 ♓	0 P 12	2 ♉	4 P 56
3 ♏	6 P 47	4 ♑	6 A 30	3 ♑	0 P 11	4 ♓	7 A 16	3 ♈	10 P 54	5 ♊	5 A 37
5 ♐	8 P 41	6 ♒	10 A 48	5 ♒	5 P 36	6 ♈	5 P 09	6 ♉	11 A 00	7 ♋	5 P 45
7 ♑	10 P 48	8 ♓	5 P 11	7 ♓	11 P 59	9 ♉	4 A 44	8 ♊	11 P 36	10 ♌	4 A 18
10 ♒	2 A 07	11 ♈	2 A 14	10 ♈	10 A 14	11 ♊	5 P 27	11 ♋	0 N 00	12 ♍	1 P 06
12 ♓	7 A 56	13 ♉	1 P 37	12 ♉	9 P 29	14 ♋	5 A 45	13 ♌	10 P 52	14 ♎	6 P 47
14 ♈	5 P 21	16 ♊	2 A 32	15 ♊	10 A 12	16 ♌	4 P 08	16 ♍	6 A 47	16 ♏	9 P 32
17 ♉	5 A 45	18 ♋	1 P 54	17 ♋	10 P 28	18 ♍	10 P 20	18 ♎	11 A 00	18 ♐	9 P 59
19 ♊	6 P 16	20 ♌	9 P 42	20 ♌	7 A 21	21 ♎	1 A 03	20 ♏	0 P 10	20 ♑	10 P 07
22 ♋	4 A 46	23 ♍	2 A 04	22 ♍	3 P 30	23 ♏	1 A 16	22 ♐	11 A 24	22 ♒	11 P 20
24 ♌	0 P 33	25 ♎	4 A 44	24 ♎	2 P 36	25 ♐	0 A 49	24 ♑	11 A 22	25 ♓	3 A 42
26 ♍	5 P 27	27 ♏	6 A 22	26 ♏	2 P 36	27 ♑	1 A 35	26 ♒	1 P 45	27 ♈	11 A 37
28 ♎	9 P 23			28 ♐	3 P 39	29 ♒	5 A 28	28 ♓	7 P 27	29 ♉	11 P 36
31 ♏	0 A 06			30 ♑	5 P 54			31 ♈	5 A 08		

JUL – DEC

JUL	TIME	AUG	TIME	SEPT	TIME	OCT	TIME	NOV	TIME	DEC	TIME
2 ♊	0 P 12	1 ♋	7 A 31	2 ♍	8 A 44	1 ♎	10 P 03	2 ♐	10 A 05	1 ♑	8 P 37
5 ♋	0 A 07	3 ♌	5 P 21	4 ♎	1 P 01	3 ♏	11 P 56	4 ♑	10 A 23	3 ♒	9 P 21
7 ♌	10 A 17	6 ♍	0 A 26	6 ♏	3 P 42	6 ♐	2 A 03	6 ♒	0 P 32	6 ♓	0 A 49
9 ♍	6 P 19	8 ♎	5 A 53	8 ♐	6 P 03	8 ♑	2 A 43	8 ♓	6 P 01	8 ♈	8 A 23
12 ♎	0 A 21	10 ♏	9 A 35	10 ♑	9 P 07	10 ♒	6 A 14	11 ♈	2 A 18	11 ♉	7 P 08
14 ♏	4 A 24	12 ♐	0 P 41	13 ♒	0 A 47	12 ♓	0 P 22	13 ♉	1 P 11	13 ♊	7 A 33
16 ♐	6 A 42	14 ♑	3 P 14	15 ♓	6 A 17	14 ♈	8 P 21	16 ♊	1 A 07	15 ♋	8 P 04
18 ♑	7 A 54	16 ♒	6 P 13	17 ♈	1 P 03	17 ♉	6 A 42	18 ♋	1 P 38	18 ♌	8 A 00
20 ♒	9 A 41	18 ♓	10 P 19	19 ♉	11 P 03	19 ♊	6 P 28	21 ♌	2 A 10	20 ♍	6 P 31
22 ♓	1 P 05	21 ♈	2 A 38	22 ♊	11 A 00	22 ♋	7 A 10	23 ♍	0 P 11	23 ♎	2 A 13
24 ♈	8 P 12	23 ♉	2 P 38	24 ♋	11 P 48	24 ♌	7 P 10	25 ♎	6 P 26	25 ♏	6 A 44
27 ♉	6 A 51	26 ♊	3 A 13	27 ♌	10 A 50	27 ♍	3 A 57	27 ♏	9 P 04	27 ♐	8 A 48
29 ♊	7 P 37	28 ♋	4 P 07	29 ♍	6 P 32	29 ♎	8 A 44	29 ♐	9 P 06	29 ♑	7 A 30
		31 ♌	1 A 59			31 ♏	10 A 13			31 ♒	7 A 40

1960

JAN	TIME	FEB	TIME	MAR	TIME	APR	TIME	MAY	TIME	JUN	TIME
2 ♓	10 A 00	1 ♈	0 A 49	1 ♉	6 P 10	3 ♋	2 A 02	2 ♌	10 P 05	1 ♍	5 P 00
4 ♈	3 P 57	3 ♉	9 A 28	4 ♊	5 A 09	5 ♌	2 P 22	5 ♍	9 A 17	4 ♎	1 A 34
7 ♉	1 A 42	5 ♊	9 P 22	6 ♋	5 P 54	8 ♍	0 A 22	7 ♎	4 P 23	6 ♏	5 A 53
9 ♊	2 P 14	8 ♋	10 A 12	9 ♌	5 A 53	10 ♎	6 A 27	9 ♏	7 P 36	8 ♐	7 A 25
12 ♋	2 A 52	10 ♌	9 P 30	11 ♍	3 P 07	12 ♏	9 A 59	11 ♐	8 P 43	10 ♑	7 A 57
14 ♌	2 P 33	13 ♍	6 A 55	13 ♎	9 P 19	14 ♐	11 A 41	13 ♑	8 P 59	12 ♒	6 A 59
17 ♍	0 A 34	15 ♎	2 P 11	16 ♏	2 A 35	16 ♑	1 P 31	15 ♒	10 P 25	14 ♓	8 A 47
19 ♎	8 A 32	17 ♏	7 P 38	18 ♐	4 A 07	18 ♒	4 P 17	18 ♓	2 A 03	16 ♈	2 P 02
21 ♏	2 P 05	19 ♐	11 P 15	20 ♑	4 A 30	20 ♓	8 P 48	20 ♈	8 A 16	18 ♉	10 P 44
23 ♐	4 P 47	22 ♑	1 A 45	22 ♒	5 A 58	23 ♈	2 A 45	22 ♉	5 P 15	21 ♊	10 A 12
25 ♑	5 P 53	24 ♒	3 A 41	24 ♓	10 A 13	25 ♉	10 A 53	25 ♊	4 A 08	23 ♋	10 P 35
27 ♒	6 P 22	26 ♓	6 A 23	26 ♈	5 P 16	27 ♊	9 P 24	27 ♋	4 P 06	26 ♌	11 A 12
29 ♓	8 P 20	28 ♈	8 A 58	29 ♉	2 A 38	30 ♋	9 A 36	30 ♌	5 A 09	28 ♍	11 P 13
				31 ♊	1 P 35						

JUL	TIME	AUG	TIME	SEPT	TIME	OCT	TIME	NOV	TIME	DEC	TIME
2 ♎	8 A 49	2 ♐	1 A 52	2 ♒	0 P 50	1 ♓	10 P 34	2 ♉	3 P 22	2 ♊	7 A 02
3 ♏	2 P 40	4 ♑	3 A 51	4 ♓	2 P 21	4 ♈	2 A 10	4 ♊	11 P 50	4 ♋	6 P 00
5 ♐	5 P 31	6 ♒	3 A 42	6 ♈	4 P 48	6 ♉	7 A 17	7 ♋	10 A 37	7 ♌	6 A 31
7 ♑	5 P 51	8 ♓	4 A 20	8 ♉	9 P 49	8 ♊	3 P 37	9 ♌	11 P 05	9 ♍	7 P 16
9 ♒	5 P 08	10 ♈	6 A 30	11 ♊	6 A 32	11 ♋	2 A 34	12 ♍	11 A 37	12 ♎	6 A 05
11 ♓	5 P 03	12 ♉	0 P 45	13 ♋	6 P 31	13 ♌	3 P 05	14 ♎	9 P 17	14 ♏	1 P 03
13 ♈	9 P 27	14 ♊	10 P 41	16 ♌	7 A 12	16 ♍	3 A 01	17 ♏	2 A 52	16 ♐	4 P 07
16 ♉	4 A 54	17 ♋	11 A 23	18 ♍	6 P 28	18 ♎	11 A 39	19 ♐	5 A 27	18 ♑	4 P 39
18 ♊	4 P 00	19 ♌	11 P 42	21 ♎	2 A 51	20 ♏	5 P 03	21 ♑	6 A 38	20 ♒	4 P 35
21 ♋	4 A 41	22 ♍	10 A 50	23 ♏	8 A 58	22 ♐	8 P 17	23 ♒	7 A 38	22 ♓	5 P 21
23 ♌	5 P 03	24 ♎	8 P 10	25 ♐	1 P 53	24 ♑	10 P 52	25 ♓	10 A 10	24 ♈	9 P 00
26 ♍	4 A 44	27 ♏	2 A 59	27 ♑	5 P 15	27 ♒	1 A 06	27 ♈	2 P 55	27 ♉	3 A 38
28 ♎	2 P 38	29 ♐	8 A 29	29 ♒	7 P 36	29 ♓	4 A 31	29 ♉	9 P 57	29 ♊	1 P 11
30 ♏	10 P 02	31 ♑	11 A 31			31 ♈	9 A 04				

1961

JAN	TIME	FEB	TIME	MAR	TIME	APR	TIME	MAY	TIME	JUN	TIME
1 ♋	0 A 49	2 ♍	7 A 58	1 ♍	2 P 34	2 ♏	4 P 37	2 ♐	5 A 14	2 ♒	6 P 11
3 ♌	1 P 24	4 ♎	7 P 32	4 ♎	1 A 26	4 ♐	10 P 56	4 ♑	8 A 56	4 ♓	8 P 11
6 ♍	1 A 49	7 ♏	5 A 04	6 ♏	10 A 29	7 ♑	3 A 29	6 ♒	0 N 00	6 ♈	11 P 51
8 ♎	1 P 22	9 ♐	10 A 58	8 ♐	5 P 13	9 ♒	7 A 08	8 ♓	2 P 35	9 ♉	4 A 58
10 ♏	10 P 05	11 ♑	2 P 06	10 ♑	9 P 46	11 ♓	8 A 53	10 ♈	6 P 05	11 ♊	0 P 11
13 ♐	2 A 32	13 ♒	2 P 14	12 ♒	11 P 41	13 ♈	11 A 00	12 ♉	10 P 30	13 ♋	9 P 22
15 ♑	3 A 57	15 ♓	2 P 04	15 ♓	0 A 20	15 ♉	2 P 27	15 ♊	4 A 48	16 ♌	8 A 36
17 ♒	3 A 20	17 ♈	2 P 43	17 ♈	1 A 25	17 ♊	7 P 49	17 ♋	1 P 34	18 ♍	9 P 17
19 ♓	2 A 59	19 ♉	6 P 22	19 ♉	4 A 10	20 ♋	5 A 16	20 ♌	1 A 08	21 ♎	9 A 25
21 ♈	4 A 53	22 ♊	1 A 55	21 ♊	10 A 23	22 ♌	5 P 08	22 ♍	1 P 38	23 ♏	6 P 51
23 ♉	9 A 04	24 ♋	1 P 26	23 ♋	8 P 48	25 ♍	5 A 57	25 ♎	1 A 21	26 ♐	0 A 16
25 ♊	6 P 54	27 ♌	2 A 00	26 ♌	9 A 22	27 ♎	4 P 09	27 ♏	9 A 30	28 ♑	2 A 28
28 ♋	7 A 02			28 ♍	9 P 55	30 ♏	0 A 26	29 ♐	2 P 30	30 ♒	2 A 43
30 ♌	7 P 30			31 ♎	8 A 09			31 ♑	4 P 36		

JUL	TIME	AUG	TIME	SEPT	TIME	OCT	TIME	NOV	TIME	DEC	TIME
2 ♓	3 A 02	2 ♉	4 P 08	1 ♊	5 A 58	3 ♌	9 A 49	2 ♍	6 A 33	2 ♎	3 A 13
4 ♈	5 A 04	4 ♊	10 P 53	3 ♋	3 P 01	5 ♍	10 P 53	4 ♎	6 P 38	4 ♏	1 P 41
6 ♉	10 A 00	7 ♋	9 A 00	6 ♌	3 A 13	8 ♎	11 A 00	7 ♏	4 A 37	6 ♐	8 P 30
8 ♊	5 P 29	9 ♌	9 P 17	8 ♍	4 P 00	10 ♏	8 P 54	9 ♐	0 N 00	9 ♑	2 A 32
11 ♋	3 A 25	12 ♍	9 A 48	11 ♎	3 A 56	13 ♐	5 A 18	11 ♑	5 P 15	11 ♒	5 A 18
13 ♌	2 P 50	14 ♎	10 P 05	13 ♏	2 P 41	15 ♑	11 A 18	13 ♒	9 P 03	13 ♓	7 A 52
16 ♍	4 A 04	17 ♏	9 A 30	15 ♐	11 P 39	17 ♒	3 P 42	16 ♓	0 A 11	15 ♈	10 A 29
18 ♎	4 P 15	19 ♐	5 P 47	18 ♑	5 A 53	19 ♓	6 P 01	18 ♈	3 A 03	17 ♉	0 P 32
21 ♏	3 A 00	21 ♑	10 P 28	20 ♒	8 A 58	21 ♈	7 P 34	20 ♉	5 A 58	19 ♊	5 P 51
23 ♐	9 A 53	23 ♒	11 P 37	22 ♓	9 A 46	23 ♉	9 P 23	22 ♊	10 A 05	22 ♋	1 A 14
25 ♑	0 P 49	25 ♓	11 P 23	24 ♈	9 A 54	26 ♊	0 A 43	24 ♋	4 P 43	24 ♌	10 A 39
27 ♒	1 P 17	27 ♈	11 P 08	26 ♉	11 A 00	28 ♋	7 A 21	27 ♌	2 A 07	26 ♍	10 P 30
29 ♓	0 P 38	30 ♉	0 A 55	28 ♊	2 P 55	30 ♌	5 P 48	29 ♍	2 P 27	29 ♎	11 A 24
31 ♈	1 P 10			30 ♋	10 P 39					31 ♏	10 P 39

1962

JAN	TIME	FEB	TIME	MAR	TIME	APR	TIME	MAY	TIME	JUN	TIME
3 ♐	6 A 53	1 ♑	9 P 13	1 ♑	6 A 42	1 ♓	8 P 27	1 ♈	6 A 00	1 ♊	6 P 00
5 ♑	10 A 38	3 ♒	11 P 02	3 ♒	9 A 52	3 ♈	8 P 27	3 ♉	6 A 40	3 ♋	10 P 24
7 ♒	0 P 20	5 ♓	10 P 57	5 ♓	9 A 47	5 ♉	8 P 09	5 ♊	8 A 20	6 ♌	5 A 27
9 ♓	1 P 09	7 ♈	10 P 24	7 ♈	9 A 07	7 ♊	10 P 08	7 ♋	0 P 22	8 ♍	3 P 51
11 ♈	2 P 23	10 ♉	0 A 26	9 ♉	9 A 37	10 ♋	3 A 23	9 ♌	8 P 29	11 ♎	4 A 49
13 ♉	5 P 50	12 ♊	5 A 30	11 ♊	0 P 54	12 ♌	0 P 48	12 ♍	8 A 10	13 ♏	4 P 53
16 ♊	0 A 04	14 ♋	1 P 46	13 ♋	7 P 56	15 ♍	0 A 20	14 ♎	9 P 05	16 ♐	2 A 21
18 ♋	7 A 53	17 ♌	0 A 42	16 ♌	6 A 39	17 ♎	1 P 20	17 ♏	8 A 53	18 ♑	8 A 47
20 ♌	6 P 10	19 ♍	0 P 37	18 ♍	6 P 43	20 ♏	1 A 49	19 ♐	6 P 12	20 ♒	1 P 02
23 ♍	5 A 55	22 ♎	1 A 02	21 ♎	7 A 33	22 ♐	1 A 49	22 ♑	1 A 32	22 ♓	4 P 03
25 ♎	6 P 31	24 ♏	1 P 46	23 ♏	7 P 27	24 ♑	11 A 49	24 ♒	6 A 50	24 ♈	7 P 03
28 ♏	7 A 01	26 ♐	11 P 54	26 ♐	5 A 54	27 ♒	7 P 56	26 ♓	10 A 38	26 ♉	9 P 53
30 ♐	4 P 00			28 ♑	2 P 18	29 ♓	1 A 40	28 ♈	1 P 36	29 ♊	1 A 45
				30 ♒	6 P 45		4 A 52	30 ♉	5 P 07		

JUL	TIME	AUG	TIME	SEPT	TIME	OCT	TIME	NOV	TIME	DEC	TIME
1 ♋	6 A 50	2 ♍	7 A 43	1 ♎	2 A 36	3 ♐	9 A 36	2 ♑	1 A 20	1 ♒	2 P 31
3 ♌	2 P 06	4 ♎	7 P 52	3 ♏	3 P 37	5 ♑	7 P 40	4 ♒	9 A 02	3 ♓	7 P 52
6 ♍	0 A 54	7 ♏	8 A 33	6 ♐	3 A 21	8 ♒	2 A 07	6 ♓	1 P 40	5 ♈	11 P 00
8 ♎	0 P 25	9 ♐	7 P 50	8 ♑	0 P 33	10 ♓	5 A 00	8 ♈	3 P 27	8 ♉	0 A 54
11 ♏	1 A 00	12 ♑	3 A 24	10 ♒	5 P 28	12 ♈	5 A 33	10 ♉	3 P 51	10 ♊	2 A 14
13 ♐	11 A 27	14 ♒	6 A 59	12 ♓	7 P 02	14 ♉	4 A 55	12 ♊	4 P 00	12 ♋	4 A 47
15 ♑	5 P 48	16 ♓	8 A 16	14 ♈	6 P 48	16 ♊	5 A 36	14 ♋	6 P 23	14 ♌	9 A 30
17 ♒	9 P 09	18 ♈	8 A 16	16 ♉	6 P 22	18 ♋	8 A 39	17 ♌	0 A 10	16 ♍	5 P 57
19 ♓	11 P 06	20 ♉	9 A 43	18 ♊	7 P 55	20 ♌	3 P 50	19 ♍	9 A 49	19 ♎	5 A 45
22 ♈	0 A 28	22 ♊	0 P 43	21 ♋	0 A 55	23 ♍	2 A 44	21 ♎	10 P 11	21 ♏	6 P 40
24 ♉	3 A 13	24 ♋	7 P 01	23 ♌	9 A 17	25 ♎	3 P 26	24 ♏	10 A 48	24 ♐	6 A 03
26 ♊	7 A 24	27 ♌	3 A 53	25 ♍	8 P 32	28 ♏	3 A 52	26 ♐	9 P 57	26 ♑	2 P 34
28 ♋	1 P 40	29 ♍	2 P 35	28 ♎	9 A 10	30 ♐	3 P 10	29 ♑	7 A 16	28 ♒	8 P 53
30 ♌	9 P 43			30 ♏	9 P 34					31 ♓	1 A 29

1963

JAN	TIME	FEB	TIME	MAR	TIME	APR	TIME	MAY	TIME	JUN	TIME
2 ♈	4 A 41	2 ♊	4 P 14	1 ♊	10 P 08	2 ♌	2 P 54	2 ♍	6 A 12	1 ♎	0 A 13
4 ♉	7 A 43	4 ♋	9 P 04	4 ♋	2 A 42	5 ♍	0 A 35	4 ♎	5 P 51	3 ♏	1 P 12
6 ♊	10 A 19	7 ♌	3 A 09	6 ♌	9 A 27	7 ♎	0 N 00	7 ♏	6 A 33	6 ♐	1 A 18
8 ♋	2 P 15	9 ♍	11 A 38	8 ♍	6 P 35	10 ♏	0 A 25	9 ♐	6 P 57	8 ♑	0 P 24
10 ♌	7 P 07	11 ♎	10 P 13	11 ♎	5 A 30	12 ♐	1 P 12	12 ♑	6 A 18	10 ♒	9 P 22
13 ♍	3 A 03	14 ♏	10 A 24	13 ♏	5 P 51	15 ♑	0 A 53	14 ♒	3 P 59	13 ♓	4 A 26
15 ♎	1 P 37	16 ♐	11 P 08	16 ♐	6 A 45	17 ♒	9 A 57	16 ♓	10 P 25	15 ♈	9 A 03
18 ♏	2 A 27	19 ♑	8 A 59	18 ♑	5 P 44	19 ♓	2 P 32	19 ♈	1 A 40	17 ♉	11 A 22
20 ♐	2 P 21	21 ♒	3 P 24	21 ♒	1 A 03	21 ♈	4 P 12	21 ♉	2 A 26	19 ♊	0 P 10
22 ♑	11 P 11	23 ♓	5 P 50	23 ♓	4 A 27	23 ♉	3 P 40	23 ♊	2 A 04	21 ♋	1 P 11
25 ♒	4 A 49	25 ♈	6 P 52	25 ♈	5 A 16	25 ♊	3 P 31	25 ♋	2 A 44	23 ♌	4 P 00
27 ♓	8 A 05	27 ♉	7 P 57	27 ♉	4 A 57	27 ♋	4 P 50	27 ♌	6 A 03	25 ♍	9 P 54
29 ♈	10 A 18			29 ♊	5 A 36	29 ♌	9 P 36	29 ♍	1 P 21	28 ♎	7 A 48
31 ♉	0 P 52			31 ♋	8 A 32					30 ♏	8 P 04

JUL	TIME	AUG	TIME	SEPT	TIME	OCT	TIME	NOV	TIME	DEC	TIME
3 ♐	9 A 00	2 ♑	3 A 25	3 ♓	1 A 23	2 ♈	1 P 49	1 ♉	0 A 57	2 ♋	11 A 31
5 ♑	7 P 03	4 ♒	11 A 18	5 ♈	3 A 54	4 ♉	2 P 33	3 ♊	0 A 43	4 ♌	0 P 52
8 ♒	3 A 34	6 ♓	4 P 23	7 ♉	5 A 23	6 ♊	2 P 29	5 ♋	0 A 58	6 ♍	5 P 36
10 ♓	9 A 40	8 ♈	8 P 04	9 ♊	7 A 03	8 ♋	4 P 29	7 ♌	3 A 46	9 ♎	2 A 24
12 ♈	2 P 15	10 ♉	10 P 41	11 ♋	10 A 08	10 ♌	8 P 55	9 ♍	10 A 10	11 ♏	2 P 26
14 ♉	5 P 28	13 ♊	1 A 31	13 ♌	3 P 36	13 ♍	4 A 37	11 ♎	8 P 13	14 ♐	3 A 07
16 ♊	7 P 48	15 ♋	4 A 56	15 ♍	10 P 53	15 ♎	2 P 23	14 ♏	8 A 23	16 ♑	3 P 43
18 ♋	10 P 13	17 ♌	9 A 21	18 ♎	7 A 57	18 ♏	1 A 56	16 ♐	8 P 48	19 ♒	2 A 18
21 ♌	1 A 35	19 ♍	3 P 44	20 ♏	7 P 13	20 ♐	2 P 38	19 ♑	9 A 11	21 ♓	11 A 16
23 ♍	7 A 07	22 ♎	0 A 18	23 ♐	7 A 45	23 ♑	2 A 53	21 ♒	8 P 37	23 ♈	5 P 29
25 ♎	3 P 56	24 ♏	11 A 24	25 ♑	8 P 09	25 ♒	2 P 05	24 ♓	5 A 09	25 ♉	8 P 50
28 ♏	3 A 44	27 ♐	0 A 19	28 ♒	5 A 57	27 ♓	9 P 19	26 ♈	10 A 17	27 ♊	9 P 58
30 ♐	4 P 39	29 ♑	0 P 12	30 ♓	11 A 29	30 ♈	0 A 38	28 ♉	0 N 00	29 ♋	10 P 16
		31 ♒	8 P 33					30 ♊	11 A 32	31 ♌	11 P 20

1964

JAN	TIME	FEB	TIME	MAR	TIME	APR	TIME	MAY	TIME	JUN	TIME
3 ♍	2 A 50	1 ♎	7 P 21	2 ♏	1 P 48	1 ♐	9 A 59	1 ♑	5 A 37	2 ♓	10 A 52
5 ♎	10 A 19	4 ♏	5 A 24	5 ♐	1 A 56	3 ♑	10 P 47	3 ♒	6 P 04	4 ♈	6 P 20
7 ♏	9 P 29	6 ♐	5 P 54	7 ♑	2 P 58	6 ♒	10 A 26	6 ♓	3 A 34	6 ♉	9 P 17
10 ♐	10 A 24	9 ♑	6 A 30	10 ♒	1 A 20	8 ♓	6 P 38	8 ♈	9 A 05	8 ♊	9 P 59
12 ♑	10 P 34	11 ♒	4 P 41	12 ♓	8 A 47	10 ♈	10 P 59	10 ♉	11 A 10	10 ♋	9 P 22
15 ♒	8 A 35	13 ♓	11 P 54	14 ♈	1 P 12	13 ♉	0 A 34	12 ♊	11 A 16	12 ♌	9 P 38
17 ♓	4 P 54	16 ♈	5 A 11	16 ♉	3 P 41	15 ♊	1 A 33	14 ♋	10 A 43	15 ♍	0 A 14
19 ♈	11 P 08	18 ♉	8 A 56	18 ♊	5 P 50	17 ♋	2 A 34	16 ♌	0 P 21	17 ♎	6 A 57
22 ♉	3 A 26	20 ♊	0 N 00	20 ♋	8 P 20	19 ♌	5 A 39	18 ♍	4 P 50	19 ♏	5 P 12
24 ♊	5 A 52	22 ♋	2 P 53	23 ♌	0 A 08	21 ♍	11 A 29	21 ♎	0 A 58	22 ♐	5 A 31
26 ♋	7 A 45	24 ♌	5 P 48	25 ♍	5 A 33	23 ♎	7 P 25	23 ♏	11 A 36	24 ♑	6 P 14
28 ♌	9 A 32	26 ♍	10 P 14	27 ♎	0 P 46	26 ♏	5 A 27	25 ♐	11 P 30	27 ♒	6 A 15
30 ♍	0 P 43	29 ♎	4 A 35	29 ♏	10 P 17	28 ♐	5 P 18	28 ♑	0 N 00	29 ♓	4 P 47
								30 ♒	0 A 30		

JUL	TIME	AUG	TIME	SEPT	TIME	OCT	TIME	NOV	TIME	DEC	TIME
2 ♈	1 A 00	2 ♊	3 P 42	1 ♋	0 A 06	2 ♍	0 P 22	1 ♎	0 A 23	3 ♐	2 A 13
4 ♉	6 A 06	4 ♋	5 P 14	3 ♌	1 A 50	4 ♎	5 P 51	3 ♏	8 A 46	5 ♑	1 P 49
6 ♊	7 A 55	6 ♌	6 P 06	5 ♍	5 A 15	7 ♏	1 A 08	5 ♐	6 P 54	8 ♒	2 A 39
8 ♋	8 A 02	8 ♍	7 P 51	7 ♎	9 A 33	9 ♐	11 A 14	8 ♑	7 A 02	10 ♓	2 P 46
10 ♌	7 A 58	10 ♎	11 P 50	9 ♏	4 P 14	11 ♑	11 P 18	10 ♒	7 P 47	13 ♈	0 A 10
12 ♍	9 A 43	13 ♏	7 A 24	12 ♐	2 A 50	14 ♒	0 P 12	13 ♓	7 A 18	15 ♉	5 A 34
14 ♎	2 P 36	15 ♐	6 P 52	14 ♑	3 P 17	16 ♓	10 P 43	15 ♈	3 P 24	17 ♊	7 A 26
16 ♏	11 P 41	18 ♑	7 A 46	17 ♒	3 A 44	19 ♈	5 A 19	17 ♉	7 P 14	19 ♋	7 A 06
19 ♐	11 A 48	20 ♒	7 P 32	19 ♓	1 P 18	21 ♉	8 A 40	19 ♊	8 P 27	21 ♌	6 A 46
22 ♑	0 A 43	23 ♓	4 A 53	21 ♈	7 P 56	23 ♊	10 A 29	21 ♋	8 P 21	23 ♍	7 A 54
24 ♒	0 P 24	25 ♈	0 P 22	23 ♉	11 P 55	25 ♋	11 A 41	23 ♌	9 P 15	25 ♎	0 P 22
26 ♓	10 P 18	27 ♉	5 P 29	26 ♊	3 A 03	27 ♌	2 P 04	26 ♍	0 A 05	27 ♏	8 P 37
29 ♈	6 A 31	29 ♊	9 P 23	28 ♋	5 A 45	29 ♍	6 P 16	28 ♎	6 A 02	30 ♐	7 A 51
31 ♉	0 P 31			30 ♌	8 A 44			30 ♏	2 P 45		

1965

JAN

JAN	TIME
1 ♑	8 P 21
4 ♒	8 A 59
6 ♓	9 P 02
9 ♈	7 A 23
11 ♉	2 P 18
13 ♊	5 P 43
15 ♋	6 P 32
17 ♌	5 P 25
19 ♍	6 P 03
21 ♎	8 P 56
24 ♏	3 A 40
26 ♐	2 P 13
29 ♑	2 A 52
31 ♒	3 P 16

FEB

FEB	TIME
3 ♓	2 A 53
5 ♈	0 P 57
7 ♉	8 P 51
10 ♊	1 A 44
12 ♋	4 A 04
14 ♌	4 A 32
16 ♍	4 A 55
18 ♎	6 A 56
20 ♏	0 P 11
22 ♐	9 P 27
25 ♑	9 A 45
27 ♒	10 P 30

MAR

MAR	TIME
2 ♓	9 A 39
4 ♈	7 P 08
7 ♉	2 A 15
9 ♊	7 A 39
11 ♋	10 A 41
13 ♌	1 P 00
15 ♍	2 P 50
17 ♎	5 P 10
19 ♏	9 P 49
22 ♐	5 A 52
24 ♑	5 P 30
27 ♒	6 A 01
29 ♓	5 P 37

APR

APR	TIME
1 ♈	2 A 31
3 ♉	8 A 55
5 ♊	1 P 14
7 ♋	4 P 53
9 ♌	7 P 25
11 ♍	10 P 26
14 ♎	2 A 07
16 ♏	7 A 10
18 ♐	2 P 54
21 ♑	1 A 24
23 ♒	2 P 15
26 ♓	2 A 25
28 ♈	11 A 38
30 ♉	5 P 20

MAY

MAY	TIME
2 ♊	9 P 33
4 ♋	10 P 27
7 ♌	0 A 49
9 ♍	3 A 54
11 ♎	8 A 35
13 ♏	2 P 37
15 ♐	11 P 03
18 ♑	9 A 17
20 ♒	9 P 46
23 ♓	10 A 24
25 ♈	8 P 47
28 ♉	3 A 11
30 ♊	6 A 08

JUN

JUN	TIME
1 ♋	6 A 47
3 ♌	7 A 47
5 ♍	9 A 41
7 ♎	1 P 58
9 ♏	8 P 31
12 ♐	5 A 40
14 ♑	4 P 37
17 ♒	4 A 57
19 ♓	5 P 40
22 ♈	4 A 58
24 ♉	1 P 03
26 ♊	4 P 28
28 ♋	5 P 27
30 ♌	5 P 05

JUL

JUL	TIME
2 ♍	5 P 10
4 ♎	7 P 59
7 ♏	1 A 53
9 ♐	11 A 03
11 ♑	10 P 54
14 ♒	10 A 48
16 ♓	11 P 36
19 ♈	11 A 37
21 ♉	8 P 49
24 ♊	2 A 10
26 ♋	3 A 58
28 ♌	3 A 55
30 ♍	3 A 16

AUG

AUG	TIME
1 ♎	4 A 14
3 ♏	8 A 35
5 ♐	4 P 44
8 ♑	4 A 24
10 ♒	5 P 06
13 ♓	5 A 33
15 ♈	5 P 04
18 ♉	2 A 44
20 ♊	9 A 39
22 ♋	1 P 10
24 ♌	2 P 13
26 ♍	1 P 47
28 ♎	2 P 39
30 ♏	5 P 29

SEPT

SEPT	TIME
2 ♐	0 A 11
4 ♑	10 A 49
6 ♒	11 P 42
9 ♓	0 N 00
11 ♈	0 P 52
14 ♉	8 A 02
16 ♊	3 P 13
18 ♋	8 P 01
20 ♌	10 P 43
22 ♍	11 P 45
25 ♎	0 A 54
27 ♏	3 A 20
29 ♐	9 A 00

OCT

OCT	TIME
1 ♑	6 P 33
4 ♒	6 A 55
6 ♓	7 P 33
9 ♈	6 A 23
11 ♉	2 P 46
13 ♊	8 P 48
16 ♋	1 A 29
18 ♌	4 A 17
20 ♍	7 A 17
22 ♎	9 A 52
24 ♏	1 P 14
26 ♐	6 P 34
29 ♑	3 A 07
31 ♒	2 P 40

NOV

NOV	TIME
3 ♓	3 A 48
5 ♈	2 P 51
7 ♉	10 P 59
10 ♊	4 A 10
12 ♋	7 A 43
14 ♌	10 A 29
16 ♍	1 P 02
18 ♎	4 P 21
20 ♏	9 P 04
23 ♐	3 A 18
25 ♑	11 A 38
27 ♒	10 P 47
30 ♓	11 A 36

DEC

DEC	TIME
2 ♈	11 P 41
5 ♉	8 A 32
7 ♊	1 P 52
9 ♋	4 P 07
11 ♌	5 P 33
13 ♍	7 P 03
15 ♎	10 P 13
18 ♏	3 A 21
20 ♐	10 A 19
22 ♑	7 P 24
25 ♒	6 A 37
27 ♓	6 P 59
30 ♈	7 A 46

1966

JAN	TIME	FEB	TIME	MAR	TIME	APR	TIME	MAY	TIME	JUN	TIME
1 ♉	6 P 15	2 ♋	1 P 11	1 ♋	10 P 26	2 ♍	10 A 31	1 ♎	7 P 46	2 ♐	9 A 55
4 ♊	0 A 05	4 ♌	1 P 55	4 ♌	0 A 24	4 ♎	10 A 52	3 ♏	9 P 48	4 ♑	4 P 06
6 ♋	2 A 28	6 ♍	1 P 25	6 ♍	0 A 24	6 ♏	11 A 50	6 ♐	0 A 57	7 ♒	1 A 17
8 ♌	3 A 03	8 ♎	1 P 29	7 ♎	11 P 58	8 ♐	3 P 04	8 ♑	7 A 04	9 ♓	1 P 01
10 ♍	3 A 03	10 ♏	3 P 55	10 ♏	1 A 26	10 ♑	10 P 13	10 ♒	4 P 46	12 ♈	2 A 02
12 ♎	4 A 37	12 ♐	10 P 08	12 ♐	5 A 33	13 ♒	9 A 02	13 ♓	5 A 18	14 ♉	0 P 57
14 ♏	8 A 38	15 ♑	7 A 41	14 ♑	2 P 00	15 ♓	9 P 58	15 ♈	5 P 54	16 ♊	8 P 40
16 ♐	4 P 03	17 ♒	7 P 41	17 ♒	2 A 12	18 ♈	10 A 02	18 ♉	4 A 01	19 ♋	0 A 47
19 ♑	1 A 50	20 ♓	8 A 20	19 ♓	2 P 50	20 ♉	8 P 29	20 ♊	11 A 39	21 ♌	3 A 24
21 ♒	1 P 36	22 ♈	8 P 36	22 ♈	2 A 53	23 ♊	4 A 38	22 ♋	4 P 42	23 ♍	5 A 21
24 ♓	1 A 51	25 ♉	8 A 06	24 ♉	1 P 44	25 ♋	10 A 57	24 ♌	8 P 35	25 ♎	7 A 43
26 ♈	2 P 25	27 ♊	4 P 57	26 ♊	10 P 48	27 ♌	3 P 07	26 ♍	11 P 40	27 ♏	11 A 29
29 ♉	1 A 44			29 ♋	5 A 25	29 ♍	6 P 13	29 ♎	2 A 22	29 ♐	4 P 33
31 ♊	9 A 19			31 ♌	8 A 58			31 ♏	5 A 29		

JUL	TIME	AUG	TIME	SEPT	TIME	OCT	TIME	NOV	TIME	DEC	TIME
1 ♑	11 P 48	3 ♓	3 A 40	1 ♈	10 P 23	1 ♉	4 P 46	2 ♋	5 P 41	2 ♌	5 A 11
4 ♒	9 A 28	5 ♈	4 P 17	4 ♉	11 A 00	4 ♊	3 A 33	4 ♌	11 P 39	4 ♍	9 A 04
6 ♓	8 P 45	8 ♉	4 A 50	6 ♊	9 P 48	6 ♋	0 N 00	7 ♍	3 A 26	6 ♎	0 P 10
9 ♈	9 A 23	10 ♊	2 P 37	9 ♋	5 A 23	8 ♌	5 P 20	9 ♎	5 A 12	8 ♏	2 P 31
11 ♉	9 P 27	12 ♋	8 P 38	11 ♌	9 A 07	10 ♍	7 P 49	11 ♏	6 A 22	10 ♐	5 P 30
14 ♊	6 A 06	14 ♌	10 P 51	13 ♍	9 A 46	12 ♎	8 P 03	13 ♐	7 A 52	12 ♑	9 P 36
16 ♋	10 A 38	16 ♍	11 P 02	15 ♎	9 A 16	14 ♏	7 P 59	15 ♑	11 A 49	15 ♒	4 A 19
18 ♌	0 P 20	18 ♎	10 P 36	17 ♏	9 A 18	16 ♐	9 P 34	17 ♒	6 P 59	17 ♓	2 P 23
20 ♍	1 P 09	20 ♏	11 P 51	19 ♐	11 A 31	19 ♑	2 A 01	20 ♓	6 A 13	20 ♈	3 A 04
22 ♎	2 P 00	23 ♐	3 A 54	21 ♑	5 P 41	21 ♒	10 A 39	22 ♈	7 P 00	22 ♉	3 P 21
24 ♏	4 P 44	25 ♑	11 A 38	24 ♒	3 A 48	23 ♓	10 P 28	25 ♉	6 A 53	25 ♊	1 A 19
26 ♐	10 P 18	27 ♒	10 P 05	26 ♓	4 P 04	26 ♈	11 A 36	27 ♊	4 P 30	27 ♋	7 A 52
29 ♑	6 A 08	30 ♓	10 A 12	29 ♈	4 A 57	28 ♉	11 P 13	29 ♋	11 P 45	29 ♌	0 N 00
31 ♒	4 P 05					31 ♊	9 A 23			31 ♍	3 P 03

1967

JAN	TIME	FEB	TIME	MAR	TIME	APR	TIME	MAY	TIME	JUN	TIME
2 ♎	5 P 42	1 ♏	2 A 18	2 ♐	0 P 11	1 ♑	0 A 20	3 ♓	1 A 19	1 ♈	8 P 39
4 ♏	8 P 35	3 ♐	6 A 18	4 ♑	5 P 54	3 ♒	8 A 12	5 ♈	1 P 49	4 ♉	9 A 14
7 ♐	0 A 37	5 ♑	0 P 11	7 ♒	2 A 36	5 ♓	7 P 24	8 ♉	2 A 24	6 ♊	8 P 42
9 ♑	5 A 51	7 ♒	8 P 29	9 ♓	1 P 12	8 ♈	7 A 46	10 ♊	1 P 58	9 ♋	6 A 20
11 ♒	1 P 08	10 ♓	6 A 30	12 ♈	1 A 19	10 ♉	8 P 17	12 ♋	11 P 54	11 ♌	1 P 48
13 ♓	10 P 49	12 ♈	6 P 28	14 ♉	2 P 02	13 ♊	8 A 23	15 ♌	7 A 59	13 ♍	7 P 15
16 ♈	11 A 00	15 ♉	7 A 29	17 ♊	2 A 05	15 ♋	6 P 49	17 ♍	1 P 12	15 ♎	10 P 48
18 ♉	11 P 36	17 ♊	7 P 02	19 ♋	11 A 49	18 ♌	1 A 52	19 ♎	3 P 47	18 ♏	0 A 35
21 ♊	10 A 39	20 ♋	3 A 18	21 ♌	5 P 40	20 ♍	5 A 54	21 ♏	4 P 32	20 ♐	2 A 30
23 ♋	5 P 40	22 ♌	7 A 52	23 ♍	7 P 56	22 ♎	6 A 47	23 ♐	4 P 50	22 ♑	5 A 02
25 ♌	9 P 11	24 ♍	9 A 07	25 ♎	7 P 47	24 ♏	6 A 18	25 ♑	6 P 51	24 ♒	9 A 21
27 ♍	11 P 01	26 ♎	9 A 10	27 ♏	7 P 25	26 ♐	6 A 18	27 ♒	11 P 48	26 ♓	5 P 04
30 ♎	0 A 04	28 ♏	9 A 43	29 ♐	8 P 13	28 ♑	9 A 05	30 ♓	8 A 40	29 ♈	4 A 20
						30 ♒	3 P 20				

JUL	TIME	AUG	TIME	SEPT	TIME	OCT	TIME	NOV	TIME	DEC	TIME
1 ♉	5 P 00	2 ♋	10 P 24	1 ♌	2 P 25	1 ♍	4 A 04	1 ♏	3 P 40	1 ♐	2 A 04
4 ♊	4 A 34	5 ♌	4 A 21	3 ♍	5 P 33	3 ♎	5 A 02	3 ♐	3 P 14	3 ♑	2 A 44
6 ♋	1 P 39	7 ♍	4 A 52	5 ♎	6 P 19	5 ♏	4 A 31	5 ♑	4 P 04	5 ♒	5 A 22
8 ♌	7 P 56	9 ♎	9 A 43	7 ♏	7 P 08	7 ♐	4 A 47	7 ♒	8 P 15	7 ♓	11 A 49
11 ♍	0 A 14	11 ♏	11 A 41	9 ♐	8 P 34	9 ♑	7 A 10	10 ♓	3 A 56	9 ♈	10 P 15
13 ♎	3 A 40	13 ♐	2 P 45	12 ♑	0 A 37	11 ♒	0 P 45	12 ♈	3 P 25	12 ♉	10 A 59
15 ♏	6 A 25	15 ♑	7 P 17	14 ♒	7 A 09	13 ♓	9 P 52	15 ♉	4 A 04	14 ♊	11 P 18
17 ♐	9 A 15	18 ♒	1 A 29	16 ♓	4 P 07	16 ♈	9 A 24	17 ♊	4 P 37	17 ♋	10 A 26
19 ♑	1 P 04	20 ♓	9 A 33	19 ♈	2 A 53	18 ♉	9 P 29	20 ♋	4 A 00	19 ♌	7 P 25
21 ♒	6 P 11	22 ♈	7 P 56	21 ♉	3 P 26	21 ♊	10 A 24	22 ♌	1 P 52	22 ♍	2 A 42
24 ♓	2 A 01	25 ♉	8 A 33	24 ♊	4 A 04	23 ♋	10 P 15	24 ♍	8 P 53	24 ♎	7 A 39
26 ♈	0 P 12	27 ♊	9 P 00	26 ♋	3 P 37	26 ♌	7 A 41	27 ♎	0 A 50	26 ♏	10 A 41
29 ♉	0 A 55	30 ♋	7 A 39	28 ♌	0 M 00	28 ♍	1 P 33	29 ♏	2 A 10	28 ♐	11 A 50
31 ♊	1 P 11					30 ♎	3 P 44			30 ♑	1 P 00

1968

JAN	TIME	FEB	TIME	MAR	TIME	APR	TIME	MAY	TIME	JUN	TIME
1 ♒	3 P 47	2 ♈	2 P 46	3 ♉	10 A 24	2 ♊	6 A 21	2 ♋	1 A 37	3 ♍	4 A 08
3 ♓	8 P 55	5 ♉	2 A 15	5 ♊	10 P 53	4 ♋	7 P 00	4 ♌	1 P 09	5 ♎	9 A 53
6 ♈	6 A 15	7 ♊	3 P 14	8 ♋	11 A 24	7 ♌	5 A 40	6 ♍	8 P 57	7 ♏	0 P 29
8 ♉	6 P 22	10 ♋	2 A 31	10 ♌	8 P 30	9 ♍	0 P 11	9 ♎	1 A 06	9 ♐	0 P 19
11 ♊	6 A 51	12 ♌	10 A 54	13 ♍	1 A 53	11 ♎	2 P 56	11 ♏	2 A 10	11 ♑	0 P 19
13 ♋	5 P 58	14 ♍	4 P 29	15 ♎	4 A 24	13 ♏	3 P 14	13 ♐	1 A 34	13 ♒	1 P 12
16 ♌	2 A 21	16 ♎	7 P 39	17 ♏	5 A 38	15 ♐	3 P 16	15 ♑	1 A 28	15 ♓	5 P 08
18 ♍	8 A 29	18 ♏	10 P 17	19 ♐	6 A 54	17 ♑	4 P 34	17 ♒	3 A 40	18 ♈	1 A 04
20 ♎	1 P 13	21 ♐	0 A 47	21 ♑	9 A 47	19 ♒	8 P 19	19 ♓	9 A 02	20 ♉	0 P 49
22 ♏	4 P 32	23 ♑	4 A 14	23 ♒	2 P 35	22 ♓	3 A 23	21 ♈	6 P 33	23 ♊	1 A 30
24 ♐	7 P 06	25 ♒	8 A 47	25 ♓	9 P 42	24 ♈	1 P 23	24 ♉	6 A 33	25 ♋	1 P 47
26 ♑	9 P 42	27 ♓	3 P 07	28 ♈	6 A 55	27 ♉	0 A 42	26 ♊	7 P 13	28 ♌	0 A 41
29 ♒	1 A 06	29 ♈	11 P 24	30 ♉	6 P 00	29 ♊	1 P 00	29 ♋	7 A 36	30 ♍	9 A 45
31 ♓	6 A 32							31 ♌	6 P 51		

JUL	TIME	AUG	TIME	SEPT	TIME	OCT	TIME	NOV	TIME	DEC	TIME
2 ♎	3 P 56	1 ♏	1 A 53	1 ♑	1 P 02	3 ♓	3 A 30	1 ♈	4 P 58	1 ♉	9 A 02
4 ♏	8 P 13	3 ♐	4 A 52	3 ♒	4 P 21	5 ♈	10 A 52	4 ♉	3 A 05	3 ♊	9 P 05
6 ♐	9 P 52	5 ♑	7 A 02	5 ♓	9 P 00	7 ♉	8 P 12	6 ♊	2 P 36	6 ♋	9 A 36
8 ♑	10 P 31	7 ♒	8 A 53	8 ♈	3 A 07	10 ♊	7 A 25	9 ♋	3 A 07	8 ♌	10 P 00
10 ♒	11 P 35	9 ♓	0 P 21	10 ♉	0 N 00	12 ♋	8 P 09	11 ♌	3 P 49	11 ♍	9 A 06
13 ♓	2 A 26	11 ♈	6 P 07	12 ♊	11 P 36	15 ♌	8 A 35	14 ♍	2 A 04	13 ♎	5 P 01
15 ♈	9 A 11	14 ♉	3 A 25	15 ♋	0 P 25	17 ♍	5 P 17	16 ♎	8 A 22	15 ♏	9 P 15
17 ♉	7 P 37	16 ♊	3 P 52	17 ♌	11 P 49	19 ♎	10 P 12	18 ♏	11 A 01	17 ♐	10 P 09
20 ♊	8 A 10	19 ♋	4 A 24	20 ♍	7 A 44	22 ♏	0 A 09	20 ♐	11 A 01	19 ♑	9 P 33
22 ♋	8 P 41	21 ♌	3 P 02	22 ♎	0 N 00	24 ♐	0 A 34	22 ♑	10 A 43	21 ♒	9 P 32
25 ♌	7 A 11	24 ♍	0 A 19	24 ♏	2 P 48	26 ♑	1 A 25	24 ♒	11 A 22	23 ♓	11 P 34
27 ♍	3 P 20	26 ♎	6 A 33	26 ♐	4 P 20	28 ♒	3 A 46	26 ♓	1 P 15	26 ♈	5 A 14
29 ♎	9 P 34	28 ♏	7 A 32	28 ♑	6 P 39	30 ♓	8 A 56	28 ♈	10 P 30	28 ♉	3 P 01
		30 ♐	10 A 18	30 ♒	10 P 16					31 ♊	3 A 11

1969

JAN	TIME		FEB	TIME		MAR	TIME
2 ♋	4 P 04		1 ♌	10 A 37		3 ♍	4 A 19
5 ♌	4 A 01		3 ♍	9 P 04		5 ♎	11 A 38
7 ♍	3 P 05		6 ♎	5 A 09		7 ♏	4 P 57
9 ♎	11 P 32		8 ♏	11 A 18		9 ♐	8 P 56
12 ♏	5 A 23		10 ♐	3 P 06		11 ♑	11 P 51
14 ♐	7 A 52		12 ♑	5 P 31		14 ♒	2 A 16
16 ♑	8 A 32		14 ♒	6 P 25		16 ♓	5 A 29
18 ♒	8 A 16		16 ♓	8 P 20		18 ♈	9 A 22
20 ♓	9 A 50		18 ♈	11 P 50		20 ♉	3 P 59
22 ♈	1 P 50		21 ♉	6 A 40		23 ♊	1 A 57
24 ♉	10 P 23		23 ♊	5 P 42		25 ♋	2 P 16
27 ♊	9 A 49		26 ♋	6 A 28		28 ♌	2 A 58
29 ♋	10 P 48		28 ♌	6 P 38		30 ♍	1 P 07

APR	TIME		MAY	TIME		JUN	TIME
1 ♎	7 P 59		1 ♏	9 A 10		1 ♑	9 P 04
4 ♏	0 A 16		3 ♐	11 A 00		3 ♒	9 P 22
6 ♐	2 A 56		5 ♑	0 N 00		5 ♓	11 P 34
8 ♑	5 A 24		7 ♒	1 P 43		8 ♈	4 A 55
10 ♒	8 A 16		9 ♓	5 P 29		10 ♉	1 P 10
12 ♓	0 P 21		11 ♈	11 P 26		13 ♊	0 A 07
14 ♈	5 P 31		14 ♉	7 A 26		15 ♋	0 P 12
17 ♉	0 A 46		16 ♊	5 P 43		18 ♌	0 A 37
19 ♊	10 A 14		19 ♋	5 A 24		20 ♍	1 P 00
21 ♋	10 P 13		21 ♌	6 P 16		22 ♎	11 P 04
24 ♌	11 A 12		24 ♍	6 A 18		25 ♏	5 A 14
26 ♍	10 P 07		26 ♎	2 P 54		27 ♐	7 A 47
29 ♎	5 A 40		28 ♏	7 P 44		29 ♑	8 A 02
			30 ♐	9 P 13			

JUL	TIME		AUG	TIME		SEPT	TIME
1 ♒	7 A 06		1 ♈	8 P 01		2 ♊	7 P 21
3 ♓	7 A 45		4 ♉	1 A 57		5 ♋	7 A 10
5 ♈	11 A 19		6 ♊	11 A 37		7 ♌	8 P 04
7 ♉	6 P 53		9 ♋	0 A 19		10 ♍	7 A 31
10 ♊	5 A 37		11 ♌	1 P 00		12 ♎	6 P 18
12 ♋	6 P 16		14 ♍	0 A 24		15 ♏	0 A 04
15 ♌	6 A 43		16 ♎	10 A 39		17 ♐	5 A 23
17 ♍	6 P 33		18 ♏	6 P 14		19 ♑	9 A 04
20 ♎	5 A 15		20 ♐	11 P 59		21 ♒	11 A 31
22 ♏	0 P 54		23 ♑	2 A 54		23 ♓	1 P 41
24 ♐	5 P 12		25 ♒	3 A 58		25 ♈	4 P 09
26 ♑	6 P 22		27 ♓	4 A 23		27 ♉	8 P 30
28 ♒	6 P 05		29 ♈	6 A 25		30 ♊	3 A 52
30 ♓	6 P 03		31 ♉	10 A 41			

OCT	TIME		NOV	TIME		DEC	TIME
2 ♋	4 P 41		1 ♌	11 A 38		1 ♍	8 A 10
5 ♌	5 A 24		4 ♍	0 A 13		3 ♎	7 P 11
7 ♍	4 P 58		6 ♎	10 A 08		6 ♏	2 A 25
10 ♎	1 A 00		8 ♏	4 P 18		8 ♐	5 A 48
12 ♏	6 A 37		10 ♐	7 P 33		10 ♑	6 A 47
14 ♐	10 A 27		12 ♑	9 P 26		12 ♒	7 A 04
16 ♑	1 P 31		14 ♒	11 P 12		14 ♓	8 A 20
18 ♒	3 P 55		17 ♓	1 A 58		16 ♈	0 P 11
20 ♓	7 P 15		19 ♈	6 A 22		18 ♉	2 P 49
22 ♈	11 P 39		21 ♉	0 P 34		20 ♊	11 P 43
25 ♉	5 A 28		23 ♊	8 P 42		23 ♋	10 A 37
27 ♊	1 P 23		26 ♋	7 A 02		26 ♌	2 A 32
30 ♋	0 A 43		28 ♌	7 P 23		28 ♍	3 P 13
						31 ♎	3 A 01

1970

JAN	TIME	FEB	TIME	MAR	TIME	APR	TIME	MAY	TIME	JUN	TIME
2 ♏	0N00	1 ♐	1A40	2 ♑	1P01	3 ♓	0A17	2 ♈	9A28	3 ♊	2A35
4 ♐	4P30	3 ♑	4A24	4 ♒	2P52	5 ♈	1A38	4 ♉	1P03	5 ♋	10A42
6 ♑	5P41	5 ♒	4A19	6 ♓	2P37	7 ♉	4A00	6 ♊	6P16	7 ♌	9P37
8 ♒	5P25	7 ♓	3A58	8 ♈	3P10	9 ♊	8A55	9 ♋	2A17	10 ♍	10A00
10 ♓	5P17	9 ♈	4A54	10 ♉	5P40	11 ♋	5P54	11 ♌	1P37	12 ♎	10P33
12 ♈	7P15	11 ♉	8A29	12 ♊	11P39	14 ♌	5A57	14 ♍	2A21	15 ♏	8A06
15 ♉	0A38	13 ♊	3P53	15 ♋	9A49	16 ♍	6P36	16 ♎	2P07	17 ♐	1P52
17 ♊	9A19	16 ♋	3A09	17 ♌	10P11	19 ♎	5A46	18 ♏	10P39	19 ♑	4P11
19 ♋	8P48	18 ♌	3P39	20 ♍	10A48	21 ♏	2P12	21 ♐	4A10	21 ♒	5P33
22 ♌	9A11	21 ♍	4A04	22 ♎	9P57	23 ♐	8P22	23 ♑	7A17	23 ♓	6P31
24 ♍	9P41	23 ♎	3P33	25 ♏	7A08	26 ♑	1A02	25 ♒	10A10	25 ♈	9P16
27 ♎	9A49	26 ♏	1A25	27 ♐	2P20	28 ♒	4A31	27 ♓	0P31	28 ♉	2A01
29 ♏	7P27	28 ♐	8A53	29 ♑	7P27	30 ♓	7A03	29 ♈	3P48	30 ♊	9A00
				31 ♒	10P38			31 ♉	8P22		

JUL	TIME	AUG	TIME	SEPT	TIME	OCT	TIME	NOV	TIME	DEC	TIME
2 ♋	5P34	1 ♌	11A02	2 ♎	6P14	2 ♏	11A14	1 ♐	2A27	2 ♒	7P36
5 ♌	4A52	3 ♍	11P30	5 ♏	5A30	4 ♐	8P33	3 ♑	8A56	4 ♓	10P07
7 ♍	5P15	6 ♎	0P12	7 ♐	3P07	7 ♑	3A10	5 ♒	1P23	7 ♈	1A01
10 ♎	5A49	8 ♏	11P43	9 ♑	9P03	9 ♒	7A34	7 ♓	4P42	9 ♉	4A25
12 ♏	4P43	11 ♐	8A28	12 ♒	0A01	11 ♓	9A34	9 ♈	6P42	11 ♊	8A58
14 ♐	11P33	13 ♑	0P41	14 ♓	0A03	13 ♈	10A23	11 ♉	8P53	13 ♋	2P58
17 ♑	2A40	15 ♒	1P55	15 ♈	11P58	15 ♉	11A12	14 ♊	0A08	15 ♌	11P49
19 ♒	3A13	17 ♓	1P25	18 ♉	0A45	17 ♊	2P07	16 ♋	5A50	18 ♍	11A12
21 ♓	2A57	19 ♈	1P09	20 ♊	4A29	19 ♋	8P20	18 ♌	2P47	20 ♎	0M00
23 ♈	4A00	21 ♉	3P04	22 ♋	0N00	22 ♌	6A39	21 ♍	3A07	23 ♏	11A37
25 ♉	7A36	23 ♊	8P08	24 ♌	11P18	24 ♍	7P27	23 ♎	3P49	25 ♐	7P38
27 ♊	2P17	26 ♋	5A21	27 ♍	0P12	27 ♎	7A48	26 ♏	2A24	28 ♑	0A16
29 ♋	11P53	28 ♌	5P12	30 ♎	0A25	29 ♏	6P10	28 ♐	10A21	30 ♒	2A54
		31 ♍	5A45					30 ♑	3P10		

1971

JAN	TIME		FEB	TIME		MAR	TIME		APR	TIME		MAY	TIME		JUN	TIME
1 ♓	4 A 37		1 ♉	4 P 00		1 ♉	0 A 07		1 ♋	5 P 14		1 ♌	9 A 33		2 ♎	5 P 30
3 ♈	6 A 46		3 ♊	9 P 36		3 ♊	3 A 28		4 ♌	2 A 33		3 ♍	9 P 17		5 ♏	5 A 49
5 ♉	9 A 59		6 ♋	4 A 37		5 ♋	10 A 08		6 ♍	2 P 40		6 ♎	10 A 12		7 ♐	3 P 47
7 ♊	3 P 26		8 ♌	2 P 42		7 ♌	8 P 24		9 ♎	3 A 25		8 ♏	10 P 01		9 ♑	10 P 56
9 ♋	10 P 30		11 ♍	1 A 57		10 ♍	8 A 24		11 ♏	3 P 45		11 ♐	8 A 12		12 ♒	4 A 25
12 ♌	7 A 55		13 ♎	2 P 14		12 ♎	9 P 07		14 ♐	2 A 18		13 ♑	4 P 33		14 ♓	8 A 07
14 ♍	7 P 04		16 ♏	3 A 15		15 ♏	9 A 24		16 ♑	11 A 16		15 ♒	10 P 39		16 ♈	11 A 10
17 ♎	7 A 35		18 ♐	2 P 03		17 ♐	8 P 33		18 ♒	5 P 13		18 ♓	2 A 55		18 ♉	2 P 01
19 ♏	7 P 59		20 ♑	8 P 43		20 ♑	4 A 58		20 ♓	8 P 07		20 ♈	5 A 23		20 ♊	5 P 10
22 ♐	5 A 18		22 ♒	11 P 35		22 ♒	9 A 34		22 ♈	8 P 59		22 ♉	6 A 33		22 ♋	9 P 04
24 ♑	10 A 58		24 ♓	11 P 54		24 ♓	10 A 51		24 ♉	9 P 01		24 ♊	8 A 27		25 ♌	3 A 41
26 ♒	0 P 39		26 ♈	11 P 17		26 ♈	10 A 36		26 ♊	10 P 13		26 ♋	11 A 39		27 ♍	1 P 12
28 ♓	1 P 18					28 ♉	10 A 12		29 ♋	2 A 09		28 ♌	6 P 28		30 ♎	1 A 30
30 ♈	1 P 49					30 ♊	11 A 50					31 ♍	4 A 44			

JUL	TIME		AUG	TIME		SEPT	TIME		OCT	TIME		NOV	TIME		DEC	TIME
2 ♏	2 P 00		1 ♐	9 A 06		2 ♒	7 A 01		1 ♓	7 P 31		2 ♉	6 A 02		1 ♊	4 P 53
5 ♐	0 A 11		3 ♑	4 P 50		4 ♓	8 A 58		3 ♈	7 P 51		4 ♊	6 A 10		3 ♋	6 P 45
7 ♑	7 A 19		5 ♒	8 P 53		6 ♈	8 A 53		5 ♉	7 P 11		6 ♋	8 A 07		5 ♌	10 P 49
9 ♒	11 A 31		7 ♓	10 P 40		8 ♉	8 A 51		7 ♊	7 P 36		8 ♌	1 P 29		8 ♍	7 A 02
11 ♓	2 P 21		9 ♈	11 P 26		10 ♊	10 A 41		9 ♋	10 P 47		10 ♍	10 P 54		10 ♎	6 P 34
13 ♈	4 P 24		12 ♉	1 A 00		12 ♋	3 P 40		12 ♌	5 A 57		13 ♎	11 A 24		13 ♏	7 A 23
15 ♉	7 P 29		14 ♊	4 A 14		15 ♌	0 A 01		14 ♍	4 P 17		15 ♏	11 P 54		15 ♐	7 P 10
17 ♊	11 P 11		16 ♋	10 A 13		17 ♍	10 A 37		17 ♎	4 A 53		18 ♐	11 A 48		18 ♑	4 A 40
20 ♋	4 A 36		18 ♌	6 P 25		19 ♎	10 P 35		19 ♏	5 P 27		20 ♑	9 P 55		20 ♒	11 A 49
22 ♌	11 A 37		21 ♍	4 A 31		22 ♏	11 A 12		22 ♐	5 A 21		23 ♒	5 A 39		22 ♓	5 P 13
24 ♍	9 P 15		23 ♎	4 P 04		24 ♐	11 P 48		24 ♑	4 P 12		25 ♓	11 A 29		24 ♈	9 P 03
27 ♎	9 A 00		26 ♏	4 A 53		27 ♑	9 A 55		27 ♒	0 A 05		27 ♈	2 P 49		26 ♉	11 P 36
29 ♏	9 P 53		28 ♐	5 P 04		29 ♒	4 P 40		29 ♓	4 A 41		29 ♉	4 P 03		29 ♊	1 A 50
			31 ♑	2 A 12					31 ♈	6 A 18					31 ♋	4 A 21

1972

JAN	TIME	FEB	TIME	MAR	TIME	APR	TIME	MAY	TIME	JUN	TIME
2 ♌	8 A 38	1 ♍	0 A 46	1 ♎	7 P 02	3 ♐	2 A 44	2 ♑	8 P 36	1 ♒	0 P 12
4 ♍	4 P 01	3 ♎	10 A 50	4 ♏	7 A 02	5 ♑	2 P 46	5 ♒	6 A 42	3 ♓	7 P 52
6 ♎	2 A 32	5 ♏	11 P 18	6 ♐	7 P 41	7 ♒	11 P 42	7 ♓	1 P 24	6 ♈	0 A 31
9 ♏	3 P 16	8 ♐	0 N 00	9 ♑	7 A 02	10 ♓	4 A 21	9 ♈	4 P 21	8 ♉	2 A 31
12 ♐	3 A 33	10 ♑	10 P 03	11 ♒	2 P 38	12 ♈	6 A 10	11 ♉	4 P 44	10 ♊	2 A 37
14 ♑	0 P 56	13 ♒	4 A 32	13 ♓	6 P 12	14 ♉	5 A 44	13 ♊	4 P 00	12 ♋	3 A 11
16 ♒	7 P 18	15 ♓	7 A 55	15 ♈	7 P 17	16 ♊	5 A 35	15 ♋	4 P 40	14 ♌	5 A 10
18 ♓	11 P 30	17 ♈	9 A 53	17 ♉	7 P 27	18 ♋	7 A 09	17 ♌	7 P 45	16 ♍	11 A 05
21 ♈	2 A 35	19 ♉	11 A 21	19 ♊	8 P 34	20 ♌	0 P 11	20 ♍	2 A 50	18 ♎	8 P 44
23 ♉	5 A 18	21 ♊	2 P 03	21 ♋	11 P 49	22 ♍	8 P 33	22 ♎	1 P 59	21 ♏	9 A 10
25 ♊	8 A 32	23 ♋	6 P 13	24 ♌	6 A 06	25 ♎	8 A 10	25 ♏	2 A 32	23 ♐	9 P 48
27 ♋	0 P 11	26 ♌	0 A 27	26 ♍	2 P 55	27 ♏	8 P 25	27 ♐	2 P 48	26 ♑	9 A 02
29 ♌	5 P 28	28 ♍	8 A 24	29 ♎	1 A 42	30 ♐	8 A 46	30 ♑	2 A 33	28 ♒	6 P 12
				31 ♏	1 P 50						

JUL	TIME	AUG	TIME	SEPT	TIME	OCT	TIME	NOV	TIME	DEC	TIME
1 ♓	1 A 09	1 ♉	3 P 02	2 ♋	2 A 24	1 ♌	0 P 22	2 ♎	10 A 28	2 ♏	4 A 12
3 ♈	6 A 24	3 ♊	5 P 45	4 ♌	7 A 00	3 ♍	7 P 31	4 ♏	10 P 00	4 ♐	4 P 53
5 ♉	9 A 41	5 ♋	8 P 31	6 ♍	0 P 56	6 ♎	4 A 27	7 ♐	10 A 24	7 ♑	5 A 12
7 ♊	11 A 41	8 ♌	0 A 08	8 ♎	9 P 36	8 ♏	3 P 26	9 ♑	11 P 05	9 ♒	4 P 50
9 ♋	0 P 51	10 ♍	5 A 19	11 ♏	8 A 12	11 ♐	3 A 52	12 ♒	10 A 50	12 ♓	2 A 21
11 ♌	3 P 27	12 ♎	1 P 10	13 ♐	8 P 28	13 ♑	4 P 37	14 ♓	7 P 38	14 ♈	8 A 38
13 ♍	8 P 19	15 ♏	0 A 06	16 ♑	9 A 02	16 ♒	3 A 38	17 ♈	0 A 30	16 ♉	0 N 00
16 ♎	4 A 39	17 ♐	0 P 49	18 ♒	7 P 05	18 ♓	11 A 08	19 ♉	1 A 57	18 ♊	0 P 38
18 ♏	4 P 27	20 ♑	0 A 53	21 ♓	1 A 02	20 ♈	2 P 36	21 ♊	1 A 39	20 ♋	0 P 10
21 ♐	5 A 12	22 ♒	9 A 49	23 ♈	3 A 47	22 ♉	3 P 03	23 ♋	1 A 19	22 ♌	0 P 51
23 ♑	4 P 26	24 ♓	3 P 27	25 ♉	4 A 57	24 ♊	2 P 44	25 ♌	2 A 49	24 ♍	4 P 18
26 ♒	1 A 12	26 ♈	6 P 33	27 ♊	5 A 41	26 ♋	3 P 21	27 ♍	7 A 28	26 ♎	11 P 24
28 ♓	7 A 40	28 ♉	9 P 03	29 ♋	8 A 04	28 ♌	6 P 43	29 ♎	4 P 21	29 ♏	10 A 37
30 ♈	0 N 00	30 ♊	11 P 12			31 ♍	0 A 46			31 ♐	11 P 24

1973

JAN	TIME	FEB	TIME	MAR	TIME	APR	TIME	MAY	TIME	JUN	TIME
3 ♑	0 N 00	2 ♒	5 A 52	1 ♒	2 P 27	2 ♈	0 P 31	2 ♉	0 A 49	2 ♋	11 A 24
5 ♒	10 P 46	4 ♓	2 P 14	3 ♓	10 P 24	4 ♉	3 P 10	4 ♊	1 A 16	4 ♌	11 A 50
8 ♓	8 A 02	6 ♈	8 P 22	6 ♈	3 A 19	6 ♊	4 P 25	6 ♋	1 A 37	6 ♍	2 P 32
10 ♈	11 A 29	9 ♉	1 A 12	8 ♉	7 A 14	8 ♋	6 P 25	8 ♌	3 A 37	8 ♎	9 P 17
12 ♉	7 P 25	11 ♊	4 A 21	10 ♊	9 A 59	10 ♌	9 P 39	10 ♍	8 A 06	11 ♏	7 A 15
14 ♊	9 P 32	13 ♋	6 A 38	12 ♋	0 P 41	13 ♍	2 A 59	12 ♎	3 P 32	13 ♐	7 P 16
16 ♋	10 P 38	15 ♌	8 A 58	14 ♌	3 P 53	15 ♎	10 A 08	15 ♏	1 A 35	16 ♑	7 A 48
18 ♌	11 P 39	17 ♍	0 P 21	16 ♍	8 P 35	17 ♏	7 P 15	17 ♐	1 P 00	18 ♒	7 P 59
21 ♍	2 A 24	19 ♎	5 P 44	19 ♎	2 A 45	20 ♐	6 A 25	20 ♑	1 A 32	21 ♓	7 A 28
23 ♎	8 A 10	22 ♏	2 A 45	21 ♏	11 A 25	22 ♑	6 P 55	22 ♒	2 P 11	23 ♈	4 P 10
25 ♏	6 P 10	24 ♐	2 P 39	23 ♐	10 P 30	25 ♒	7 A 25	25 ♓	1 A 08	25 ♉	9 P 07
28 ♐	6 A 50	27 ♑	3 A 13	26 ♑	11 A 23	27 ♓	5 P 11	27 ♈	8 A 24	27 ♊	10 P 32
30 ♑	7 P 09			28 ♒	11 P 19	29 ♈	10 P 52	29 ♉	11 A 40	29 ♋	10 P 27
				31 ♓	7 A 37			31 ♊	0 N 00		

JUL	TIME	AUG	TIME	SEPT	TIME	OCT	TIME	NOV	TIME	DEC	TIME
1 ♌	9 P 51	2 ♎	0 P 55	1 ♏	5 A 20	3 ♑	0 N 00	2 ♒	8 A 33	2 ♓	4 A 24
3 ♍	11 P 34	4 ♏	8 P 33	3 ♐	3 P 37	6 ♒	0 A 37	4 ♓	8 P 17	4 ♈	2 P 00
6 ♎	4 A 04	7 ♐	7 A 39	6 ♑	4 A 04	8 ♓	11 A 37	7 ♈	4 A 38	6 ♉	7 P 12
8 ♏	1 P 00	9 ♑	8 P 39	8 ♒	4 P 32	10 ♈	6 P 31	9 ♉	8 A 47	8 ♊	9 P 17
11 ♐	1 A 13	12 ♒	8 A 40	11 ♓	2 A 36	12 ♉	10 P 52	11 ♊	10 A 31	10 ♋	9 P 22
13 ♑	1 P 49	14 ♓	6 P 53	13 ♈	9 A 50	15 ♊	1 A 40	13 ♋	11 A 22	12 ♌	9 P 11
16 ♒	2 A 10	17 ♈	3 A 16	15 ♉	3 P 19	17 ♋	3 A 37	15 ♌	0 P 31	14 ♍	10 P 42
18 ♓	0 P 57	19 ♉	9 A 10	17 ♊	7 P 09	19 ♌	6 A 06	17 ♍	3 P 43	17 ♎	3 A 07
20 ♈	9 P 48	21 ♊	1 P 41	19 ♋	10 P 04	21 ♍	10 A 15	19 ♎	9 P 13	19 ♏	11 A 03
23 ♉	4 A 01	23 ♋	4 P 20	22 ♌	0 A 47	23 ♎	3 P 20	22 ♏	5 A 22	21 ♐	9 P 50
25 ♊	7 A 27	25 ♌	5 P 55	24 ♍	4 A 07	25 ♏	10 P 29	24 ♐	3 P 33	24 ♑	9 A 57
27 ♋	8 A 24	27 ♍	7 P 48	26 ♎	8 A 13	28 ♐	8 A 06	27 ♑	2 A 59	26 ♒	10 P 18
29 ♌	8 A 51	29 ♎	10 P 27	28 ♏	2 P 38	30 ♑	7 P 52	29 ♒	3 P 42	29 ♓	10 A 37
31 ♍	9 A 52			30 ♐	11 P 47					31 ♈	9 P 25

1974

JAN	TIME	FEB	TIME	MAR	TIME	APR	TIME	MAY	TIME	JUN	TIME
3 ♉	4 A 39	1 ♊	4 P 46	3 ♋	2 A 53	1 ♌	11 A 31	2 ♎	11 P 49	1 ♏	11 A 29
5 ♊	7 A 59	3 ♋	6 P 50	5 ♌	4 A 20	3 ♍	2 P 00	5 ♏	4 A 58	3 ♐	7 P 42
7 ♋	8 A 16	5 ♌	6 P 43	7 ♍	5 A 10	5 ♎	4 P 26	7 ♐	0 P 12	6 ♑	5 A 53
9 ♌	7 A 54	7 ♍	6 P 39	9 ♎	6 A 46	7 ♏	8 P 48	9 ♑	10 P 15	8 ♒	5 P 51
11 ♍	7 A 55	9 ♎	8 P 31	11 ♏	10 A 46	10 ♐	3 A 34	12 ♒	10 A 24	11 ♓	6 A 55
13 ♎	10 A 48	12 ♏	1 A 21	13 ♐	6 P 28	12 ♑	1 P 50	14 ♓	11 P 05	13 ♈	6 P 14
15 ♏	5 P 32	14 ♐	10 A 16	16 ♑	6 A 01	15 ♒	2 A 54	17 ♈	9 A 33	16 ♉	2 A 09
18 ♐	3 A 33	16 ♑	10 P 47	18 ♒	6 P 40	17 ♓	2 P 57	19 ♉	4 P 23	18 ♊	5 A 54
20 ♑	4 P 15	19 ♒	11 A 12	21 ♓	6 A 34	20 ♈	0 A 28	21 ♊	7 P 52	20 ♋	7 A 26
23 ♒	4 A 37	21 ♓	11 P 19	23 ♈	3 P 59	22 ♉	7 A 12	23 ♋	9 P 35	22 ♌	7 A 11
25 ♓	4 P 34	24 ♈	9 A 09	25 ♉	11 P 22	24 ♊	11 A 19	25 ♌	11 P 01	24 ♍	8 A 13
28 ♈	3 A 22	26 ♉	5 P 25	28 ♊	4 A 54	26 ♋	2 P 13	28 ♍	1 A 23	26 ♎	10 A 58
30 ♉	11 A 49	28 ♊	11 P 22	30 ♋	8 A 35	28 ♌	5 P 15	30 ♎	5 A 28	28 ♏	5 P 01
						30 ♍	7 P 57				

JUL	TIME	AUG	TIME	SEPT	TIME	OCT	TIME	NOV	TIME	DEC	TIME
1 ♐	1 A 36	2 ♒	6 A 33	1 ♓	1 A 19	3 ♉	4 A 50	1 ♊	6 P 32	1 ♋	6 A 25
3 ♑	0 P 24	4 ♓	7 P 04	3 ♈	0 P 52	5 ♊	0 N 00	3 ♋	11 P 06	3 ♌	8 A 40
6 ♒	0 A 25	7 ♈	7 A 11	5 ♉	10 P 52	7 ♋	5 P 15	6 ♌	2 A 22	5 ♍	11 A 00
8 ♓	1 P 24	9 ♉	5 P 27	8 ♊	6 A 32	9 ♌	8 P 50	8 ♍	5 A 07	7 ♎	2 P 05
11 ♈	1 A 18	12 ♊	0 A 14	10 ♋	11 A 40	11 ♍	11 P 01	10 ♎	8 A 07	9 ♏	6 P 35
13 ♉	10 A 43	14 ♋	3 A 37	12 ♌	1 P 48	14 ♎	0 A 24	12 ♏	11 A 49	12 ♐	0 A 44
15 ♊	4 P 06	16 ♌	4 A 20	14 ♍	2 P 24	16 ♏	3 A 00	14 ♐	4 P 57	14 ♑	8 A 59
17 ♋	5 P 53	18 ♍	3 A 46	16 ♎	2 P 39	18 ♐	7 A 41	17 ♑	0 A 41	16 ♒	7 P 27
19 ♌	5 P 41	20 ♎	4 A 07	18 ♏	4 P 46	20 ♑	3 P 32	19 ♒	11 A 13	19 ♓	7 A 46
21 ♍	5 P 11	22 ♏	6 A 51	20 ♐	10 P 10	23 ♒	3 A 07	22 ♓	0 A 06	21 ♈	8 P 32
23 ♎	6 P 28	24 ♐	1 P 32	23 ♑	7 A 10	25 ♓	4 P 02	24 ♈	0 P 12	24 ♉	6 A 51
25 ♏	11 P 01	27 ♑	0 A 25	25 ♒	7 P 33	28 ♈	3 A 33	26 ♉	9 P 17	26 ♊	1 P 21
28 ♐	7 A 02	29 ♒	0 P 49	28 ♓	8 A 33	30 ♉	0 P 22	29 ♊	2 A 58	28 ♋	4 P 09
30 ♑	6 P 25			30 ♈	7 P 36					30 ♌	4 P 52

1975

JAN		TIME	FEB		TIME	MAR		TIME	APR		TIME	MAY		TIME	JUN		TIME
1	♍	6 P 03	2	♏	6 A 38	1	♏	3 P 04	2	♑	11 A 16	2	♒	5 A 37	1	♓	1 A 44
3	♎	8 P 01	4	♐	0 P 34	3	♐	7 P 38	4	♒	10 P 13	4	♓	6 P 04	3	♈	2 P 47
6	♏	0 A 21	6	♑	10 P 10	6	♑	4 A 08	7	♓	11 A 12	7	♈	6 A 43	6	♉	1 A 46
8	♐	7 A 12	9	♒	9 A 25	8	♒	3 P 49	9	♈	11 P 24	9	♉	5 P 18	8	♊	9 A 59
10	♑	4 P 09	11	♓	10 P 09	11	♓	4 A 16	12	♉	10 A 37	12	♊	1 A 46	10	♋	3 P 06
13	♒	3 A 05	14	♈	10 A 36	13	♈	4 P 46	14	♊	7 P 34	14	♋	8 A 05	12	♌	6 P 42
15	♓	3 P 26	16	♉	10 P 29	16	♉	4 A 17	17	♋	2 A 31	16	♌	0 P 51	14	♍	9 P 28
18	♈	4 A 00	19	♊	7 A 33	18	♊	1 P 52	19	♌	7 A 22	18	♍	3 P 52	17	♎	0 A 15
20	♉	3 P 37	21	♋	0 P 51	20	♋	8 P 46	21	♍	10 A 02	20	♎	6 P 33	19	♏	3 A 43
22	♊	11 P 01	23	♌	2 P 36	23	♌	0 A 12	23	♎	10 A 51	22	♏	8 P 58	21	♐	7 A 59
25	♋	3 A 03	25	♍	2 P 22	25	♍	1 A 10	25	♏	0 N 00	25	♐	0 A 16	23	♑	2 P 03
27	♌	3 A 42	27	♎	1 P 58	27	♎	0 A 49	27	♐	2 P 30	27	♑	5 A 23	25	♒	10 P 44
29	♍	3 A 20				29	♏	1 A 25	29	♑	8 P 17	29	♒	2 P 09	28	♓	9 A 49
31	♎	3 A 20				31	♐	4 A 25							30	♈	10 P 18

JUL		TIME	AUG		TIME	SEPT		TIME	OCT		TIME	NOV		TIME	DEC		TIME
3	♉	10 A 26	2	♊	4 A 00	2	♌	11 P 05	2	♍	10 A 12	2	♏	8 P 53	2	♐	7 A 50
5	♊	7 P 04	4	♋	10 A 15	4	♍	11 P 48	4	♎	10 A 08	4	♐	9 P 46	4	♑	11 A 10
8	♋	0 A 09	6	♌	0 P 40	6	♎	11 P 17	6	♏	9 A 46	7	♑	0 A 14	6	♒	5 P 16
10	♌	2 A 40	8	♍	1 P 07	8	♏	11 P 21	8	♐	11 A 12	9	♒	7 A 49	9	♓	3 A 13
12	♍	4 A 07	10	♎	1 P 10	11	♐	2 A 01	10	♑	3 P 32	11	♓	7 P 04	11	♈	1 P 26
14	♎	5 A 39	12	♏	1 P 17	13	♑	8 A 08	13	♒	0 A 07	14	♈	7 A 46	14	♉	1 A 53
16	♏	8 A 44	14	♐	7 P 04	15	♒	5 P 48	15	♓	0 N 00	16	♉	8 P 05	16	♊	2 P 27
18	♐	1 P 49	17	♑	2 A 29	18	♓	5 A 55	18	♈	0 A 43	19	♊	6 A 14	18	♋	9 P 46
20	♑	8 P 59	19	♒	0 P 12	20	♈	6 P 28	20	♉	1 P 00	21	♋	2 P 35	21	♌	3 A 15
23	♒	6 A 00	21	♓	11 P 30	23	♉	6 A 37	22	♊	11 P 49	23	♌	8 P 50	23	♍	6 A 54
25	♓	5 P 12	24	♈	0 P 12	25	♊	6 P 14	25	♋	8 A 49	26	♍	1 A 17	25	♎	10 A 00
28	♈	5 A 51	27	♉	0 A 49	28	♋	3 A 02	27	♌	3 P 20	28	♎	4 A 04	27	♏	0 P 51
30	♉	6 P 19	29	♊	0 P 11	30	♌	8 A 19	29	♍	7 P 01	30	♏	5 A 52	29	♐	3 P 59
			31	♋	7 P 37				31	♎	8 P 17				31	♑	8 P 19

1976

JAN	TIME	FEB	TIME	MAR	TIME	APR	TIME	MAY	TIME	JUN	TIME
3 ♒	2 A 28	1 ♓	8 P 03	2 ♈	2 P 39	1 ♉	9 A 36	1 ♊	4 A 01	2 ♌	4 A 30
5 ♓	11 A 37	4 ♈	7 A 33	5 ♉	3 A 20	3 ♊	10 P 24	3 ♋	2 P 41	4 ♍	10 A 32
7 ♈	11 P 29	6 ♉	8 P 17	7 ♊	3 P 47	6 ♋	9 A 06	5 ♌	11 P 11	6 ♎	2 P 13
10 ♉	0 P 36	9 ♊	8 A 14	10 ♋	1 A 43	8 ♌	4 P 44	8 ♍	4 A 32	8 ♏	4 P 05
12 ♊	11 P 24	11 ♋	4 P 45	12 ♌	7 A 33	10 ♍	8 P 10	10 ♎	6 A 54	10 ♐	5 P 17
15 ♋	6 A 47	13 ♌	9 P 15	14 ♍	9 A 53	12 ♎	9 P 04	12 ♏	7 A 00	12 ♑	6 P 42
17 ♌	11 A 20	15 ♍	11 P 08	16 ♎	9 A 55	14 ♏	8 P 24	14 ♐	6 A 57	14 ♒	10 P 34
19 ♍	1 P 49	17 ♎	11 P 51	18 ♏	9 A 38	16 ♐	8 P 31	16 ♑	8 A 27	17 ♓	5 A 57
21 ♎	3 P 52	20 ♏	0 A 45	20 ♐	10 A 39	18 ♑	10 P 52	18 ♒	0 P 56	19 ♈	4 P 56
23 ♏	6 P 11	22 ♐	3 A 50	22 ♑	3 P 03	21 ♒	5 A 03	20 ♓	9 P 50	22 ♉	2 A 21
25 ♐	9 P 57	24 ♑	8 A 55	24 ♒	10 P 34	23 ♓	3 P 02	23 ♈	9 A 45	25 ♊	2 P 33
28 ♑	3 A 15	26 ♒	5 P 06	27 ♓	9 A 02	26 ♈	3 A 20	25 ♉	10 P 38	27 ♋	11 P 49
30 ♒	10 A 32	29 ♓	3 A 05	29 ♈	9 P 17	28 ♉	4 P 02	28 ♊	10 A 14	29 ♌	7 A 25
								30 ♋	8 P 23		

JUL	TIME	AUG	TIME	SEPT	TIME	OCT	TIME	NOV	TIME	DEC	TIME
1 ♍	3 P 50	2 ♏	3 A 57	2 ♑	4 P 18	1 ♒	3 A 38	3 ♈	5 A 12	2 ♉	0 M 00
3 ♎	7 P 46	4 ♐	6 A 54	4 ♒	10 P 24	4 ♓	0 P 24	5 ♉	5 P 40	5 ♊	0 P 48
5 ♏	10 P 31	6 ♑	10 A 38	7 ♓	6 A 29	6 ♈	11 P 13	8 ♊	6 A 09	8 ♋	0 A 18
8 ♐	1 A 15	8 ♒	4 P 00	9 ♈	4 P 32	9 ♉	11 A 12	10 ♋	6 P 10	10 ♌	10 A 17
10 ♑	3 A 57	10 ♓	11 P 19	12 ♉	4 A 37	11 ♊	0 M 00	13 ♌	4 A 39	12 ♍	6 P 11
12 ♒	8 A 08	13 ♈	9 A 02	14 ♊	5 P 20	14 ♋	0 N 00	15 ♍	11 A 49	14 ♎	11 P 28
14 ♓	2 P 52	15 ♉	9 P 10	17 ♋	4 A 59	16 ♌	9 P 57	17 ♎	3 P 54	17 ♏	1 A 54
17 ♈	0 A 53	18 ♊	9 A 49	19 ♌	1 P 26	18 ♍	3 A 34	19 ♏	4 P 29	19 ♐	2 A 40
19 ♉	1 P 14	20 ♋	8 P 46	21 ♍	5 P 33	21 ♎	5 A 49	21 ♐	4 P 08	21 ♑	3 A 15
22 ♊	1 A 57	23 ♌	3 A 39	23 ♎	7 P 05	23 ♏	5 A 39	23 ♑	4 P 11	23 ♒	5 A 02
24 ♋	11 A 49	25 ♍	7 A 18	25 ♏	7 P 00	25 ♐	5 A 16	25 ♒	6 P 54	25 ♓	10 A 00
26 ♌	6 P 23	27 ♎	9 A 07	27 ♐	7 P 33	27 ♑	6 A 01	28 ♓	1 A 14	27 ♈	6 P 57
28 ♍	10 P 38	29 ♏	10 A 21	29 ♑	10 P 13	29 ♒	10 A 13	30 ♈	11 A 24	30 ♉	7 A 02
31 ♎	1 A 36	31 ♐	0 P 21			31 ♓	5 P 58				

1977

JAN	TIME	FEB	TIME	MAR	TIME	APR	TIME	MAY	TIME	JUN	TIME
1 ♊	7 P 47	3 ♌	0 A 23	2 ♌	9 A 23	1 ♍	1 A 24	2 ♏	4 P 00	1 ♐	2 A 37
4 ♋	7 A 10	5 ♍	6 A 32	4 ♍	3 P 37	3 ♎	4 A 37	4 ♐	3 P 46	3 ♑	1 A 57
6 ♌	4 P 33	7 ♎	11 A 10	6 ♎	6 P 48	5 ♏	5 A 26	6 ♑	3 P 47	5 ♒	2 A 56
8 ♍	11 P 54	9 ♏	3 P 03	8 ♏	8 P 46	7 ♐	6 A 20	8 ♒	6 P 16	7 ♓	6 A 53
11 ♎	5 A 15	11 ♐	5 P 45	10 ♐	10 P 48	9 ♑	7 A 52	10 ♓	11 P 48	9 ♈	2 P 55
13 ♏	8 A 47	13 ♑	8 P 34	13 ♑	1 A 47	11 ♒	11 A 49	13 ♈	9 A 06	12 ♉	2 A 21
15 ♐	9 A 39	15 ♒	11 P 59	15 ♒	6 A 26	13 ♓	6 P 25	15 ♉	8 P 36	14 ♊	3 P 02
17 ♑	0 P 40	18 ♓	4 A 52	17 ♓	0 P 23	16 ♈	3 A 33	18 ♊	8 A 46	17 ♋	3 A 32
19 ♒	3 P 18	20 ♈	0 P 35	19 ♈	8 P 42	18 ♉	2 P 23	20 ♋	9 P 29	19 ♌	2 P 57
21 ♓	7 P 42	22 ♉	11 P 00	22 ♉	7 A 06	21 ♊	2 P 39	23 ♌	9 A 16	22 ♍	0 A 46
24 ♈	3 A 27	25 ♊	11 A 36	24 ♊	7 P 30	23 ♋	3 P 26	25 ♍	6 P 48	24 ♎	7 A 52
26 ♉	2 P 51	27 ♋	11 P 59	27 ♋	8 A 00	26 ♌	2 A 59	28 ♎	0 A 31	26 ♏	11 A 40
29 ♊	3 A 32			29 ♌	6 P 43	28 ♍	11 A 16	30 ♏	2 A 36	28 ♐	1 P 07
31 ♋	3 P 18					30 ♎	3 P 09			30 ♑	0 P 48

JUL	TIME	AUG	TIME	SEPT	TIME	OCT	TIME	NOV	TIME	DEC	TIME
2 ♒	1 P 10	1 ♓	1 A 53	2 ♉	0 A 47	1 ♊	8 P 20	3 ♌	5 A 12	2 ♍	11 P 14
4 ♓	3 P 53	3 ♈	7 A 04	4 ♊	0 P 24	4 ♋	8 A 58	5 ♍	3 P 30	5 ♎	7 A 19
6 ♈	10 P 19	5 ♉	4 P 21	7 ♋	1 A 08	6 ♌	9 P 07	7 ♎	10 P 06	7 ♏	11 A 29
9 ♉	8 A 40	8 ♊	4 A 32	9 ♌	0 P 35	9 ♍	6 A 28	10 ♏	0 A 38	9 ♐	0 P 10
11 ♊	9 P 34	10 ♋	5 P 15	11 ♍	8 P 55	11 ♎	0 N 00	12 ♐	1 A 16	11 ♑	11 A 41
14 ♋	10 A 00	13 ♌	4 A 15	14 ♎	2 A 16	13 ♏	2 P 09	14 ♑	1 A 02	13 ♒	11 A 31
16 ♌	8 P 55	15 ♍	0 P 44	16 ♏	5 A 43	15 ♐	3 P 36	16 ♒	2 A 30	15 ♓	1 P 55
19 ♍	6 A 10	17 ♎	6 P 38	18 ♐	8 A 11	17 ♑	4 P 50	18 ♓	6 A 10	17 ♈	7 P 40
21 ♎	1 P 05	19 ♏	11 P 25	20 ♑	11 A 00	19 ♒	7 P 35	20 ♈	1 P 32	20 ♉	4 A 56
23 ♏	6 P 18	22 ♐	2 A 46	22 ♒	2 P 15	22 ♓	0 A 43	22 ♉	11 P 08	22 ♊	4 P 53
25 ♐	9 P 07	24 ♑	5 A 18	24 ♓	6 P 52	24 ♈	7 A 41	25 ♊	11 A 38	25 ♋	5 A 33
27 ♑	10 P 17	26 ♒	7 A 59	27 ♈	1 A 01	26 ♉	4 P 44	27 ♋	11 P 05	27 ♌	5 P 51
29 ♒	11 P 36	28 ♓	11 A 20	29 ♉	9 A 23	29 ♊	3 A 48	30 ♌	11 A 37	30 ♍	5 A 25
		30 ♈	4 P 35			31 ♋	4 P 19				

1978

JAN	TIME	FEB	TIME	MAR	TIME	APR	TIME	MAY	TIME	JUN	TIME
1 ♎	2 P 43	2 ♐	7 A 03	1 ♐	1 P 01	2 ♒	0 A 30	1 ♓	9 A 23	2 ♉	4 A 01
3 ♏	8 P 18	4 ♑	8 A 34	3 ♑	4 P 00	4 ♓	3 A 09	3 ♈	2 P 54	4 ♊	1 P 58
5 ♐	10 P 38	6 ♒	9 A 08	5 ♒	6 P 06	6 ♈	8 A 08	5 ♉	9 P 40	7 ♋	1 A 37
7 ♑	10 P 51	8 ♓	10 A 00	7 ♓	8 P 04	8 ♉	2 P 15	8 ♊	7 A 22	9 ♌	2 P 14
9 ♒	10 P 16	10 ♈	0 P 55	9 ♈	11 P 18	10 ♊	11 P 24	10 ♋	6 P 31	12 ♍	2 A 44
11 ♓	11 P 35	12 ♉	7 P 50	12 ♉	5 A 05	13 ♋	10 A 59	13 ♌	7 A 20	14 ♎	0 P 56
14 ♈	3 A 24	15 ♊	6 A 33	14 ♊	2 P 35	15 ♌	11 P 54	15 ♍	7 P 27	16 ♏	7 P 15
16 ♉	11 A 38	17 ♋	7 P 16	17 ♋	2 A 58	18 ♍	11 A 02	18 ♎	4 A 15	18 ♐	9 P 45
18 ♊	11 P 24	20 ♌	7 A 46	19 ♌	3 P 35	20 ♎	6 P 49	20 ♏	9 A 14	20 ♑	9 P 59
21 ♋	0 N 00	22 ♍	5 P 54	22 ♍	2 A 01	22 ♏	11 P 12	22 ♐	11 A 41	22 ♒	9 P 20
24 ♌	0 A 19	25 ♎	2 A 12	24 ♎	9 A 49	25 ♐	1 A 50	24 ♑	11 A 12	24 ♓	10 P 27
26 ♍	11 A 13	27 ♏	8 A 35	26 ♏	2 P 56	27 ♑	3 A 40	26 ♒	0 P 30	27 ♈	2 A 21
28 ♎	8 P 17			28 ♐	6 P 37	29 ♒	6 A 06	28 ♓	2 P 59	29 ♉	9 A 22
31 ♏	2 A 50			30 ♑	9 P 44			30 ♈	8 P 17		

JUL	TIME	AUG	TIME	SEPT	TIME	OCT	TIME	NOV	TIME	DEC	TIME
1 ♊	7 P 37	3 ♌	2 A 21	1 ♍	8 P 44	1 ♎	2 P 15	2 ♐	9 A 59	1 ♑	9 P 04
4 ♋	7 A 48	5 ♍	2 P 13	4 ♎	7 A 02	3 ♏	9 P 33	4 ♑	0 P 51	3 ♒	10 P 14
6 ♌	8 P 09	8 ♎	1 A 15	6 ♏	3 P 18	6 ♐	2 A 50	6 ♒	3 P 15	5 ♓	0 M 00
9 ♍	8 A 36	10 ♏	9 A 57	8 ♐	9 P 27	8 ♑	6 A 51	8 ♓	6 P 13	8 ♈	3 A 50
11 ♎	7 P 50	12 ♐	3 P 37	11 ♑	1 A 17	10 ♒	9 A 41	10 ♈	10 P 03	10 ♉	9 A 40
14 ♏	3 A 38	14 ♑	6 P 08	13 ♒	3 A 21	12 ♓	0 P 30	13 ♉	3 A 30	12 ♊	5 P 47
16 ♐	7 A 35	16 ♒	6 P 32	15 ♓	4 A 37	14 ♈	3 P 18	15 ♊	10 A 43	15 ♋	4 A 01
18 ♑	8 A 40	18 ♓	6 P 37	17 ♈	6 A 20	16 ♉	7 P 20	17 ♋	8 P 12	17 ♌	3 P 49
20 ♒	8 A 05	20 ♈	7 P 54	19 ♉	9 A 43	19 ♊	2 A 00	20 ♌	8 A 20	20 ♍	4 A 25
22 ♓	8 A 00	23 ♉	0 A 11	21 ♊	4 P 47	21 ♋	11 A 39	22 ♍	8 P 57	22 ♎	4 P 21
24 ♈	10 A 14	25 ♊	8 A 23	24 ♋	3 A 44	24 ♌	0 A 19	25 ♎	8 A 08	25 ♏	1 A 12
26 ♉	3 P 48	27 ♋	8 P 04	26 ♌	4 P 17	26 ♍	0 P 59	27 ♏	3 P 33	27 ♐	5 A 53
29 ♊	1 A 42	30 ♌	9 A 11	29 ♍	4 A 31	28 ♎	11 P 04	29 ♐	7 P 20	29 ♑	7 A 18
31 ♋	1 P 49					31 ♏	5 A 40			31 ♒	7 A 25

1979

JAN

Date	Sign	TIME
2	♓	7 A 40
4	♈	10 A 00
6	♉	3 P 12
9	♊	0 A 13
11	♋	11 A 37
13	♌	11 P 24
16	♍	11 A 14
18	♎	11 P 31
21	♏	9 A 42
23	♐	3 P 39
25	♑	6 P 24
27	♒	6 P 12
29	♓	5 P 45
31	♈	6 P 25

FEB

Date	Sign	TIME
2	♉	10 P 06
5	♊	5 A 33
7	♋	4 P 37
10	♌	4 A 44
12	♍	5 P 37
15	♎	5 A 37
17	♏	4 P 03
19	♐	11 P 36
22	♑	4 A 00
24	♒	5 A 02
26	♓	5 A 03
28	♈	4 A 50

MAR

Date	Sign	TIME
2	♉	6 A 46
4	♊	0 P 46
6	♋	10 P 59
9	♌	11 A 23
12	♍	0 A 13
14	♎	11 A 37
16	♏	9 P 38
19	♐	5 A 39
21	♑	11 A 19
23	♒	1 P 59
25	♓	3 P 04
27	♈	3 P 28
29	♉	5 P 18
31	♊	9 P 58

APR

Date	Sign	TIME
3	♋	6 A 30
5	♌	6 P 22
8	♍	7 A 23
10	♎	6 P 38
13	♏	4 A 29
15	♐	11 A 29
17	♑	8 P 23
19	♒	11 P 06
21	♓	0 A 56
24	♈	3 A 40
26	♉	7 A 42
28	♊	3 P 05
30	♋	

MAY

Date	Sign	TIME
3	♌	1 A 56
5	♍	2 P 47
8	♎	2 A 24
10	♏	11 A 27
12	♐	6 P 13
14	♑	11 P 16
17	♒	1 A 47
19	♓	4 A 30
21	♈	7 A 37
23	♉	11 A 19
25	♊	4 P 33
27	♋	11 P 55
30	♌	10 A 03

JUN

Date	Sign	TIME
1	♍	10 P 41
4	♎	11 A 00
6	♏	8 P 47
9	♐	3 A 01
11	♑	6 A 25
13	♒	8 A 23
15	♓	10 A 11
17	♈	1 P 02
19	♉	5 P 31
21	♊	11 P 38
24	♋	7 A 49
26	♌	6 P 07
29	♍	6 A 21

JUL

Date	Sign	TIME
1	♎	6 P 49
4	♏	5 A 52
6	♐	0 P 53
8	♑	4 P 18
10	♒	5 P 12
12	♓	5 P 41
14	♈	7 P 03
16	♉	10 P 39
19	♊	5 A 02
21	♋	2 P 08
24	♌	0 A 49
26	♍	1 P 01
29	♎	1 A 56
31	♏	1 P 44

AUG

Date	Sign	TIME
2	♐	10 P 01
5	♑	2 A 16
7	♒	3 A 38
9	♓	3 A 17
11	♈	3 A 21
13	♉	5 A 16
15	♊	10 A 33
17	♋	7 P 28
20	♌	6 A 51
22	♍	7 P 13
25	♎	7 A 46
27	♏	7 P 37
30	♐	5 A 27

SEPT

Date	Sign	TIME
1	♑	11 A 49
3	♒	2 P 08
5	♓	2 P 12
7	♈	1 P 45
9	♉	2 P 21
11	♊	6 P 02
14	♋	1 A 31
16	♌	0 P 48
19	♍	1 A 26
21	♎	1 P 59
24	♏	1 A 15
26	♐	6 P 46
28	♑	10 P 52
30	♒	

OCT

Date	Sign	TIME
3	♓	0 A 24
5	♈	0 A 28
7	♉	0 A 56
9	♊	3 A 26
11	♋	9 A 23
13	♌	7 P 30
16	♍	8 A 19
18	♎	8 P 36
21	♏	7 A 43
23	♐	4 P 56
25	♑	0 M 00
28	♒	5 A 18
30	♓	8 A 27

NOV

Date	Sign	TIME
1	♈	9 A 53
3	♉	11 A 21
5	♊	1 P 35
7	♋	6 P 48
10	♌	3 A 36
12	♍	3 P 39
15	♎	4 A 20
17	♏	3 P 37
19	♐	11 P 53
22	♑	6 A 10
24	♒	11 A 08
26	♓	2 P 03
28	♈	5 P 03
30	♉	7 P 35

DEC

Date	Sign	TIME
2	♊	11 P 06
5	♋	4 A 21
7	♌	0 P 35
9	♍	11 P 30
12	♎	0 P 25
15	♏	0 A 18
17	♐	8 A 51
19	♑	2 P 15
21	♒	5 P 33
23	♓	8 P 01
25	♈	10 P 31
28	♉	1 A 59
30	♊	6 A 30

1980

JAN

Date	Sign	Time
1	♋	0P56
3	♌	9P07
6	♍	8A00
8	♎	8P39
11	♏	8A52
13	♐	6P37
16	♑	0A06
18	♒	2A12
20	♓	3A11
22	♈	4A27
24	♉	6A56
26	♊	0P11
28	♋	7P21
31	♌	4A56

FEB

Date	Sign	Time
2	♍	3P26
5	♎	3A56
7	♏	4P48
10	♐	3A27
12	♑	10A23
14	♒	1P28
16	♓	1P55
18	♈	1P46
20	♉	2P43
22	♊	6P20
25	♋	1A08
27	♌	10A39
29	♍	10P13

MAR

Date	Sign	Time
3	♎	10A36
5	♏	11P18
8	♐	10A50
10	♑	7P18
12	♒	11P35
15	♓	0A19
17	♈	0A04
19	♉	2A04
21	♊	7A15
23	♋	4P32
25	♌	4A20
28	♍	4P53
30	♎	

APR

Date	Sign	Time
2	♏	5A24
4	♐	5P00
7	♑	2A27
9	♒	8A22
11	♓	11A12
13	♈	11A23
15	♉	11A04
17	♊	11A50
19	♋	3P18
21	♌	11P19
24	♍	10A47
26	♎	11P30
29	♏	11A48

MAY

Date	Sign	Time
1	♐	10P29
4	♑	7A30
6	♒	2P30
8	♓	6P45
10	♈	8P39
12	♉	9P23
14	♊	10P07
17	♋	1A06
19	♌	7A25
21	♍	5P45
24	♎	6A21
26	♏	6P54
29	♐	1P39
31	♑	

JUN

Date	Sign	Time
2	♒	7P43
5	♓	0A26
7	♈	3A30
9	♉	5A40
11	♊	7A50
13	♋	10A58
15	♌	4P49
18	♍	1A46
20	♎	2P02
23	♏	2A50
25	♐	1P13
27	♑	9P04
30	♒	2A22

JUL

Date	Sign	Time
2	♓	5A43
4	♈	8A56
6	♉	11A31
8	♊	2P56
10	♋	7P20
13	♌	1A28
15	♍	10A28
17	♎	9P41
20	♏	10A36
22	♐	10P04
25	♑	6A12
27	♒	10A38
29	♓	1P29
31	♈	2P49

AUG

Date	Sign	Time
2	♉	4P53
4	♊	8P21
7	♋	1A32
9	♌	8A51
11	♍	6P07
14	♎	5A12
16	♏	6P04
19	♐	6A26
21	♑	3P40
23	♒	8P38
25	♓	10P50
27	♈	11P18
29	♉	11P56

SEPT

Date	Sign	Time
1	♊	1A58
3	♋	7A07
5	♌	2P47
8	♍	0A41
10	♎	0N00
13	♏	0A49
15	♐	1P24
17	♑	11P49
20	♒	6A41
22	♓	9A34
24	♈	9A04
26	♉	9A53
28	♊	1P26
30	♋	

OCT

Date	Sign	Time
2	♌	8P07
5	♍	6A27
7	♎	6P31
10	♏	6A51
12	♐	7P27
15	♑	6A43
17	♒	2P52
19	♓	7P22
21	♈	8P33
23	♉	8P06
25	♊	7P59
27	♋	9P46
30	♌	3A09

NOV

Date	Sign	Time
1	♍	0P36
4	♎	0A43
6	♏	1P14
9	♐	1A35
11	♑	0P35
13	♒	9P04
16	♓	3A22
18	♈	6A01
20	♉	6A59
22	♊	6A44
24	♋	8A02
26	♌	11A49
28	♍	7P53

DEC

Date	Sign	Time
1	♎	7A23
3	♏	8P28
6	♐	8A03
8	♑	6P38
11	♒	2A53
13	♓	8A58
15	♈	1P12
17	♉	3P36
19	♊	4P38
21	♋	6P40
23	♌	10P03
26	♍	4A35
28	♎	3P25
31	♏	3A48

1981

JAN	TIME	FEB	TIME	MAR	TIME	APR	TIME	MAY	TIME	JUN	TIME
2 ♐	4 P 09	1 ♑	11 A 03	3 ♒	3 A 50	1 ♓	6 P 16	1 ♈	6 A 26	1 ♊	4 P 57
5 ♑	2 A 11	3 ♒	6 P 02	5 ♓	7 A 50	3 ♈	8 P 09	3 ♉	6 A 44	3 ♋	5 P 11
7 ♒	9 A 38	5 ♓	10 P 12	7 ♈	9 A 34	5 ♉	7 P 50	5 ♊	6 A 02	5 ♌	6 P 54
9 ♓	2 P 47	8 ♈	1 A 06	9 ♉	10 A 32	7 ♊	8 P 09	7 ♋	6 A 33	8 ♍	0 A 40
11 ♈	6 P 48	10 ♉	3 A 27	11 ♊	0 N 00	9 ♋	10 P 08	9 ♌	9 A 45	10 ♎	9 A 39
13 ♉	9 P 37	12 ♊	5 A 36	13 ♋	3 P 24	12 ♌	3 A 05	11 ♍	5 P 00	12 ♏	10 P 23
16 ♊	0 A 26	14 ♋	9 A 55	15 ♌	9 P 31	14 ♍	11 A 03	14 ♎	3 A 36	15 ♐	11 A 12
18 ♋	3 A 23	16 ♌	3 P 26	18 ♍	5 A 22	16 ♎	10 P 07	16 ♏	4 P 02	17 ♑	10 P 34
20 ♌	7 A 36	18 ♍	10 P 38	20 ♎	3 P 41	19 ♏	9 A 49	19 ♐	4 A 24	20 ♒	8 A 44
22 ♍	2 P 03	21 ♎	8 A 06	23 ♏	3 A 13	21 ♐	10 P 30	21 ♑	4 P 25	22 ♓	4 P 47
24 ♎	11 P 47	23 ♏	7 P 44	25 ♐	3 P 52	24 ♑	11 A 00	24 ♒	3 A 14	24 ♈	10 P 30
27 ♏	11 A 48	26 ♐	8 A 56	28 ♑	4 A 03	26 ♒	9 P 09	26 ♓	11 A 16	27 ♉	1 A 40
30 ♐	0 A 30	28 ♑	8 P 12	30 ♒	1 P 17	29 ♓	3 A 56	28 ♈	3 P 52	29 ♊	2 A 55
								30 ♉	5 P 25		

JUL	TIME	AUG	TIME	SEPT	TIME	OCT	TIME	NOV	TIME	DEC	TIME
1 ♋	3 A 26	1 ♍	6 P 55	2 ♏	8 P 57	2 ♐	4 P 56	1 ♑	0 P 48	1 ♒	7 A 01
3 ♌	5 A 12	4 ♎	1 A 59	5 ♐	9 A 22	5 ♑	5 A 37	4 ♒	0 A 47	3 ♓	5 P 04
5 ♍	9 A 21	6 ♏	0 P 37	7 ♑	9 P 55	7 ♒	5 P 04	6 ♓	9 A 38	5 ♈	11 P 27
7 ♎	5 P 31	9 ♐	1 A 38	10 ♒	8 A 14	10 ♓	0 A 20	8 ♈	2 P 31	8 ♉	2 A 28
10 ♏	5 A 01	11 ♑	1 P 34	12 ♓	2 P 36	12 ♈	4 A 04	10 ♉	4 P 08	10 ♊	2 A 48
12 ♐	6 P 04	13 ♒	10 P 48	14 ♈	5 P 47	14 ♉	5 A 07	12 ♊	3 P 48	12 ♋	2 A 24
15 ♑	5 A 43	16 ♓	5 A 28	16 ♉	7 P 54	16 ♊	5 A 25	14 ♋	3 P 34	14 ♌	2 A 55
17 ♒	3 P 10	18 ♈	9 A 31	18 ♊	9 P 21	18 ♋	6 A 33	16 ♌	5 P 01	16 ♍	6 A 03
19 ♓	10 P 14	20 ♉	0 P 51	20 ♋	0 M 00	20 ♌	9 A 43	18 ♍	10 P 01	18 ♎	0 P 58
22 ♈	3 A 43	22 ♊	3 P 35	23 ♌	4 A 21	22 ♍	3 P 47	21 ♎	6 A 29	21 ♏	0 A 07
24 ♉	7 A 41	24 ♋	6 P 39	25 ♍	10 A 23	25 ♎	0 A 57	23 ♏	6 P 00	23 ♐	0 P 49
26 ♊	10 A 19	26 ♌	10 P 21	27 ♎	6 P 14	27 ♏	11 A 37	26 ♐	6 A 21	26 ♑	1 A 19
28 ♋	0 P 30	29 ♍	3 A 46	30 ♏	4 A 59	29 ♐	11 P 54	28 ♑	6 P 49	28 ♒	0 P 47
30 ♌	2 P 54	31 ♎	10 A 53							30 ♓	10 P 47

1982

JAN	TIME	FEB	TIME	MAR	TIME	APR	TIME	MAY	TIME	JUN	TIME
2 ♈	6 A 31	2 ♊	8 P 31	2 ♊	2 A 12	2 ♌	1 P 45	1 ♍	11 P 45	2 ♏	9 P 31
4 ♉	11 A 00	4 ♋	10 P 14	4 ♋	4 A 58	4 ♍	6 P 25	4 ♎	6 A 37	5 ♐	9 A 02
6 ♊	0 P 49	6 ♌	11 P 40	6 ♌	7 A 29	7 ♎	0 A 40	6 ♏	3 P 33	7 ♑	9 P 29
8 ♋	1 P 08	9 ♍	2 A 08	8 ♍	11 A 20	9 ♏	8 A 46	9 ♐	2 A 36	10 ♒	10 A 00
10 ♌	1 P 19	11 ♎	6 A 55	10 ♎	4 P 25	11 ♐	7 P 30	11 ♑	3 P 02	12 ♓	9 P 41
12 ♍	3 P 50	13 ♏	3 P 21	13 ♏	0 A 17	14 ♑	7 A 48	14 ♒	3 A 44	15 ♈	6 A 45
14 ♎	9 P 22	16 ♐	3 A 20	15 ♐	11 A 00	16 ♒	8 P 32	16 ♓	2 P 51	17 ♉	11 A 20
17 ♏	7 A 15	18 ♑	3 P 51	17 ♑	11 P 54	19 ♓	6 A 08	18 ♈	9 P 59	19 ♊	0 P 48
19 ♐	7 P 36	21 ♒	3 A 18	20 ♒	0 N 00	21 ♈	0 P 21	21 ♉	1 A 14	21 ♋	0 P 29
22 ♑	8 A 12	23 ♓	11 A 49	22 ♓	8 P 51	23 ♉	2 P 57	23 ♊	2 A 04	23 ♌	0 N 00
24 ♒	7 P 32	25 ♈	6 P 10	25 ♈	2 A 26	25 ♊	4 P 05	25 ♋	1 A 45	25 ♍	1 P 34
27 ♓	4 A 35	27 ♉	10 P 46	27 ♉	5 A 39	27 ♋	5 P 07	27 ♌	2 A 24	27 ♎	6 P 19
29 ♈	0 N 00			29 ♊	8 A 11	29 ♌	7 P 20	29 ♍	5 A 45	30 ♏	3 A 18
31 ♉	5 P 03			31 ♋	10 A 19			31 ♎	0 N 00		

JUL	TIME	AUG	TIME	SEPT	TIME	OCT	TIME	NOV	TIME	DEC	TIME
2 ♐	2 P 40	1 ♑	9 A 49	2 ♓	3 P 51	2 ♈	8 A 08	3 ♊	1 A 00	2 ♋	11 A 23
5 ♑	3 A 32	3 ♒	10 P 15	5 ♈	0 A 17	4 ♉	1 P 35	5 ♋	2 A 28	4 ♌	11 A 50
7 ♒	4 P 00	6 ♓	8 A 53	7 ♉	6 A 38	6 ♊	5 P 28	7 ♌	4 A 17	6 ♍	1 P 44
10 ♓	3 A 14	8 ♈	6 P 12	9 ♊	11 A 10	8 ♋	8 P 27	9 ♍	7 A 42	8 ♎	6 P 31
12 ♈	1 P 07	11 ♉	1 A 06	11 ♋	2 P 31	10 ♌	11 P 08	11 ♎	1 P 05	11 ♏	2 A 06
14 ♉	7 P 14	13 ♊	5 A 39	13 ♌	4 P 42	13 ♍	2 A 24	13 ♏	7 P 56	13 ♐	11 A 47
16 ♊	10 P 29	15 ♋	8 A 02	15 ♍	7 P 06	15 ♎	6 A 50	16 ♐	5 A 10	15 ♑	11 P 30
18 ♋	11 P 02	17 ♌	8 A 58	17 ♎	10 P 16	17 ♏	0 P 33	18 ♑	4 P 13	18 ♒	11 A 48
20 ♌	10 P 47	19 ♍	9 A 34	20 ♏	4 A 18	19 ♐	8 P 59	21 ♒	5 A 42	21 ♓	0 A 30
22 ♍	11 P 20	21 ♎	0 P 21	22 ♐	0 P 24	22 ♑	8 A 00	23 ♓	5 P 12	23 ♈	11 A 27
25 ♎	2 A 53	23 ♏	6 P 25	25 ♑	0 A 36	24 ♒	8 P 52	26 ♈	3 A 06	25 ♉	6 P 29
27 ♏	9 A 57	26 ♐	4 A 19	27 ♒	1 P 24	27 ♓	8 A 29	28 ♉	8 A 50	27 ♊	9 P 51
29 ♐	9 P 13	28 ♑	5 P 00	30 ♓	0 A 11	29 ♈	5 P 39	30 ♊	11 A 01	29 ♋	10 P 09
		31 ♒	5 A 33			31 ♉	10 P 17			31 ♌	9 P 41

1983

JAN	TIME	FEB	TIME	MAR	TIME	APR	TIME	MAY	TIME	JUN	TIME
2 ♍	10 P 13	1 ♎	10 A 10	3 ♏	0 A 10	1 ♐	4 P 33	1 ♑	11 A 02	2 ♓	7 P 33
5 ♎	1 A 14	3 ♏	3 P 09	5 ♐	7 A 37	4 ♑	2 A 41	3 ♒	11 P 05	5 ♈	7 A 16
7 ♏	7 A 37	6 ♐	0 A 01	7 ♑	7 P 04	6 ♒	3 P 28	6 ♓	0 N 00	7 ♉	3 P 25
9 ♐	4 P 32	8 ♑	0 N 00	10 ♒	7 A 46	9 ♓	3 A 44	8 ♈	10 P 24	9 ♊	7 P 33
12 ♑	4 A 08	11 ♒	0 A 55	12 ♓	7 P 50	11 ♈	2 P 02	11 ♉	5 A 40	11 ♋	9 P 23
14 ♒	4 P 29	13 ♓	0 P 59	15 ♈	6 A 12	13 ♉	9 P 13	13 ♊	10 A 08	13 ♌	10 P 07
17 ♓	6 A 39	15 ♈	11 P 43	17 ♉	2 P 22	16 ♊	2 A 27	15 ♋	0 P 41	15 ♍	11 P 32
19 ♈	6 P 00	18 ♉	8 A 51	19 ♊	8 P 31	18 ♋	6 A 30	17 ♌	2 P 50	18 ♎	2 A 43
22 ♉	2 A 32	20 ♊	2 P 59	22 ♋	1 A 00	20 ♌	9 A 26	19 ♍	5 P 32	20 ♏	8 A 23
24 ♊	7 A 32	22 ♋	6 P 06	24 ♌	3 A 27	22 ♍	0 P 10	21 ♎	9 P 19	22 ♐	4 P 23
26 ♋	9 A 07	24 ♌	7 P 17	26 ♍	4 A 50	24 ♎	3 P 19	24 ♏	2 A 38	25 ♑	2 A 25
28 ♌	8 A 53	26 ♍	7 P 20	28 ♎	6 A 46	26 ♏	7 P 25	26 ♐	9 A 39	27 ♒	2 P 02
30 ♍	8 A 32	28 ♎	8 P 30	30 ♏	9 A 59	29 ♐	1 A 53	28 ♑	7 P 27	30 ♓	2 A 52
								31 ♒	7 A 02		

JUL	TIME	AUG	TIME	SEPT	TIME	OCT	TIME	NOV	TIME	DEC	TIME
2 ♈	2 P 58	1 ♉	7 A 41	2 ♋	2 A 41	1 ♌	0 P 40	1 ♎	11 P 45	1 ♏	10 A 04
5 ♉	0 A 23	3 ♊	2 P 56	4 ♌	4 A 50	3 ♍	2 P 16	4 ♏	2 A 29	3 ♐	3 P 26
7 ♊	5 A 55	5 ♋	6 P 03	6 ♍	4 A 35	5 ♎	3 P 16	6 ♐	6 A 41	5 ♑	10 P 24
9 ♋	7 A 47	7 ♌	6 P 29	8 ♎	4 A 32	7 ♏	4 P 52	8 ♑	1 P 22	8 ♒	8 A 30
11 ♌	8 A 00	9 ♍	5 P 45	10 ♏	6 A 18	9 ♐	9 P 48	10 ♒	0 M 00	10 ♓	8 P 37
13 ♍	8 A 34	11 ♎	6 P 08	12 ♐	11 A 29	12 ♑	4 A 24	13 ♓	0 P 37	13 ♈	9 A 34
15 ♎	9 A 18	13 ♏	8 P 56	14 ♑	8 P 20	14 ♒	3 P 54	16 ♈	0 A 53	15 ♉	7 P 53
17 ♏	1 P 39	16 ♐	3 A 49	17 ♒	8 A 58	17 ♓	4 A 44	18 ♉	10 A 30	18 ♊	2 A 39
19 ♐	9 P 48	18 ♑	9 P 22	19 ♓	9 P 22	19 ♈	4 P 32	20 ♊	5 P 06	20 ♋	5 A 54
22 ♑	9 A 15	21 ♒	2 A 21	22 ♈	9 A 04	22 ♉	1 A 59	22 ♋	9 P 07	22 ♌	7 A 47
24 ♒	8 P 37	23 ♓	2 P 51	24 ♉	7 P 25	24 ♊	9 A 17	25 ♌	0 A 26	24 ♍	9 A 24
27 ♓	9 A 34	26 ♈	2 A 58	27 ♊	3 A 16	26 ♋	2 P 48	27 ♍	3 A 03	26 ♎	11 A 31
29 ♈	9 P 46	28 ♉	1 P 54	29 ♋	9 A 21	28 ♌	6 P 28	29 ♎	6 A 01	28 ♏	3 P 47
		30 ♊	9 P 56			30 ♍	9 P 11			30 ♐	9 P 55

1984

JAN	TIME	FEB	TIME	MAR	TIME	APR	TIME	MAY	TIME	JUN	TIME
2 ♑	6 A 20	3 ♓	11 A 36	1 ♓	5 P 51	3 ♉	0 A 30	2 ♊	3 P 59	1 ♋	5 A 39
4 ♒	4 P 42	6 ♈	0 A 19	4 ♈	6 A 25	5 ♊	10 A 27	4 ♋	11 P 22	3 ♌	10 A 15
7 ♓	4 A 20	8 ♉	0 P 35	6 ♉	6 P 25	7 ♋	6 P 01	7 ♌	4 A 46	5 ♍	1 P 42
9 ♈	5 P 15	10 ♊	8 P 57	9 ♊	4 A 46	9 ♌	10 P 57	9 ♍	8 A 05	7 ♎	4 P 24
12 ♉	4 A 56	13 ♋	2 A 39	11 ♋	11 A 39	12 ♍	1 A 13	11 ♎	10 A 19	9 ♏	7 P 16
14 ♊	0 P 43	15 ♌	4 A 07	13 ♌	3 P 06	14 ♎	1 A 35	13 ♏	11 A 41	11 ♐	11 P 02
16 ♋	4 P 38	17 ♍	4 A 35	15 ♍	3 P 38	16 ♏	2 A 08	15 ♐	2 P 13	14 ♑	4 A 00
18 ♌	5 P 41	19 ♎	4 A 01	17 ♎	2 P 52	18 ♐	4 A 07	17 ♑	6 P 34	16 ♒	11 A 49
20 ♍	5 P 58	21 ♏	5 A 24	19 ♏	3 P 13	20 ♑	9 A 28	20 ♒	2 A 57	18 ♓	10 P 13
22 ♎	6 P 40	23 ♐	9 A 51	21 ♐	6 P 02	22 ♒	6 P 45	22 ♓	2 P 16	21 ♈	11 A 00
24 ♏	9 P 38	25 ♑	6 P 14	24 ♑	0 A 46	25 ♓	7 A 05	25 ♈	3 A 20	23 ♉	11 P 19
27 ♐	3 A 53	28 ♒	5 A 24	26 ♒	11 A 37	27 ♈	7 P 52	27 ♉	2 P 34	26 ♊	8 A 27
29 ♑	0 P 35			29 ♓	0 A 13	30 ♉	6 A 55	29 ♊	11 P 32	28 ♋	2 P 06
31 ♒	11 P 18			31 ♈	0 P 25					30 ♌	5 P 21

JUL	TIME	AUG	TIME	SEPT	TIME	OCT	TIME	NOV	TIME	DEC	TIME
2 ♍	7 P 25	1 ♎	4 A 23	1 ♐	4 P 44	1 ♑	5 A 25	2 ♓	8 A 00	2 ♈	4 A 16
4 ♎	9 P 37	3 ♏	6 A 13	3 ♑	10 P 44	3 ♒	1 P 57	4 ♈	8 P 52	4 ♉	4 P 46
7 ♏	0 A 46	5 ♐	10 A 37	6 ♒	7 A 57	6 ♓	1 A 29	7 ♉	9 A 23	7 ♊	3 A 33
9 ♐	5 A 18	7 ♑	5 P 27	8 ♓	7 P 43	8 ♈	2 P 14	9 ♊	8 P 17	9 ♋	0 P 11
11 ♑	11 A 39	10 ♒	2 A 18	11 ♈	7 A 57	11 ♉	2 A 44	12 ♋	5 A 33	11 ♌	6 P 25
13 ♒	7 P 47	12 ♓	1 P 12	13 ♉	8 P 28	13 ♊	2 P 09	14 ♌	0 P 22	13 ♍	10 P 46
16 ♓	6 A 15	15 ♈	1 A 38	16 ♊	8 A 30	15 ♋	11 P 49	16 ♍	5 P 18	16 ♎	2 A 22
18 ♈	6 P 36	17 ♉	2 P 15	18 ♋	5 P 31	18 ♌	6 A 08	18 ♎	7 P 46	18 ♏	4 A 40
21 ♉	7 A 15	20 ♊	1 A 37	20 ♌	10 P 41	20 ♍	10 A 10	20 ♏	8 P 53	20 ♐	7 A 09
23 ♊	5 P 27	22 ♋	9 A 30	23 ♍	0 A 29	22 ♎	11 A 03	22 ♐	9 P 57	22 ♑	10 A 17
25 ♋	11 P 49	24 ♌	1 P 00	25 ♎	0 A 19	24 ♏	10 A 43	25 ♑	0 A 30	24 ♒	3 P 52
28 ♌	2 A 46	26 ♍	1 P 55	26 ♏	11 P 51	26 ♐	11 A 12	27 ♒	6 A 01	27 ♓	0 A 17
30 ♍	3 A 44	28 ♎	1 P 36	29 ♐	1 A 06	28 ♑	2 P 19	29 ♓	3 P 47	29 ♈	0 P 12
		30 ♏	1 P 51			30 ♒	9 P 17				

1985

JAN
Date	Sign	TIME
1	♉	0 A 49
3	♊	0 P 23
5	♋	8 P 13
8	♌	1 A 33
10	♍	5 A 10
12	♎	4 A 57
14	♏	10 A 19
16	♐	1 P 55
18	♑	6 P 32
21	♒	0 A 34
23	♓	8 A 55
25	♈	8 P 17
28	♉	8 A 58
30	♊	9 P 07

FEB
Date	Sign	TIME
2	♋	5 A 47
4	♌	10 A 58
6	♍	1 P 30
8	♎	2 P 56
10	♏	4 P 17
12	♐	7 P 35
15	♑	0 A 43
17	♒	7 A 45
19	♓	4 P 46
22	♈	4 A 00
24	♉	4 P 29
27	♊	4 A 52

MAR
Date	Sign	TIME
1	♋	3 P 09
3	♌	9 P 12
5	♍	11 P 26
7	♎	11 P 58
10	♏	0 A 15
12	♐	3 A 10
14	♑	8 A 05
16	♒	1 P 21
18	♓	11 P 25
21	♈	10 A 48
23	♉	11 P 17
26	♊	0 N 00
28	♋	11 P 09
31	♌	6 A 30

APR
Date	Sign	TIME
2	♍	10 A 19
4	♎	11 A 03
6	♏	10 A 26
8	♐	10 A 32
10	♑	1 P 04
12	♒	7 P 31
15	♓	5 A 16
17	♈	5 P 06
20	♉	2 A 46
22	♊	3 P 11
25	♋	2 A 31
27	♌	11 A 27
29	♍	4 P 46

MAY
Date	Sign	TIME
1	♎	9 P 17
3	♏	9 P 13
5	♐	8 P 43
7	♑	10 P 12
10	♒	2 A 38
12	♓	11 A 03
14	♈	11 P 11
17	♉	0 N 00
19	♊	11 P 59
22	♋	10 A 50
24	♌	8 P 03
27	♍	2 A 20
29	♎	6 A 01
31	♏	7 A 18

JUN
Date	Sign	TIME
2	♐	7 A 25
4	♑	8 A 32
6	♒	11 A 40
8	♓	6 P 56
11	♈	6 A 01
13	♉	6 P 52
16	♊	7 A 03
18	♋	5 P 16
21	♌	1 A 40
23	♍	7 A 33
25	♎	0 P 11
27	♏	3 P 04
29	♐	4 P 47

JUL
Date	Sign	TIME
1	♑	6 P 18
3	♒	9 P 39
6	♓	3 A 41
8	♈	1 P 47
11	♉	2 A 15
13	♊	2 P 35
16	♋	1 A 02
18	♌	8 A 23
20	♍	1 P 35
22	♎	5 P 36
24	♏	8 P 41
26	♐	11 P 10
29	♑	2 A 37
31	♒	6 A 38

AUG
Date	Sign	TIME
2	♓	0 P 33
4	♈	9 P 57
7	♉	9 A 57
9	♊	10 P 30
12	♋	9 A 33
14	♌	4 P 59
16	♍	9 P 28
18	♎	11 P 56
21	♏	2 A 04
23	♐	4 A 24
25	♑	8 A 19
27	♒	1 P 39
29	♓	8 P 41

SEPT
Date	Sign	TIME
1	♈	6 A 00
3	♉	5 P 50
6	♊	6 A 09
8	♋	6 P 14
11	♌	2 A 47
13	♍	7 A 16
15	♎	9 A 00
17	♏	2 P 03
19	♐	1 P 09
21	♑	1 P 41
23	♒	4 P 57
26	♓	3 A 08
28	♈	1 P 11

OCT
Date	Sign	TIME
1	♉	0 A 43
3	♊	1 P 26
6	♋	1 A 42
8	♌	11 A 38
10	♍	5 P 24
12	♎	7 P 38
14	♏	7 P 50
16	♐	7 P 25
18	♑	8 P 37
21	♒	1 A 04
23	♓	8 A 35
25	♈	7 P 09
28	♉	7 A 11
30	♊	7 P 36

NOV
Date	Sign	TIME
2	♋	8 A 12
4	♌	8 A 12
7	♍	2 A 34
9	♎	6 A 14
11	♏	6 A 53
13	♐	6 A 12
15	♑	6 A 10
17	♒	8 A 54
19	♓	3 P 04
22	♈	1 A 00
24	♉	1 P 37
27	♊	2 A 02
29	♋	1 P 59

DEC
Date	Sign	TIME
2	♌	1 A 04
4	♍	9 A 38
6	♎	2 P 44
8	♏	5 P 05
10	♐	5 P 11
12	♑	5 P 03
14	♒	6 P 39
16	♓	11 P 21
19	♈	7 A 55
21	♉	8 P 09
24	♊	8 A 46
26	♋	8 P 41
29	♌	6 A 51
31	♍	3 P 06

1986

JAN	TIME	FEB	TIME	MAR	TIME	APR	TIME	MAY	TIME	JUN	TIME
2 ♎	8 P 08	1 ♏	6 A 38	2 ♐	3 P 03	3 ♒	3 A 39	2 ♓	2 P 49	1 ♈	5 A 01
5 ♏	0 A 42	3 ♐	9 A 35	4 ♑	6 P 02	5 ♓	9 A 39	4 ♈	11 P 36	3 ♉	4 P 13
7 ♐	2 A 28	5 ♑	11 A 50	6 ♒	9 P 59	7 ♈	5 P 54	7 ♉	10 A 26	6 ♊	4 A 37
9 ♑	3 A 31	7 ♒	2 P 44	9 ♓	3 A 10	10 ♉	3 A 56	9 ♊	10 P 24	8 ♋	5 P 12
11 ♒	5 A 18	9 ♓	6 P 49	11 ♈	10 A 30	12 ♊	3 P 51	12 ♋	11 A 12	11 ♌	5 A 09
13 ♓	8 A 36	12 ♈	1 A 30	13 ♉	8 P 16	15 ♋	4 A 49	14 ♌	11 P 05	13 ♍	3 P 35
15 ♈	4 P 19	14 ♉	11 A 37	16 ♊	8 A 10	17 ♌	4 P 25	17 ♍	9 A 12	15 ♎	10 P 51
18 ♉	3 A 32	17 ♊	0 A 19	18 ♋	8 P 57	20 ♍	0 A 37	19 ♎	2 P 45	18 ♏	2 A 36
20 ♊	4 P 25	19 ♋	0 P 36	21 ♌	7 A 45	22 ♎	4 A 52	21 ♏	4 P 50	20 ♐	3 A 22
23 ♋	4 A 19	21 ♌	10 P 24	23 ♍	2 P 49	24 ♏	6 A 10	23 ♐	4 P 38	22 ♑	3 A 00
25 ♌	1 P 52	24 ♍	5 A 15	25 ♎	6 P 16	26 ♐	6 A 18	25 ♑	4 P 10	24 ♒	3 A 11
27 ♍	9 P 04	26 ♎	9 A 13	27 ♏	8 P 07	28 ♑	6 A 54	27 ♒	5 P 18	26 ♓	5 A 47
30 ♎	2 A 39	28 ♏	0 P 30	29 ♐	9 P 32	30 ♒	9 A 33	29 ♓	9 P 23	28 ♈	0 N 00
				31 ♑	11 P 34					30 ♉	10 P 13

JUL	TIME	AUG	TIME	SEPT	TIME	OCT	TIME	NOV	TIME	DEC	TIME
3 ♊	10 A 47	2 ♋	6 A 09	1 ♌	1 A 21	3 ♎	1 A 14	1 ♏	2 P 21	1 ♐	2 A 04
5 ♋	11 P 13	4 ♌	5 P 19	3 ♍	10 A 30	5 ♏	4 A 37	3 ♐	3 P 25	3 ♑	1 A 54
8 ♌	10 A 50	7 ♍	2 A 44	5 ♎	4 P 27	7 ♐	6 A 46	5 ♑	4 P 05	5 ♒	1 A 57
10 ♍	8 P 57	9 ♎	2 A 12	7 ♏	9 P 12	9 ♑	8 A 41	7 ♒	5 P 47	7 ♓	4 A 32
13 ♎	4 A 44	11 ♏	3 P 20	10 ♐	4 A 34	11 ♒	11 A 49	9 ♓	9 P 44	9 ♈	10 A 00
15 ♏	10 A 22	13 ♐	6 P 53	12 ♑	5 A 41	13 ♓	4 P 17	12 ♈	4 A 35	11 ♉	7 P 27
17 ♐	0 P 30	15 ♑	9 P 21	14 ♒	5 A 45	15 ♈	10 P 38	14 ♉	1 P 12	14 ♊	6 A 51
19 ♑	1 P 18	17 ♒	10 P 50	16 ♓	9 A 55	18 ♉	6 A 39	17 ♊	0 A 30	16 ♋	7 P 13
21 ♒	1 P 39	20 ♓	1 A 38	18 ♈	2 P 55	20 ♊	5 P 00	19 ♋	0 P 25	19 ♌	7 A 45
23 ♓	3 P 35	22 ♈	5 A 47	20 ♉	10 P 30	23 ♋	5 A 21	22 ♌	1 A 13	21 ♍	7 P 50
25 ♈	8 P 26	24 ♉	1 P 46	23 ♊	8 A 53	25 ♌	6 P 04	24 ♍	0 P 57	24 ♎	5 A 11
28 ♉	5 A 30	27 ♊	0 A 55	25 ♋	9 P 46	28 ♍	4 A 42	26 ♎	9 P 00	26 ♏	10 A 51
30 ♊	5 P 27	29 ♋	1 P 49	28 ♌	10 A 00	30 ♎	11 A 29	29 ♏	1 A 06	28 ♐	1 P 08
				30 ♍	7 P 25					30 ♑	0 P 47

1987

JAN	TIME	FEB	TIME	MAR	TIME	APR	TIME	MAY	TIME	JUN	TIME
1 ♒	0 P 29	2 ♈	2 A 31	1 ♈	0 P 42	2 ♊	0 N 00	2 ♋	7 A 25	1 ♌	3 A 20
3 ♓	1 P 22	4 ♉	9 A 00	3 ♉	6 P 16	4 ♋	11 P 30	4 ♌	8 P 09	3 ♍	4 P 11
5 ♈	5 P 17	6 ♊	7 P 33	6 ♊	3 A 17	7 ♌	0 P 36	7 ♍	8 A 14	6 ♎	2 A 21
8 ♉	1 A 31	9 ♋	8 A 20	8 ♋	3 P 29	9 ♍	11 P 41	9 ♎	5 P 19	8 ♏	8 A 50
10 ♊	0 P 49	11 ♌	8 P 48	11 ♌	4 A 20	12 ♎	8 A 11	11 ♏	10 P 48	10 ♐	11 A 41
13 ♋	1 A 30	14 ♍	7 A 55	13 ♍	3 P 15	14 ♏	1 P 24	14 ♐	1 A 14	12 ♑	0 P 10
15 ♌	2 P 10	16 ♎	5 P 01	15 ♎	11 P 48	16 ♐	4 P 56	16 ♑	2 A 41	14 ♒	11 A 50
18 ♍	1 A 35	19 ♏	0 A 05	18 ♏	5 A 58	18 ♑	7 P 36	18 ♒	3 A 54	16 ♓	1 P 31
20 ♎	11 A 15	21 ♐	5 A 03	20 ♐	10 A 46	20 ♒	10 P 25	20 ♓	6 A 51	18 ♈	5 P 15
22 ♏	6 P 23	23 ♑	6 A 42	22 ♑	1 P 52	23 ♓	1 A 33	22 ♈	11 A 49	21 ♉	0 A 22
24 ♐	10 P 07	25 ♒	9 A 08	24 ♒	4 P 40	25 ♈	6 A 18	24 ♉	6 P 56	23 ♊	10 A 14
26 ♑	11 P 22	27 ♓	10 A 13	26 ♓	6 P 59	27 ♉	0 P 11	27 ♊	3 A 53	25 ♋	9 P 29
28 ♒	11 P 26			28 ♈	10 P 26	29 ♊	8 P 42	29 ♋	3 P 01	28 ♌	10 A 00
30 ♓	11 P 40			31 ♉	3 A 38					30 ♍	10 P 43

JUL	TIME	AUG	TIME	SEPT	TIME	OCT	TIME	NOV	TIME	DEC	TIME
3 ♎	10 A 02	2 ♏	0 A 49	2 ♑	5 P 03	2 ♒	2 A 00	2 ♈	1 P 45	2 ♉	0 A 58
5 ♏	5 P 50	4 ♐	6 A 35	4 ♒	6 P 39	4 ♓	4 A 04	4 ♉	6 P 02	4 ♊	8 A 08
7 ♐	9 P 46	6 ♑	8 A 41	6 ♓	6 P 59	6 ♈	5 A 48	7 ♊	0 A 10	6 ♋	5 P 07
9 ♑	10 P 36	8 ♒	8 A 53	8 ♈	8 P 04	8 ♉	9 A 04	9 ♋	9 A 17	9 ♌	4 A 37
11 ♒	10 P 15	10 ♓	8 A 32	10 ♉	11 P 11	10 ♊	3 P 01	11 ♌	8 P 52	11 ♍	5 P 27
13 ♓	10 P 03	12 ♈	9 A 34	13 ♊	5 A 49	13 ♋	0 A 35	14 ♍	9 A 48	14 ♎	5 A 19
16 ♈	0 A 21	14 ♉	1 P 39	15 ♋	4 P 37	15 ♌	1 P 00	16 ♎	9 P 09	16 ♏	2 P 34
18 ♉	6 A 09	16 ♊	9 P 52	18 ♌	5 A 18	18 ♍	1 A 30	19 ♏	4 A 44	18 ♐	7 P 16
20 ♊	3 P 35	19 ♋	9 A 25	20 ♍	5 P 40	20 ♎	0 P 11	21 ♐	9 A 14	20 ♑	9 P 18
23 ♋	3 A 29	21 ♌	10 P 24	23 ♎	3 A 56	22 ♏	7 P 31	23 ♑	11 A 50	22 ♒	9 P 45
25 ♌	4 P 13	24 ♍	10 A 37	25 ♏	0 P 22	25 ♐	0 A 47	25 ♒	1 P 31	24 ♓	10 P 48
28 ♍	4 A 32	26 ♎	9 P 22	27 ♐	6 P 28	27 ♑	4 A 34	27 ♓	3 P 51	27 ♈	1 A 17
30 ♎	3 P 55	29 ♏	6 A 34	29 ♑	10 P 57	29 ♒	7 A 35	29 ♈	7 P 37	29 ♉	6 A 38
		31 ♐	1 P 04			31 ♓	10 A 19			31 ♊	2 P 29

1988

JAN	TIME	FEB	TIME	MAR	TIME	APR	TIME	MAY	TIME	JUN	TIME
3 ♋	0 A 30	1 ♌	6 P 31	2 ♍	1 P 26	1 ♎	8 A 12	1 ♏	1 A 24	1 ♑	8 P 51
5 ♌	0 N 00	4 ♍	7 A 10	4 ♎	1 A 29	3 ♏	6 P 28	3 ♐	8 A 40	3 ♒	11 P 48
8 ♍	0 A 37	6 ♎	7 P 27	7 ♏	0 P 35	6 ♐	2 A 28	5 ♑	1 P 55	6 ♓	2 A 16
10 ♎	1 P 12	9 ♏	6 A 38	9 ♐	8 P 59	8 ♑	8 A 38	7 ♒	6 P 08	8 ♈	5 A 16
12 ♏	11 P 21	11 ♐	2 P 19	12 ♑	2 A 35	10 ♒	0 P 41	9 ♓	8 P 50	10 ♉	9 A 12
15 ♐	5 A 28	13 ♑	6 P 20	14 ♒	5 A 06	12 ♓	2 P 46	11 ♈	11 P 20	12 ♊	2 P 22
17 ♑	8 A 20	15 ♒	7 P 22	16 ♓	5 A 30	14 ♈	3 P 39	14 ♉	2 A 22	14 ♋	9 P 42
19 ♒	8 A 08	17 ♓	6 P 43	18 ♈	5 A 30	16 ♉	5 P 26	16 ♊	6 A 24	17 ♌	7 A 10
21 ♓	7 A 58	19 ♈	6 P 39	20 ♉	6 A 56	18 ♊	8 P 48	18 ♋	0 P 46	19 ♍	7 P 04
23 ♈	8 A 32	21 ♉	8 P 56	22 ♊	10 A 58	21 ♋	4 A 04	20 ♌	10 P 54	22 ♎	7 A 59
25 ♉	0 P 54	24 ♊	2 A 42	24 ♋	7 P 36	23 ♌	2 P 51	23 ♍	11 A 12	24 ♏	6 P 59
27 ♊	7 P 53	26 ♋	0 P 36	27 ♌	7 A 23	26 ♍	3 A 44	25 ♎	11 P 55	27 ♐	2 A 21
30 ♋	6 A 39	29 ♌	0 A 50	29 ♍	8 P 13	28 ♎	3 P 55	28 ♏	10 A 03	29 ♑	6 A 06
								30 ♐	4 P 44		

JUL	TIME	AUG	TIME	SEPT	TIME	OCT	TIME	NOV	TIME	DEC	TIME
1 ♒	7 A 38	1 ♈	5 P 48	2 ♊	8 A 08	1 ♋	10 P 43	3 ♍	4 A 25	3 ♎	1 A 13
3 ♓	8 A 52	3 ♉	8 P 12	4 ♋	3 P 50	4 ♌	9 A 00	5 ♎	5 P 15	5 ♏	0 P 47
5 ♈	10 A 41	6 ♊	1 A 34	7 ♌	2 A 32	6 ♍	9 P 22	8 ♏	4 A 39	7 ♐	10 P 10
7 ♉	2 P 31	8 ♋	10 A 07	9 ♍	3 P 02	9 ♎	10 A 00	10 ♐	1 P 53	10 ♑	5 A 53
9 ♊	8 P 17	10 ♌	8 P 57	12 ♎	3 A 32	11 ♏	9 P 34	12 ♑	9 P 23	12 ♒	9 A 04
12 ♋	4 A 29	13 ♍	8 A 37	14 ♏	3 P 25	14 ♐	7 A 35	15 ♒	2 A 46	14 ♓	0 P 10
14 ♌	2 P 25	15 ♎	9 P 26	17 ♐	2 A 01	16 ♑	3 P 38	17 ♓	6 A 37	16 ♈	2 P 53
17 ♍	2 A 24	18 ♏	9 A 37	19 ♑	9 A 40	18 ♒	9 P 07	19 ♈	8 A 50	18 ♉	5 P 50
19 ♎	3 P 04	20 ♐	7 P 49	21 ♒	2 P 09	20 ♓	11 P 56	21 ♉	10 A 41	20 ♊	9 P 48
22 ♏	3 A 01	22 ♑	1 A 45	23 ♓	2 P 45	23 ♈	0 A 49	23 ♊	1 P 13	23 ♋	2 A 42
24 ♐	0 N 00	25 ♒	4 A 20	25 ♈	2 P 33	25 ♉	1 A 22	25 ♋	5 P 36	25 ♌	10 A 08
26 ♑	4 P 15	27 ♓	4 A 14	27 ♉	2 P 30	27 ♊	3 A 07	28 ♌	1 A 04	27 ♍	8 P 36
28 ♒	5 P 58	29 ♈	3 A 45	29 ♊	5 P 01	29 ♋	7 A 42	30 ♍	0 P 12	30 ♎	8 A 58
30 ♓	5 P 45	31 ♉	4 A 30			31 ♌	4 P 25				

1989

JAN		TIME	FEB		TIME	MAR		TIME	APR		TIME	MAY		TIME	JUN		TIME
1	♏	9 P 27	2	♑	11 P 31	2	♑	8 A 53	3	♓	1 A 13	2	♈	11 A 41	2	♊	9 P 56
4	♐	7 A 26	5	♒	2 A 40	4	♒	1 P 31	5	♈	1 A 15	4	♉	11 A 22	5	♋	0 A 26
6	♑	1 P 24	7	♓	3 A 54	6	♓	2 P 26	7	♉	0 A 49	6	♊	11 A 41	7	♌	5 A 36
8	♒	4 P 44	9	♈	4 A 26	8	♈	2 P 13	9	♊	1 A 35	8	♋	2 P 18	9	♍	2 P 13
10	♓	6 P 40	11	♉	5 A 45	10	♉	2 P 09	11	♋	5 A 07	10	♌	8 P 31	12	♎	2 A 54
12	♈	8 P 58	13	♊	9 A 30	12	♊	4 P 21	13	♌	0 P 47	13	♍	6 A 27	14	♏	3 P 14
14	♉	11 P 34	15	♋	4 P 08	14	♋	9 P 42	16	♍	0 A 13	15	♎	7 P 20	17	♐	2 A 18
17	♊	4 A 03	18	♌	0 A 52	17	♌	6 A 43	18	♎	0 P 48	18	♏	7 A 39	19	♑	10 A 43
19	♋	9 A 50	20	♍	11 A 48	19	♍	6 P 00	21	♏	1 A 19	20	♐	6 P 59	21	♒	5 P 08
21	♌	6 P 10	22	♎	11 P 42	22	♎	6 A 25	23	♐	0 P 36	23	♑	4 A 04	23	♓	9 P 44
24	♍	4 A 31	25	♏	0 P 48	24	♏	6 P 52	25	♑	10 P 35	25	♒	11 A 18	26	♈	1 A 18
26	♎	4 P 39	28	♐	0 A 24	27	♐	7 A 01	28	♒	6 A 09	27	♓	4 A 31	28	♉	3 A 50
29	♏	5 A 33				29	♑	4 P 49	30	♓	10 A 10	29	♈	7 P 30	30	♊	6 A 34
31	♐	4 P 21				31	♒	10 P 46				31	♉	8 P 50			

JUL		TIME	AUG		TIME	SEPT		TIME	OCT		TIME	NOV		TIME	DEC		TIME
2	♋	9 A 34	3	♍	7 A 22	2	♎	1 A 23	1	♏	8 P 17	3	♑	2 A 53	2	♒	5 P 47
4	♌	2 P 55	5	♎	6 P 00	4	♏	1 P 50	4	♐	9 A 11	5	♒	0 P 11	5	♓	0 A 33
6	♍	10 P 49	8	♏	6 A 50	7	♐	2 A 44	6	♑	8 P 37	7	♓	6 P 02	7	♈	4 A 52
9	♎	10 A 00	10	♐	5 P 50	9	♑	1 P 29	9	♒	5 A 05	9	♈	8 P 50	9	♉	6 A 38
11	♏	10 P 53	13	♑	4 A 26	11	♒	8 P 09	11	♓	9 A 25	11	♉	8 P 56	11	♊	7 A 26
14	♐	10 A 28	15	♒	10 A 05	13	♓	11 P 01	13	♈	10 A 32	13	♊	8 P 43	13	♋	8 A 13
16	♑	7 P 07	17	♓	0 P 40	15	♈	11 P 43	15	♉	10 A 05	15	♋	9 P 33	15	♌	11 A 10
19	♒	0 A 35	19	♈	1 P 50	17	♉	11 P 22	17	♊	9 A 46	18	♌	1 A 20	17	♍	5 P 27
21	♓	4 A 11	21	♉	3 P 00	20	♊	0 A 35	19	♋	11 A 31	20	♍	8 A 56	20	♎	3 A 52
23	♈	6 A 30	23	♊	5 P 46	22	♋	4 A 07	21	♌	5 P 01	22	♎	8 P 24	22	♏	4 P 27
25	♉	9 A 07	25	♋	10 P 34	24	♌	10 A 53	24	♍	2 A 14	25	♏	9 A 11	25	♐	5 A 01
27	♊	0 P 21	28	♌	5 A 33	26	♍	8 P 32	26	♎	2 P 01	27	♐	9 P 31	27	♑	3 P 18
29	♋	5 P 08	30	♍	2 P 31	29	♎	8 A 03	29	♏	2 A 50	30	♑	8 A 31	29	♒	11 P 42
31	♌	11 P 04							31	♐	3 P 11						

1990

JAN	TIME	FEB	TIME	MAR	TIME	APR	TIME	MAY	TIME	JUN	TIME
1 ♓	6 A 07	1 ♉	7 P 25	1 ♉	1 A 38	1 ♋	1 P 03	1 ♌	0 A 27	1 ♎	11 P 25
3 ♈	10 A 48	3 ♊	10 P 21	3 ♊	3 A 53	3 ♌	6 P 11	3 ♍	7 A 08	4 ♏	11 A 37
5 ♉	1 P 51	6 ♋	1 A 33	5 ♋	7 A 14	6 ♍	1 A 59	5 ♎	5 P 24	7 ♐	0 A 19
7 ♊	4 P 00	8 ♌	5 A 58	7 ♌	0 P 44	8 ♎	11 A 47	7 ♏	5 A 33	9 ♑	0 P 24
9 ♋	5 P 54	10 ♍	0 N 00	9 ♍	7 P 43	10 ♏	11 P 18	10 ♐	6 P 04	11 ♒	11 P 09
11 ♌	9 P 26	12 ♎	8 P 59	12 ♎	5 A 08	13 ♐	0 N 00	13 ♑	6 A 25	14 ♓	7 A 56
14 ♍	2 A 47	15 ♏	8 A 20	14 ♏	4 P 04	16 ♑	0 A 25	15 ♒	5 P 44	16 ♈	2 P 04
16 ♎	0 P 12	17 ♐	9 P 05	17 ♐	4 A 57	18 ♒	10 A 52	18 ♓	1 A 42	18 ♉	4 P 47
19 ♏	0 A 19	20 ♑	8 A 40	19 ♑	5 P 09	20 ♓	5 P 43	20 ♈	6 A 19	20 ♊	5 P 32
21 ♐	1 P 00	22 ♒	4 P 40	22 ♒	2 A 12	22 ♈	8 P 20	22 ♉	7 A 27	22 ♋	5 P 29
23 ♑	11 P 38	24 ♓	9 P 23	24 ♓	7 A 42	24 ♉	8 P 46	24 ♊	6 A 57	24 ♌	6 P 39
26 ♒	0 P 42	26 ♈	11 P 56	26 ♈	9 A 52	26 ♊	8 P 06	26 ♋	6 A 40	26 ♍	10 P 39
28 ♓	4 P 26			28 ♉	10 A 03	28 ♋	8 P 58	28 ♌	8 A 47	29 ♎	6 A 38
30 ♈				30 ♊	10 A 51			30 ♍	2 P 02		

JUL	TIME	AUG	TIME	SEPT	TIME	OCT	TIME	NOV	TIME	DEC	TIME
1 ♏	5 P 54	3 ♑	2 A 17	1 ♒	8 P 35	1 ♓	1 P 45	2 ♉	5 A 38	1 ♊	4 P 35
4 ♐	7 A 02	5 ♒	0 P 11	4 ♓	3 A 53	3 ♈	5 P 33	4 ♊	5 A 44	3 ♋	4 P 10
6 ♑	6 P 45	7 ♓	7 P 35	6 ♈	8 A 04	5 ♉	7 P 11	6 ♋	5 A 41	5 ♌	4 P 32
9 ♒	4 A 58	10 ♈	0 A 47	8 ♉	11 A 00	7 ♊	8 P 20	8 ♌	7 A 55	7 ♍	8 P 02
11 ♓	1 P 28	12 ♉	4 A 52	10 ♊	1 P 11	9 ♋	9 P 48	10 ♍	0 P 34	10 ♎	3 A 03
13 ♈	7 P 17	14 ♊	7 A 50	12 ♋	4 P 17	12 ♌	1 A 14	12 ♎	9 P 09	12 ♏	1 P 48
15 ♉	11 P 40	16 ♋	10 A 29	14 ♌	7 P 59	14 ♍	7 A 07	15 ♏	8 A 00	15 ♐	2 A 09
18 ♊	1 A 54	18 ♌	1 P 14	17 ♍	1 A 15	16 ♎	3 P 05	17 ♐	7 P 41	17 ♑	2 P 48
20 ♋	3 A 32	20 ♍	5 P 23	19 ♎	8 A 19	19 ♏	1 A 09	20 ♑	8 A 20	20 ♒	2 A 44
22 ♌	4 A 54	22 ♎	0 M 00	21 ♏	5 P 51	21 ♐	1 P 12	22 ♒	8 P 52	22 ♓	1 P 20
24 ♍	8 A 22	25 ♏	9 A 30	24 ♐	5 A 45	24 ♑	1 A 45	25 ♓	7 A 03	24 ♈	9 P 19
26 ♎	2 P 54	27 ♐	9 P 53	26 ♑	6 P 33	26 ♒	1 P 56	27 ♈	1 P 24	27 ♉	1 A 47
29 ♏	1 A 42	30 ♑	10 A 48	29 ♒	5 A 48	28 ♓	10 P 59	29 ♉	4 P 32	29 ♊	3 A 19
31 ♐	2 P 13					31 ♈	3 A 50			31 ♋	2 A 54

SUN SIGN RELATIONSHIPS

SUN COMBINATIONS

Aries
Impetuous
Sincere
Energetic
Must win
Enthusiastic
Seeks challenges
Likes success
Heroic

Aries Sun Parent/Aries Sun Child

Aries are adventure-seeking, enthusiastic and see life as a perpetual challenge. They'll get on together like a house on fire. Two winners with a mutual respect for each other's independence and self-reliance. However, the need to compete, for this double act, will be almost impossible to resist and 'pushing each other a little too far' can become a perpetual hazard. Neither has a natural talent for knowing when to stop so arbitration by the other parent may be necessary. Individual 'rights' will need to be supported on both sides. 'Don't do as I do, do as I tell you' inconsistency will be met with 'If you can do it, so can I!'. This may become embarrassing when Junior calls Aunt Mary what you called the tax man the day before, and a reprimand will guarantee a response that will let all know that you share responsibility for the *'faux pas'*. Before getting too heavy remember that Junior will lose respect for justice that punishes for emulating his hero's behaviour. So enjoy the spirit, the nerve, the sheer bravery and the *'faux pas'*, and watch your language.

Best activities to share: lighthearted competitive games; toy car racing; anything fast (guide away from the risky as sore heads are a perpetual hazard); climbing frames; and camping.

Aries	Taurus
Impetuous	Cautious
Sincere	Steady
Energetic	Calm
Must win	Must acquire
Enthusiastic	Sensual
Seeks challenges	Seeks growth
Likes success	Likes security
Heroic	Romantic

Aries Sun Parent/Taurus Sun Child

The Aries parent is energetic, challenging, quick to act, and will immediately experience the 'different' nature of the little Taurean. For Junior is slow but sure and won't be pushed into anything, no matter how enthusiastic or encouraging the parent is, until confident that the time is right. This relationship personifies 'the tortoise and the hare' and in a competitive situation the Aries parent may be as puzzled as the hare at the outcome. Nevertheless, they share strength of will and a desire to succeed, and Aries will appreciate the steady persistence of the young Bull in overcoming and understanding each facet of a problem in order to reach a successful conclusion. Taureans absorb ideas slowly but thoroughly and respond best to first-hand experiment, putting things to practical test and getting the feel of how they work. Aries belief that 'actions speak louder than words' can fall on receptive ground with this child. Problems in this relationship will never be solved by open conflict, for Taurean obstinacy produces the immovable object to Aries' irresistible force and there is a resulting impasse. Sincere respect for each other's very different individual requirements is essential for family calm.

Best activities to share: building; gardening (Taureans are born gardeners); moulding and making things; Lego; papier mâché; cooking; mudpie making etc.

The Taurean parent is stable, calm, patient, and above all dependable. Aries will develop confidence and self-reliance as long as this parent's conscientious support is not made to appear too obvious. Little Aries' greatest need is to 'go it alone' against all odds; security and caution thrown to the wind, Commonsense Taurus will recognize the need, see the dangers, and calmly and quietly remove the hazards before Junior hits them head on. This protection can't go on for ever though, and the Taurean parent will provide smaller, safer projects with enough excitement in order for young Aries to learn the practical 'nuts and bolts' approach that aids eventual success. These two are both affectionate but their different needs may sometimes conflict. Insistence on the proper way to do things and application to the finer details, if it takes the form of a reprimand, will only result in open rebellion. 'You can't do it that way', like most negatives sets up a challenge for Aries that just can't be ignored. Sincere praise for achievements will produce better results than analysing failures.

Best activities to share: 'projects'; competitive games; getting things done; anything busy, noisy, exhausting, or nearly impossible.

ARIES / GEMINI

Aries	Gemini
Impetuous	Changeable
Sincere	Unpredictable
Energetic	Interested
Must win	Must know
Enthusiastic	Moody
Seeks challenges	Seeks to communicate
Likes success	Likes change
Heroic	Versatile

One of the best challenges for an Aries parent could be the Gemini child. Never a dull moment, and if ever the unlimited energy of Aries came in handy, now's the time. Young Geminis from a year and a half onwards are all-talking, all-moving, all-thinking sparkles of restless activity. They take to learning like a duck to water, getting the hang of things quickly and guessing the rest. It's almost better to speak of them in the plural for that's what one of these little wonders feels like. If Aries can deal with all the how?, whys?, whens? and did you knows? the rest will take care of itself. Except for one maddening thing. Young Gemini rarely focuses long enough to finish anything; and as it's hardly likely that Aries will accept a 'jack of all trades, master of none' for an offspring, some action will be necessary. If the reasoning is good, the logic unchallengable and the prospect stimulating you'll win. Play Gemini's own game for success. If you make your attitude heavy, loaded with reprimands, you'll have a nervy, abstracted little worrier to deal with (oppressed Geminis suffer skin complaints and headaches so watch out for rashes).

Best activities to share: fact finding; quiz games; music; TV; reading; writing stories; board games; jigsaws; model making; collecting; Scrabble. All done preferably in groups of two or three.

Gemini Sun Parent/Aries Sun Child

The Gemini parent never quite loses the wonder and curiosity of childhood. Bringing up little Aries will be approached with a fresh lively mind and a good sense of fun. Young Arietians are usually bright and precocious and respond well to the continuous stimulation of the Gemini household. This parent will be smart enough to recognize the different approach to learning that little Aries has. Gemini avidly grabs facts, figures and pieces of information and makes sense of the whole, Junior tests everything out with immediate action. Hammers smash eggs? So he tries it! This fearless impetuosity can land small

Aries in a barrel of trouble. But Gemini, quick on the feet, deft of hand, and fast with advice can avert the worst. The main friction points between these two arise as a result of this scatterbrained parent providing too many windmills for quixotic Junior to tilt against at the same time. Aries turns frustrated energy into destructive aggression if not allowed to bring battles to a successful conclusion. The policy one at a time but keep 'em coming works wonders.

Best activities to share: fast active games (ping-pong, stunt kite-flying, Scalextric racing); board games with a little romance (Knights in Armour, Quests etc.); and swinging, running, jumping, climbing, leaping games.

ARIES / CANCER

Aries	Cancer
Impetuous	Sensitive
Sincere	Reliable
Energetic	Devoted
Must win	Must care
Enthusiastic	Responsive
Seeks challenges	Seeks to protect
Likes success	Likes the familiar
Heroic	Caring

Aries Sun Parent/Cancer Sun Child

The Aries parent is strong, self-willed, affectionate and quick to act. Cancer always responds to the mood of the moment. This parent will encourage the child confidently to express what it feels, *when* it feels it. Cancer's radar tunes in to other people's highs and lows and shares them. With the Aries parent the wavelength is enthusiasm, and the potential positive. Powerful as they are Aries adults rarely crush others, for their belief in the right of the individual is supreme. Junior will be supported when necessary, but not hampered or over-protected when wanting to 'go it alone'. An ideal relationship to bring out this child's leadership potential. Negatively Aries' overdrive can rush and panic Cancer into unprepared-for situations with resulting emotional disaster, while Aries remains blissfully unaware that not everybody learns to swim by jumping in the deep end, and wonders why such an excellent child should suddenly turn into a nervous, apprehensive, and crabby crybaby. Develop good timing and read little Cancer's signals which are always well displayed.

Best activities to share: going places (bring back souvenirs); junk shops and jumble sales; cooking; caring for pets.

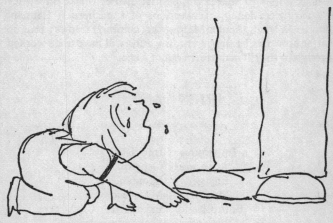

'How was I to know it was *your* earwig!'

Cancer Sun Parent/Aries Sun Child

The Cancer parent provides a warm, comfortable and caring environment in which little Aries can find safe self-expression. Safe, is the operative words as the Aries irrepressible attitude of 'let's do it and hang the consequences' is well balanced by Cancer's protective feeling for potential hazards. Cancer will

71

soon sense that in order to deal with this, the provision of another, safer but no less exciting challenge, is more effective than total frustration. Saying 'No' to Aries rarely gets willing compliance, and always makes the unattainable more desirable. Cancer will take delight in using imaginative ways to cope with Junior's boredom with routine tasks. Tough but full of affection the little Aries will blossom with sincere support and belief in his or her self-confidence. The ever-present snag to this relationship is Cancer's negative use of the protective instinct. 'You're still my baby' may produce warm satisfied feelings in some children but tiny Aries warriors will read that as a call to battle and respond to this insult to their achievements with aggression: 'Please notice I'm growing up'.

Best activities to share: competitive games (make sure they lose very occasionally); collections of superheroes, Batman, Wonder Woman, Action Men; sport; climbing frames; and, no matter how pacifist the parent, toy guns will have to be worked through or they'll make them out of Lego.

ARIES / LEO

Aries	Leo
Impetuous	Impulsive
Sincere	Generous
Energetic	Spontaneous
Must win	Must lead
Enthusiastic	Expansive
Seeks challenges	Seeks admiration
Likes success	Likes big ideas
Heroic	Dramatic

Aries Sun Parent/Leo Sun Child

This is a relationship of fire, enthusiasm, and super-creative activity with a dash of healthy competition thrown in for good measure. Big winner and little boss. Aries will soon sense, support, and enthusiastically encourage, Leo Junior's obvious leadership potential. Leo learns easily, with a natural sense of creative self-expression and backed with liberal doses of appreciation can push on to great heights. The Aries parent will delight in young Leo's firm independence and the sunny good-natured bossiness that automatically makes him head of the gang with young contemporaries. Leos need little help and possibly some subtle restraint in this direction for the pain of an overthrown tyrannical dictator can be inconsolable. With a great sense of drama, and an irresistible urge to 'show off' (showbiz is full of them) they need a good audience but a firm Aries parent can help them learn when enough is enough. There can be no open combat though, for Ram and Lion are hotheads, neither easily admitting defeat. Too many chiefs, too few Indians; smoke peacepipe, heaps better fun.

Best activities to share: making things; planning things; painting huge pictures; singing, dancing, play acting and organizing everybody.

Leo Sun Parent/Aries Sun Child

The generous Leo parent is proud, ambitious, and spares no expense where home and loved ones are concerned. Little Arietians are tough, affectionate, energetic, survivors. In the comfort of a Leo home the young Aries pioneer will be warmly encouraged and creatively stimulated. The Leo parent – a natural games player – will understand little Aries' need to approach each facet of learning as a challenge to be defeated. Danger and adventure attracts the young Ram, and these fearless exploits need careful supervision (their heads have a recurrent habit of hitting hard objects). Leos are never short of good attractive ideas with which to replace the worst of Junior's kamikaze compulsions. Both parent and child are strong leaders and there will be a strong mutual respect in this relationship that should make matters of discipline run smoothly. As with the reverse relationship between these two signs, aggressive confrontation solves nothing; us versus the world, is better than you against me.

Best activities to share: forts and toy soldiers (dainty Aries girls battle alongside the boys); heroes and heroines, from Wonder Woman to Snoopy (Snoopy *must* be Aries!); building or making the fastest, biggest, loudest, longest, tallest – you name it.

ARIES / VIRGO

Aries	Virgo
Impetuous	Conscientious
Sincere	Responsible
Energetic	Painstaking
Must win	Must perfect
Enthusiastic	Critical
Seeks challenges	Seeks order
Likes success	Likes efficiency
Heroic	Dutiful

Aries Sun Parent/Virgo Sun Child

The Aries parent is a strong but generous authority figure in home life and little Virgo is happiest with a firm well established pattern within which to grow and improve. Young Virgos learn quickly with great application and modest devotion; sifting and analysing with their sharp little minds each new piece of information. Aries parents, no lovers of routine, may find themselves organized and coopted into regular appointments for games, and educational assistance. The Virgoan love of facts, figures, and good hard work can leave Junior on the fringe of the fun but the Aries parent will encourage friendships and help young shy Virgo find confidence. Good little organizers like these are invaluable in group situations but unlike Leos, they wait to be asked. Conflicts can arise if Aries is too ambitiously pushy on Virgo's behalf. The fear of being propelled into anything risky or potentially embarrassing will evoke sharp criticism and pointed sarcasm that can deflate even an Aries ego. Timing is of the essence, they'll let you know when, in triplicate.

Best activities to share: keeping a diary; sticking things in albums and scrapbooks; pressing wild flowers; making lists; sorting out old button boxes and junk drawers; helping Mum, helping Dad.

Virgo Sun Parent/Aries Sun Child

The Virgo parent is intelligent, calmly efficient, and comfortingly reliable. Aries junior is intelligent, always excitable, and disconcertingly impetuous. Surprisingly enough, though Aries dislikes limiting routine in large doses, a few firmly laid down rules give a good and necessary anchor to all that fiery energy. Virgo will respect young Aries' independence and patiently support the sometimes rash, raw enthusiasm with a good grounding in common sense. Quiet lessons in i-dotting and t-crossing will give Junior's need to succeed at all costs more than a sporting chance. Virgo's slightly cynical sense of humour can't fail to be softened and expanded by this unabashed little clown's unexpected antics. However unselfish the intention, Virgos can sometimes let their excellent critical faculties turn them into unbearable nag-bags. Young Aries sees criticism as an attack on personal prestige and will be savagely defensive.

Best activities to share: competitive games; working models; plenty of outdoor action; outlets for excess energy (with hammer, nails, pegboards); lots of old furniture for imaginary adventures (galleons, forts, castles etc.).

Aries	Libra
Impetuous	Amenable
Sincere	Easy-going
Energetic	Cooperative
Must win	Must relate
Enthusiastic	Diplomatic
Seeks challenges	Seeks company
Likes success	Likes harmony
Heroic	Just

Aries Sun Parent/Libran Sun Child

Aries parents are affectionate, quick acting, individualists. Libran children are sociable and charming, and constantly seek and love the company of others. Their biggest social asset, always being able to see the other person's point of view, has a negative side that can drive the spontaneous Aries parent steadily up the wall. Decisions! Decisions! They just can't make them. Little Libra has an excellent logical mind that accepts nothing at face value without trying the alternatives. Great for friendly argument, social conversation and the accumulation of broad knowledge. But what to have for breakfast becomes an interminable inquiry, and which dress to wear, a two hour debate. The Aries parent can help initially by firmly limiting the options. Later, a little Aries logic – that any decision is better than no decision, may be acceptable. Don't rush though, unless you want to change your amiable, little chatterbox and devoted companion into a sulky, argumentative opponent. However, on balance, there's less rough than smooth with little Libra.

Best activities to share: anything artistic, at least a dabble with a musical instrument; board games for two (dice, but never chess!); tennis; playing on a garden swing; long conversations.

The Libran parent is easy-going, sociable, and a just and understanding friend. Little Aries is affectionate and independent; fearless and friendly. A bee in the bonnet of Junior provokes immediate action regardless of consequences. Librans, though not sharing the Aries need to continually prove themselves, will recognize the basic drive and react with support and appreciation. Junior's progress can be assisted by this parent's intelligent and logical approach. To this end physical demonstrations and interesting experiments achieve more with young Aries than balanced theoretical discussion. Libra's usually balanced outlook hits the happy medium, neither over protective nor neglectful, giving little Aries plenty of opportunity to develop self-confidence and ability. Now the bad news. Friction in this otherwise idyllic relationship may occur if Libra opens up too many options and alternatives at any given situation, for energetic Aries, seeing each one as a challenge, will want to do the lot. Exhausted Rams are never sociable. Keep the menu to the 'plat du jour' and hide the 'à la carte'.

Best activities to share: solving puzzles; competitive games (Aries will get a fair share of wins); drawing, painting, etc.

ARIES / SCORPIO

Aries	Scorpio
Impetuous	Intense
Sincere	Powerful
Energetic	Passionate
Must win	Must defeat
Enthusiastic	Penetrating
Seeks challenges	Seeks power
Likes success	Likes challenge
Heroic	Magnetic

The Aries parent may never discover that such powerful and actively strong characters as little Scorpios can be very emotionally vulnerable. They tap in to other people's thoughts and feelings almost telepathically, rarely giving away their own. The honest straightforward Aries, 'if you feel it, you show it' attitude can go a long way in helping little Scorpio to share bottled up hopes and fears confidently. They will be united by a love of challenges. Rarely childishly carefree, young Scorpio thrives on deep, passionate interests, and loves converting others to the same cause. The Aries parents will support enthusiastically when necessary but never intrusively, for their own strong self-reliance makes them respect and encourage juniors. Scorpios rarely accept domineering authority, preferring to shake off bad habits with their own strict brand of self-discipline. Hurt pride can produce sly, secretive disobedience, and brooding resentment.

Best activities to share: detective stories; problems and puzzles (Scorpios make good chess players); plenty of outdoor action, exploring ,treasure hunting; I spy; war games.

Scorpio Sun Parent/Aries Sun Child

This powerful couple have a great deal in common, both seeing life as a succession of stimulating challenges that cannot be refused. The Scorpio parent, deeply sensitive, and eternally fascinated by understanding what makes other people tick, will soon sense and admire the sheer driving spirit of little Aries. Like Cancer and Pisces, Scorpio's protective instinct is strong but will never intrude on Junior's great need to 'go it alone'. Subtle direction will guide little Aries past the more obvious pitfalls on the road to self-confidence. Little Rams are often precociously bright, needing almost continuous stimulation and diversion to prevent their unlimited energy from becoming aggressively self-destructive. Scorpio's creativity responds with imaginative projects, that excite and maintain interest. A good non-aggression pact is worth fixing early on in the relationship as in battle this couple are merciless and hurt deeply, neither accepting defeat nor giving ground. You can set up enough challenges without tackling each other.

Best activities to share: painting the ceiling of the Sistine Chapel (or woodshed); climbing Everest (or Primrose Hill); swimming the Channel (at the local baths); discovering America (with a packed lunch on Wandsworth Common).

ARIES / SAGITTARIUS

Aries	Sagittarius
Impetuous	Tolerant
Sincere	Honest
Energetic	Interested
Must win	Must understand
Enthusiastic	Outgoing
Seeks challenges	Seeks to know
Likes success	Likes adventure
Heroic	Philosophic

Aries Sun Parent/Sagittarius Sun Child

These two will share a love of activity, adventure, and the outdoors. Aries encourages with enthusiasm the expression of little Sagittarius's natural free-ranging individual approach to life. Although always active and on the move, Junior is a thinker and has to understand the truth of everything in order to develop fully. Straight answers, even if they hurt a little, are the basis and the strength of this relationship. Aries is a natural authority figure and providing there is always reason and logic behind limitations to this child's freedom the little Archer will cooperate gracefully. Both need challenges, but

Sagittarius vision is long-distance and without Aries' help may miss immediate opportunities while looking towards tomorrow. The biggest clash for these two fiery characters can come from Aries over-reacting and losing patience with Sagittarius's continual 'why?' to every order. The answer 'Because I said so' will never get results, and this normallly easy-going child can become a permanent opponent, or look for logic elsewhere.

Best activities to share: sport; hiking; camping; animals (a mongrel pup will be in good hands); quiz games.

Sagittarius Sun Parent/Aries Sun Child

The Sagittarian parent is good-humoured, freedom-loving and always active. The Aries child relates well to the Archer who provides long-range projects to soak up some of the irrepressible Ram's energy. Sagittarian understanding and good communication keeps this fiery relationship on a healthy 'learn as you play' basis. Neither child nor parent in this duo are particularly good at, or even interested in, subtle hints, white lies, or devious behaviour. Cards are dealt straight on the table for Aries and Sagittarius. Junior deals better with a strong 'yes' or 'no' delivered consistently, and the Sagittarian will rarely waver. Arietians are tough, and respect strength, in this way learning to deal on their own. Aries individuality will prove no threat to the Sagittarian fear of being fettered but clashes can occur if this parent's talent for 'home truths' hits little Aries' weaknesses too often. The Ram rarely learns from mistakes but builds the confidence for self-expression on past successes.

Best activities to share: active sports; competitive games; outdoor projects; long interesting walks.

ARIES / CAPRICORN

Aries	Capricorn
Impetuous	Cautious
Sincere	Persistent
Energetic	Ambitious
Must win	Must improve
Enthusiastic	Dutiful
Seeks challenges	Seeks achievement
Likes success	Likes authority
Heroic	Responsible

Aries Sun Parent/Capricorn Sun Child

The Aries parent, exuberant, with an almost childlike enthusiasm and love of adventure, may be taken aback by the serious and often grown-up manner of tiny Capricornians. They like to know what is expected of them and when, and set about conscientiously living up to these standards to the best of their abilities. Aries will admire this youngster's dogged ambition and attention to routine details and be delighted by sudden outbursts of zany humour that seem so out of character with the normally serious manner. The term 'Giddy Goat' must have been made for Capricornians. Anyway it makes a good safety valve for all that discipline. Aries will see that despite Junior's sober ways, this is no stick-in-the-mud child, and Arietian encouragement and enthusiasm is about all this one needs in order to aim higher and higher. The main difficulties in this relationship can come with Aries expanding and confining the rules at a moment's notice leaving Junior confused to say the least. Consistency is security to young Capricorn.

Best activities to share: making things for practical use; playing with toy soldiers; saving money; games like Monopoly and Careers; keeping diaries, etc.

The Capricorn parent is cautious, patient, ambitious and seeks a secure position in society. Aries finds security in self-reliance. Capricornian patience can be the vital link between this widely differing pair. Risk just isn't in the parent's book and there'll be a great deal of lip-biting at some of young Aries' 'fools rush in

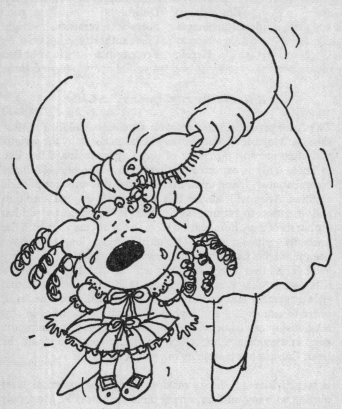

'We've given you every advantage that we didn't have, skrimped and saved, and what thanks do we get? Don't you *want* to be the prettiest girl at the party?'

where angels fear to tread' exploits. If anyone has the perseverance and subtlety necessary to get some good common sense into this irrepressible adventurer's head, then it must be the wily old Goat. This ambitious parent will recognize the leadership potential of Aries, and gently, with well-defined guidelines, encourage the more practical aspects of the child's abilities. Authority suits Capricorn well but an excess of orders can quickly put this relationship into the cold war category. Capricorn knows instinctively that success is based on good solid preparation, and an ability to bide one's time for the right moment. How infuriating that Junior can often succeed by doing exactly the opposite. Praise little Aries' forethought that shows up one time in ten and resist criticizing the nine times that it doesn't. It really works.

Best activities to share: adventure stories; hammer and nails (with background supervision); painting (plenty of red – Aries' favourite colour); model car racing.

ARIES / AQUARIUS

Aries	Aquarius
Impetuous	Unpredictable
Sincere	Spontaneous
Energetic	Humanitarian
Must win	Must be different
Enthusiastic	Changing
Seeks challenges	Seeks causes
Likes success	Likes the unusual
Heroic	Rebellious

Aries Sun Parent/Aquarius Sun Child

Aries parents are enthusiastic, optimistic, energetic and a powerhouse of support to their loved ones. Aquarians are original, inventive and masters of the unexpected. Aries will be totally involved in the challenge of keeping up with this future-orientated wonder. Young Aquarius approaches life in the spirit of the explorer accepting little at face value, questioning everything. The Aries parent's individuality will respond with admiration for the little Water Carrier's natural self-confidence that refuses to conform to the norm. In this relationship reason, respect, and logic are better peacemakers than heavy-handed authority. The Aquarius child may seem detached and even absent-minded when it comes to close family affections but you'll get your fair share. It just has to be shared with the dog, the milkman, *Star Trek*, and an ever-changing bevy of oddball 'friends'. Tie this one down to your Aries objectives and expectations and you'll find the leash strained to the limit. Encourage and support 'doing one's own thing'. It shouldn't be hard as that's what you do.

Best activities to share: plenty of junk boxes full of screws, nuts, bolts, etc.; mechanical gadgets to convert; simple science books; anything about different people and cultures.

Aquarius Sun Parent/Aries Sun Child

This parent is inventive, original, detached, and loves the new and the unusual. Junior will get plenty of stimulation and adventure here. For Aries, life centres on one's personal achievement and for Aquarius it's about trying everything on for size in order to form one's unique ideas. The Aquarian parent can develop an understanding in self-sufficient little Aries, that the world contains other people, other ideas. Authority should be no problem to these two individuals as strong mutual respect for each other's independence will produce a great feeling of friendship as well as love. Aquarius is a bit of a rebel who rarely accepts established ideas, rules and regulations without question and believes in everybody's rights including the child's. Fair this may be, but too much freedom can push little Aries into extremes of action, just to find out where the borderline is. Help Junior focus on something a little more specific than your own broad horizons.

Best activities to share: 'experiments'; mechanical toys; competitive games (you won't mind losing); Action Men; inventions.

ARIES / PISCES

Aries	Pisces
Impetuous	Sympathetic
Sincere	Helpful
Energetic	Selfless
Must win	Must give
Enthusiastic	Imaginative
Seeks challenges	Seeks ideals
Likes success	Likes fantasy
Heroic	Poetic

Aries Sun Parent/Pisces Sun Child

The generous, powerful, success orientated Aries parent may find the Pisces child an enchanting but confusing puzzle. Pisceans are sentimental, intuitive, tearful, compassionate, and responsive to every mood and feeling of everyone about them (that includes dogs, cats, goldfish and stuffed teddies). Aries will appreciate Junior's highly coloured imaginative abilities and endeavour to bring these to concrete results. But the Piscean rarely seeks personal achievement and it is in giving rather than receiving that they are most fulfilled. The deep feelings and sensitivity of the little Piscean, if allowed full range of expression, will find strength and confidence to help others creatively. However, Aries' natural admiration of personal strength and achievement may miss the point and see Piscean sensitivity as weakness. All attempts to bulldoze the Fish into becoming super-heroic will result in Junior doing a disappearing act into the world of escapist fantasy. This could waste the talents that feature so prominently in medicine, nursing, painting, writing, film and fashion.

Best activities to share: acting; making up stories (parent and child); dressing up; looking after pets; helping Mum or Dad; sailing toy boats, paddling, swimming (the fishy element).

Pisces Sun Parent/Aries Sun Child

Quick to sense and share the dreams and aspirations of loved ones the Piscean is totally at home in the imaginative world of the child. Through fact and fantasy this parent will expand and develop the little Arietian's creative potential, encouraging success and consoling failure. The gentler side of the Aries nature will be supported alongside the tough 'go-getter' aspect. The 'little boys don't cry' attitude is just not in the Piscean's book; the fish intuitively knows that strength of character comes from the unashamed expression of one's true feelings. With the Piscean parent young Aries can become a more caring individualist less likely to tread on other people's toes on the road to success. Pisces' tendency to idealize loved ones can sometimes go over the top and push a confused and over-indulged little Arietian into extremes of aggressive action. Aries must know the limits, or bust a gut trying to find them out. Draw imaginative pictures for little Aries to aspire to but define the borders.

Best activities to share: stories with strong heroes and heroines; 'exploring' (Pisces can make the beach or back streets an adventure); treasure hunts; anything risky (with a watchful eye, and a first-aid box).

TAURUS / TAURUS

Taurus
Cautious
Steady
Calm
Must acquire
Sensual
Seeks growth
Likes security
Romantic

Taurus Sun Parent/Taurus Sun Child

This is an affectionate, cosy relationship with an easy pace and calm atmosphere. Just how young Taurus likes it. Taurus senior will recognize Junior's need to explore, at leisure, the physical world, taking infinite time and pleasure in this process of discovery. Little Taureans may learn slowly but they certainly learn surely. Though it is unlikely that this patient parent would be inclined to rush or push the young Bull, the resulting impasse would soon prove it unwise. This is the most obstinate of all the twelve signs and a conflict between two 'immovable objects' would make the siege interminable. Sharing a great love of home comforts and good living, a little care is necessary in order not to put too much emphasis on self-indulgence. Junior learns by example and though potentially a steady hard worker the temptations of the easy life are always present. Good routine and familiar patterns of daily life build for little Taurus a surprisingly early self-confidence. Happy to share and take over little responsibilities, this will do much to increase the down-to-earther's abilities. Though parent and child are quite possessive, if they both respect each other's territory all should be well. After all they 'belong' to each other anyway.

Best activities to share: digging and planting the garden; messy art (finger-painting, mud sculpture etc., to get the feel of things); music and singing; nature walks; lots of cuddles.

TAURUS / GEMINI

Taurus	Gemini
Cautious	Changeable
Steady	Unpredictable
Calm	Interested
Must acquire	Must know
Sensual	Moody
Seeks growth	Seeks to communicate
Likes security	Likes change
Romantic	Versatile

Taurus Sun Parent/Gemini Sun Child

The calm, steady Taurean parent could well feel that life with a young Gemini is a perpetual game of Junior Quiztime. Gemineans are quick to learn, early talkers and walkers (unless a cautious moon sign slows down the pace) dashing hither and thither picking up snippets of information to feed their insatiable minds. Taureans have a sympathetic understanding of all growing things, and will recognize young Gemini's need for continuous mental stimulation and freedom of movement. Taurus, however, tackles one job at a time conscientiously, and may see Junior's restless diversity of interests as too scattered to be constructive. For Gemineans, though, specialization is far too limiting, and a broad span of knowledge and experience is more effective in supporting their own particular brand of self-confidence. If Junior insists that it's possible to do homework whilst watching TV, with this child you can believe it. Tying this one down to 'it'll do you good' routines will be like trying to put an octopus in a paper bag. Enjoy and encourage this versatile and always entertaining one-man band.

Best activities to share: as many musical instruments as you can afford; books; storytelling (interrupted by unlimited questions); telephoning (anybody); encyclopedias; painting; drawing; puppetry; quizzes and so on *ad infinitum*.

The Gemini parent is eternally young in heart, with a fresh and lively mind that relates well to the childhood world. Steadier, young Taureans soon dig their heels in if the Geminean breakneck pace proves too bewildering. After the parent's interesting discovery that not all quick-thinking Geminis have quick-thinking whizz-kids, they'll enthusiastically set about the fascinating business of adapting themselves to a slow-thinking whizz-kid. Taurus is a 'builder' and won't put the roof on, however novel the design, until the walls are completed. In the Gemini household, there'll be no lack of stimulating materials to expand practical young Taurus's 'feel, touch, and taste' approach to learning. The Gemini will sense that practical experiment works better than theoretical concepts with this youngster. Pressure and too many fingers in too many pies will be met with the immovable Taurean obstinacy or the Bull's second-string weapon, lethargy (it's too much to do so I won't do anything). Bottom gear on hills for this youngster.

Best activities to share: making music; making models; mud pies; cooking; making a mess; making it tidy; making anything.

TAURUS / CANCER

Taurus	*Cancer*
Cautious	Sensitive
Steady	Reliable
Calm	Devoted
Must acquire	Must care
Sensual	Responsive
Seeks growth	Seeks to protect
Likes security	Likes the familiar
Romantic	Caring

The Taurean parent is steady as a rock, materially comfortable, likes good order and lets everyone know where they stand. The Cancerian child needs a secure protective home environment which is well met in this relationship. The Taurean appreciates the Cancerian child's ability to record every experience and file it away for instant recall, making learning easy. Although often moody and clinging, this is not a sign of weakness but of great sensitivity and response to people and situations. Far from being 'shrinking violets' Cancereans have leadership qualities of the good-humoured, gentle kind, given the security that comes naturally from the Taurean parent. Conflicts can occur when Taurus's fixed and well-proven ideas come up against Cancer's inexplicable 'feelings'. With common sense and obstinacy (a good Taurean combination), the Bull may be too quick to scoff at intuitive hunches. A Crab on the defence will learn to build a thicker shell and will let the soft, sensitive nature stay on the inside.

Best activities to share: caring for pets; helping in general; dolls' houses (for both sexes); making things; collecting.

Cancer Sun Parent/Taurus Sun Child

This parent is home-loving, family conscious, and sensitive to the material welfare of the child. The Taurean child needs a secure and comfortable home. Both have an essentially easy-going nature and will share a love of beauty, art, and common sense. The Cancer parent will understand the child's slow, steady way of doing things, and appreciate the necessity to understand and become familiar with each stage of learning before proceeding with the next. To rush young Taureans is to take away the thoroughness with which they build their security. Conflict can occur if Cancer's natural desire to help becomes overprotective and takes over in an attempt to speed things up. Taurus's strong sense of possession will allow sharing but not giving up an anticipated pleasure. Such children need to be respected for standing on their own two feet, and will react with outstanding obstinacy when their sometimes painfully leisurely approach is mistaken for inability.

Best activities to share: collecting; building; growing things. Both are usually quite talented in working with their hands; the young Taurean, especially, learns well if encouraged to get the feel of things. Don't fuss if you find the child elbow- or knee-deep in water, mud, or blancmange. The Bull learns through all the senses.

TAURUS / LEO

Taurus	Leo
Cautious	Impulsive
Steady	Generous
Calm	Spontaneous
Must acquire	Must lead
Sensual	Expansive
Seeks growth	Seeks admiration
Likes security	Likes big ideas
Romantic	Dramatic

Taurus Sun Parent/Leo Sun Child

The Taurean parent has endless patience, and is rarely bored with the day to day routine of caring for home and loved ones. Generous little Leo brings more than a fair share of sparkle and sunshine to this relatively easy relationship. Lion cubs learn to deal with their own extrovert leadership potential by looking up to and emulating those for whom they can develop respect. Taurus, calm and secure, can fit the bill well. Leos respond to sincere appreciation and usually work hard to earn it, but the desire for the limelight may, without a little injection of Taurean common sense, get out of hand. Notorious 'show offs' (many are attracted to the stage), spoiled Leos can become bossy to the point of tyranny. Plenty of creative activity is a productive safety-valve for these self-expressive children and Taurean patience in this direction will be richly rewarded.

Best activities to share: artistic projects; painting; dressing-up; play acting; parties (Leo is a budding perfect host or hostess).

Leo Sun Parent/Taurus Sun Child

The Leo parent is sincere, loving, generous, affectionate and the boss. Young Taurus will live in a physically comfortable, nothing-but-the-best, glow of encouragement and high hopes. Leo's enthusiasm is contagious and no expense or time will be spared in providing little Taurus with every advantage. The pleasure and luxury will get appreciative response, but no amount of pushing will make the young Bull run before it can walk. The Taurean child is usually industrious, with good powers of concentration and a sensitive Leo will admire and encourage the practical talents of this little worker. If these talents are artistic they won't find better support than with a fireball Leo impresario. However, Leo parents can sometimes be overprotective, domineering, taking over to such an extent that little Taureans never learn just how strong their own feet are on the ground. Insecure Bulls usually find solace in the larder, become fat and lazy, and that can hit Leo where it hurts. Lions are proud, and appearance matters, 'How could Junior let me down?' If they can resist the temptation to dominate and rehearse Junior a little more thoroughly all's well that ends well.

Best activities to share: making and decorating things; gardening; cooking; collages; pressed flowers.

TAURUS / VIRGO

Taurus	Virgo
Cautious	Conscientious
Steady	Responsible
Calm	Painstaking
Must acquire	Must perfect
Sensual	Critical
Seeks growth	Seeks order
Likes security	Likes efficiency
Romantic	Dutiful

Taurus Sun Parent/Virgo Sun Child

Little Virgos are bright and intelligent, with a love of getting things right that puts them high in the ranks of quick learners. Calm Taurus has a similar down-to-earth liking for order and will respect and encourage young Virgo's neat virtuosity. Little will ruffle the smooth running of this relationship. Junior is just as hungry for knowledge and know-how as Gemini, but has the advantage of being a little more thorough. There'll be questions galore for the patient Taurean parent to answer, plus, would you believe, note-taking. Virgos back up their good memories with copious notes, lists, and schedules almost as soon as they can write ABC. Junior's natural reserve and conscientious application to work, can make for shyness and difficulty in relating to others. Little Virgo will need warm but unobtrusive encouragement in order to build the confidence to 'mix'. If you can help to establish one or two friendships for this modest little one, then you have done your job well. Unsympathetic pushing and shoving will result in the Virgo's only defence, sharp personal criticism, and nervous withdrawal.

Best activities to share: helping Mum, helping Dad (real help, that is); craftwork; collections; scrapbooks; old box files and things to sort out; country walks with maps; museums; etc.

Unlike the quick-witted Virgo parent, little Taurus is slow-thinking, slow-moving and impervious to any attempt at changing this tardy pace. Although sharing the parent's tenacity of purpose in achieving tangible results the child's methods differ. The Virgo parent will quickly understand that Junior's way is to experience in physical terms, to gain complete familiarity with, the shape, feel, and meaning of each new thing or idea. Steady, but rarely dull, the little Bull's love of the sheer pleasure of play, work, food, toys, Mum, and Dad, can fill the cool, orderly Virgoan home with warm, affectionate companionship. For young Taureans, major changes in family life (starting school, moving house, family splits) will require, more than for most, sympathetic help and gentle coaxing in order that they become familiar with, and accept, the new experience. If a dog-eared Teddy has to share the first couple of years at school so be it. There may be times when the tidy

'You'll *thank* us later for making you practise!'

analytical mind of the Virgoan won't be able to resist criticizing Junior's lethargy and self-indulgence. Nag, nag, nag, gets the line of most resistance from this immoveably obstinate Bull. The prospect of shared pleasure is a better incentive to move those lazy limbs.

Best activities to share: good solid building bricks; construction kits; planting and growing seeds and bulbs; walking in the country; visits to pig styes and palaces; lots of messy paints, mud pies and sand pits.

TAURUS / LIBRA

Taurus	Libra
Cautious	Amenable
Steady	Easy-going
Calm	Cooperative
Must acquire	Must relate
Sensual	Diplomatic
Seeks growth	Seeks company
Likes security	Likes harmony
Romantic	Just

Taurus Sun Parent/Libran Sun Child

The friendly, harmonious Libran and the affectionate, steady-as-a-rock Taurean parent should be as close as two peas in a pod. Some relationships thrive on competitive tussles, slanging matches, and slammed doors. Not so this one. The Taurean parent will soon notice how easily Junior fits in with any family plans. There's nothing weak-willed about this bright-minded child though, just a genuine desire to make you feel good. And if you feel good, so does tiny Libra. They are never 'loners' and left to their own devices, often become lazy, listless, with 'nothing to do'. But their real talent is expressed in team-work and group activity where they can develop their exceptional gifts of diplomacy. The Taurean parent will find it easier than most to deal patiently with young Libra's indecisiveness. Junior's keen sense of justice can see so easily the pros and cons, that coming down on one side or the other can take ages. Clashes should be almost non-existent in this relationship. However, the sheer luxury-loving, easy-going, natures of Taurus and Libra could deteriorate into such self-indulgent inertia, that Junior's creative potential remains unexplored.

Best activities to share: making music; having friends round; visiting; stories (especially happy-ever-after ones); painting; making things more harmonious and beautiful (own room particularly).

Libra Sun Parent/Taurus Sun Child

The Libran parent takes pleasure in understanding and relating to the needs of others. Young Taurus's leisurely pace, and sensual enjoyment of the colour, shape, touch, and taste of things, will delight Libra's own sensitive, artistic nature. The need for 'thoroughness' is shared by both parent and child. Libra exploring every intellectual possibility, and Taurus each material one. This gives the Libra parent a sympathetic approach to Junior's sometimes maddening slowness. The 'giving-in' quality of Libra may, in this relationship, need a more than usual balanced view as these two easy-going natures can easily come to a lethargic standstill. The love of harmonious, artistic and beautiful things can provide good creative outlets for getting a little action out of the team. Often surprisingly mature, the little Taurean will take a responsible attitude to school work and helping in the home, excelling in areas where steady effort shows tangible results.

Best activities to share: making anything out of plasticine; powder paints; paper, scissors and glue; building bricks; pastry and pastry cutters; digging in sandpits and flowerbeds; learning a musical instrument.

TAURUS / SCORPIO

Taurus	Scorpio
Cautious	Intense
Steady	Powerful
Calm	Passionate
Must acquire	Must defeat
Sensual	Penetrating
Seeks growth	Seeks power
Likes security	Likes challenge
Romantic	Magnetic

Taurus Sun Parent/Scorpio Sun Child

The Taurean parent is affectionate, firm but reasonable, and above all consistent. The powerful young Scorpio, so easily given to extremes of action, will learn with this parent how to control the excesses that can typify this character. Quick to learn, and highly intuitive, little Scorpios seem irresistibly drawn to the difficult rather than the easy, as if only that is a worthy challenge to their powers. The Taurean parent is usually a stickler for getting the everyday routine jobs out of the way before tackling bigger, more demanding projects. Junior's nature may resist or be totally indifferent to such 'trivialities', until they accumulate and become a Herculean task to be conquered. Scorpios, almost psychically, sense and respond to other people's thoughts and feelings, making them close, warm and loving companions. On the other side of the coin, dogmatic Taurean nagging, without just and logical reasoning, will produce deep and brooding resentment that results in cold, destructive retaliation. Respect the intense power of the little Scorpion and you'll have a positive, eternally loyal friend and never feel the sharp sting in the tail.

Best activities to share: old mechanical gadgets to take apart and reassemble; quiz and problem books (they actually like IQ tests); art (Picasso was a little Scorpio!); and later, 'roughing it' camping and junior martial arts.

The Scorpio parent has an intuitive insight into other people's thoughts and feelings. This natural psychologist will soon recognize the importance of the 'slow but sure' method in the little Taurean. The child's response to the sensual world of colour, shape, sound, and the feel of things, will be enthusiastically shared and supported. Scorpio is a born entrepreneur, sensing hidden talents and abilities and nurturing them with the right amount of creative stimulation to produce self-confidence. The young Taurean's great need for security will be well met in the calm strength of the Scorpio parent. Although the Scorpion's protective instinct is powerful, with this child it will take no great sensitivity to know when enough is enough. Little Bulls put out the firmest of signals when they're ready to stand on their own two feet. The most obvious cause for clashes with this couple can come from Scorpio's sometimes domineering manner being met with exasperating Taurean obstinacy. Sieges like this can be interminable.

Best activities to share: music and dance (loosen up those solid little legs); growing things in own garden plot or seed trays; construction kits (never too advanced for the age); small responsible duties around the house.

TAURUS / SAGITTARIUS

Taurus	Sagittarius
Cautious	Tolerant
Steady	Honest
Calm	Interested
Must acquire	Must understand
Sensual	Outgoing
Seeks growth	Seeks to know
Likes security	Likes adventure
Romantic	Philosophic

The Sagittarian child is happy-go-lucky, freedom-loving and wields disarming honesty like a blunt instrument. The Taurean parent's well organized set of rules to keep the family on an even keel, will get little respect or obedience until all the 'whys' and 'hows' are convincingly answered. Junior's natural curiosity craves and accumulates knowledge, but never without question. Taurean patience can work wonders with this delightful little intellectual adventurer, but later a couple of dozen good reference books may provide good support. Often blissfully unaware of clumsiness with word and action, Junior's 'Sorry I trod on your toe, but you've got such huge feet, Mum' will have to be endured until you've successfully explained why the obvious truth is sometimes unacceptable. This couple share a love of the outdoors, though Taurus may prefer pottering about the garden to Sagittarius's impulse to aim for the far-distant horizon. This love of freedom can make for itchy feet if Taurus becomes overpossessive and restrictive. Trust produces a more positive result.

Best activities to share: walks and romps with a dog (borrowed if necessary); travelling (anywhere); anything adventurous (within Taurean reason); boisterous fun.

Sagittarius Sun Parent/Taurus Sun Child

The Sagittarian is good-humoured, understanding, with a flexible but logical, common sense attitude to young Taurus's welfare. There is little danger that this youngster will feel insecure surrounded by so much optimism. However, Sagittarians usually hate routine or being tied down in any way so the little Taurean's lack of pace may sometimes try the Archer's patience. Once it is established that Junior, although slow and thorough, develops an early sense of independence through familiarity with predictable routines, a good compromise can be reached. Sagittarians treat children as intelligent human beings, refusing to cajole, tell white lies or put off with 'when you're older, dear'. Simple, honest answers to any question, give young Taureans the solid background of practical know-ledge that develops self-confidence and individuality. The biggest threat to the relationship is that Sagittarius, always on the move, can become distant, preoccupied, or just not around when needed. This can bring out the more possessive, de-manding nature of little Taurus and so inflate the very situation that this parent wishes to avoid. A little extra close affection between trips keeps everything friendly and free.

Best activities to share: country walks (not too fast or too far); plenty of paints, crayons, cardboard, glue, and papier mâché (Junior loves a creative mess and will enjoy clearing up just as much).

TAURUS / CAPRICORN

Taurus	Capricorn
Cautious	Cautious
Steady	Persistent
Calm	Ambitious
Must acquire	Must improve
Sensual	Dutiful
Seeks growth	Seeks achievement
Likes security	Likes authority
Romantic	Responsible

Taurus Sun Parent/Capricorn Sun Child

This is a meeting of good, practical, down-to-earth, like minds. The Taurean parent will find few problems, and achieve an easy relationship with this conscientious and serious little Capricornian. Both like system and order, and are happiest living to an efficient and comfortable routine. Young Capricorn learns steadily and keeps up well with the expected norm at each stage. The great love of home and family that this couple have in common can find good expression in shared duties around the house. Junior loves to help, and feel responsible for little jobs that show tangible results. Little Goats are sociable and mix well with other children. Though rarely pushy leader types, they establish their place amongst their fellows through their natural talent for organization. Too little experiment and imagination, however, can turn young Capricorn into a dull, bossy, 'holier than thou' child, raining 'you shoulds' and 'you oughts' on to less conscientious playmates. Not a good recipe for popularity. They have a crazy sense of humour; don't let it get buried in all that earthiness.

Best activities to share: small jobs and responsibilities; playing with toy shops; cookers; dustpans, hammer and nails; dressing-up (and clowning – encourage a little fun); visits with a little pomp and ceremony (Tower of London, Changing of the Guard etc.).

Capricorn Sun Parent/Taurus Sun Child

Capricornians are conscientious and supportive parents, providing the comfortable background of well-organized routine in which young Taureans thrive. Though ambitious for Junior's achievements, the Capricornian is endowed with unlimited patience and sense of purpose relating easily to the Taurean need for thoroughness that often makes their progress seem slow. Pushed too far and too fast, little Bulls become timid and insecure, yet can be surprisingly quick in showing self-reliance in areas where they have been given the time to completely familiarize themselves. The affectionate little Taurean responds positively to, and needs plenty of, hugs and kisses, even their natural obstinacy melting with copious doses of physical warmth. In too easy an atmosphere, their love of the sense-world can lead them to lazy self-indulgence. When this provokes the worst of Capricorn's 'lecturing' potential, Junior's stubbornness knows no bounds. Happily, unsolvable battles are few in this well-matched common sense relationship.

Best activities to share: 'helping' Mummy and Daddy; simple cooking (they make good chefs later); anything musical; mending and cleaning (with real polish); doll's prams and tricycles; building anything and digging anywhere (a special plot in the garden that's their very own).

TAURUS / AQUARIUS

Taurus	Aquarius
Cautious	Unpredictable
Steady	Spontaneous
Calm	Humanitarian
Must acquire	Must be different
Sensual	Changing
Seeks growth	Seeks causes
Likes security	Likes the unusual
Romantic	Rebellious

Taurus Sun Parent/Aquarius Sun Child

The Taurean can set up perfect routines that makes everyone's lives around them run smoothly and efficiently. Except for that of a young Aquarian. Good proven ways hold no water for this miniature revolutionary. From earliest years, small Aquarians think for themselves, mentally experimenting and communicating their controversial ideas. Taurean thoroughness (with a great deal of loosening up) can provide a firm home base for the long-range exploits of this free spirit. Little Aquarians never seem to share the average child's need to conform in order to feel secure. Indifferent to what the others wear, think and do, these young eccentrics maintain their unique individuality whilst still being a most welcome member of the 'gang'. The Taurean will find that friendly discussion achieves far more than heavy 'guidance'. Fortunately Taureans won't feel obliged to give in all the time, and the Aquarian need to fight for ideas and causes will increase the child's confidence and common sense in these day-to-day encounters. Pushed to extremes, however, and Junior can shock with continual outbursts of outrageous and anti-social behaviour. Routine yes, but a different one each day will help.

Best activities to share: concocting unusual inventions with string, kitchen utensils, old pram wheels (a junk box is a must); group games (new rules each time); dressing up and clowning; construction kits (the instruction book is quickly lost); anything space-age.

Aquarian Sun Parent/Taurus Sun Child

The Aquarian approaches parenthood with an open mind and a good knack for making unusual methods work. This avant-garde outlook may suffer a few initial set-backs when confronted by a stubborn little Taurean. In no uncertain terms, this solid little creature of habit will make it known that the only acceptable way to bring up a Bull is by routine. Junior will respond to this parent's freethinking methods as long as they are regularly maintained. Aquarians are rarely enthusiastic slaves to routine, but the bonus for making a concession in this area will be young Taurus's surprisingly early self-reliance. The child will never be punished for telling the truth, no matter how shocking. Aquarians always treat their children with respect and a friendly trust that encourages honest self-expression. Negatively, too much sudden, new and unusual stimuli can throw the little Taurean into helpless confusion. An insecure, clinging, possessive child is the freedom-loving Aquarian's worst threat. Stick to the rules of the game and Junior's happy.

Best activities to share: building kits; growing bulbs, cress and beanshoots; clay and dough modelling; musical games, toys and instruments; finger painting and simple cooking.

Taurus	Pisces
Cautious	Sympathetic
Steady	Helpful
Calm	Selfless
Must acquire	Must give
Sensual	Imaginative
Seeks growth	Seeks ideals
Likes security	Likes fantasy
Romantic	Poetic

Taurus Sun Parent/Pisces Sun Child

The down-to-earth, but caring Taurean parent will find the enchanting little Piscean a delightful enigma. Intuitive, rich in imagination and sensitivity, these small dreamers fluctuate between the worlds of fantasy and reality as if they were one. The Taurean parent will understand that only in encouraging the confident expression of these talents, can young Pisces achieve a good foothold on the material world. They are the most vulnerable and potentially the most talented children of the twelve signs. Pisceans have an extreme impressionability that enables them to quickly tune in and respond to the needs and feelings of others. This ability can produce, in practical terms, the most successful artists, poets, pop stars, doctors, nurses, fashion designers. Even with unsympathetic bulldozing they can just as sensitively adapt and selflessly become what is demanded of them. The Taurean love of beauty, harmony, and tangible results will provide invaluable support in developing this unique individuality.

Best activities to share: traditional fairy stories; music and art; small pets (at least a beloved hamster); doctors and nurses sets (plenty of bandages for teddy); caring for wounded sparrows, lame dogs, and sick earwigs *ad infinitum.*

'You just wait 'til I get you home you little devil'

Although not a natural stickler for routine the Piscean parent will sensitively feel little Taurus's need for well-ordered schedules and predictable patterns. Rarely forgetting the deep impressions of their own childhood, Pisceans easily sense the feelings and needs of their small charges. The little Bull's approach to learning can be a pleasure to observe. Everyday objects are felt, fumbled, stroked, tasted and thumped into familiarity. New distractions are ignored or stubbornly refused until this thorough exploration is complete. The Piscean talent for fantasy and storytelling can expand the imaginative side of this little realist. Magical fairyland exploits, however, may fall on stony ground in favour of the more earthy adventures of tractors and trains. Often developing early independence, Junior will still need oceans of Piscean affection. The most obstinate Taurean tantrum melts easily with a warm loving hug. The selfless Piscean need to 'give' can, if taken to extremes, bring out Junior's worst potential: inaction. Luxury-loving, self-indulgent and probably fat (Taurean sins go quickly to the waistline) your little one can become a big, big problem. Keep the routine regular and young Taurus on the move.

Best activities to share: creative pursuits with plenty of varied materials (paint, clay, pastry etc.); dance (music can get this little one moving); helping with responsible little jobs; toy cookers, vacuum cleaners, shops, woodwork sets (the more like the real thing, the better).

GEMINI / GEMINI

Gemini
Changeable
Unpredictable
Interested
Must know
Moody
Seeks to communicate
Likes change
Versatile

Gemini Sun Parent/Gemini Sun Child

If anyone could keep up with the physical and mental agility of a little Geminean, it's a big Geminean. Always carrying the sparkling curiosity of childhood into adult life, the Gemini parent will find easy and delightful affinity with this 'like mind'. Gemini households are packed with the 'tools of the trade' that stimulate and fulfil their multifaceted interests. A ready-made hunting ground for Junior. Little Gemini's early mastery of language and movement sets this busy relationship off to a quick start. Usually versatile and talented, these youngsters will need enthusiastic help in sustaining interest long enough to achieve tangible results. Gemini moods change like the wind, and two in the family running the gamut of hot, cold, interested, bored, crazy, serious, may cause a clash or two when they don't coincide. In these duels the weapons are words, often spitefully sarcastic but always quickly forgotten. The mutual need for good-companionship is too strong for long drawn out battles. The best outlet for any frustrated energies is argument, debate and discussion. The rest of the family won't get a word in edgeways.

Best activities to share: you know! Let Junior share yours.

Gemini	Cancer
Changeable	Sensitive
Unpredictable	Reliable
Interested	Devoted
Must know	Must care
Moody	Responsive
Seeks to communicate	Seeks to protect
Likes change	Likes the familiar
Versatile	Caring

Gemini Sun Parent/Cancer Sun Child

The Geminean parent is versatile, intelligent, with wide interests and an ever-changing personality. The Cancerean child learns through feeling and personal experience rather than the accumulation of intellectual knowledge. The child's sensitivity, awareness and imagination, will respond well to this parental encyclopedia of activity and information. Gemini's interest in every thing the young Cancerean sees, feels and does, will keep the child's strong need for close relationships well satisfied. The Gemini parent's own desire for constant stimulation will expand Junior's self-expressive nature. The area where clashes can occur may be found in Cancer's need to structure ideas based on past experience and Gemini's facility for dropping yesterday's truths in the light of today's discoveries. Ideas should be opened up and expanded rather than shattered and replaced. Otherwise Cancer will be totally confused.

Best activities to share: Gemini will enjoy storytelling to this avid listener; play every game under the sun, and understand the full meaning of teaching through play.

For the Gemini child the parent is above all a source of knowledge, information, and company. The Cancer parent's sensitivity will respond quickly to the ever-changing moods of this versatile child. The young Gemini's interests are broad but often short-lived and it can become a full-time job keeping up with the multitude of unfinished activities this child leaves for newer and more absorbing ones. The Cancer parent hopefully will realize that the Gemini child's quest for countless superficial snippets of experience and information are leading to a real understanding of how everything relates to everything else. On the best days (for with both, moods fluctuate) this relationship will sparkle with wit, good humour, and inexhaustible activity. Conflicts that are likely with this couple will centre around their opposite senses of direction. Nostalgic old Cancer looks back to the way things used to be, and forward-looking Gemini is three jumps ahead. Firmly established Cancerean routines produce snappy answers or sulky withdrawal from Gemini. A different way every day works better.

Best activities to share: books, books and more books; old gadgets to take apart; anything for a short while; storytelling; going anywhere.

GEMINI / LEO

Gemini	Leo
Changeable	Impulsive
Unpredictable	Generous
Interested	Spontaneous
Must know	Must lead
Moody	Expansive
Seeks to communicate	Seeks admiration
Likes change	Likes big ideas
Versatile	Dramatic

Alternating between interested friend, strict authority, sparkling entertainer, learned professor and clown, the Gemini parent is good news for little Leo. Small Lion cubs are sunny, creative, optimistic and will respond well to the continually changing stimuli of this mercurial adult. Needing only a little encouragement and plenty of appreciation, these Leo leaders confidently push themselves into the limelight. Finding the happy medium between good self-expression and over-dramatic showing off, is a knotty but worthy problem for the sharp-witted Gemini mind. Young Leo's true leadership strength lies in honest generosity and the sense of justice. The Gemini parent's broad understanding of the world can teach this child the importance of respecting other people's needs and motivations. Gemini's quick change of moods makes most parent/child clashes short-lived. Junior's penchant for 'big scenes' in stress situations will find better release in good humour than sarcastic put-downs. Punctured pride drags out the performance.

Best activities to share: anything creative as long as it's big; spare a wall in young Leo's room – for murals; dressing up; play acting; entertaining friends; planning everything.

Leo Sun Parent/Gemini Sun Child

Proud Leo parents lavish love, affection, and 'no expense spared' comforts on their grateful children. It really is like the indulgent lioness allowing her cubs to romp and play in complete freedom, but ready when necessary to apply a short, sharp cuff of the paw to keep her young ones in line. Young Geminis make the transition from cradle and cot to talkative toddler in double quick time. Precocious, amiable and superactive, this busy little companion will enjoy, but never be idle in, the luxurious Leo home. Variety is the spice of Junior's life and, without a little help in maintaining interest long enough to finish a project, attention soon wanders. The helpful Leo may have difficulty in discovering which of this versatile child's many talents to specifically encourage. All of them. The truth is that Geminis are extremely reluctant specialists. Their most successful place in life is where the brilliant all-rounder is essential. Clashes will be few if a good middle line is taken with this youngster. But over-stimulation or dogmatic restrictions can result in nervous tension (skin rashes and nervous tics are obvious signals) or black, black moods.

Best activities to share: picture books and story books; frequent short visits here, here and everywhere; plenty of friends to tea; things for nimble fingers (crafts, gadgetry, and musical instruments).

GEMINI / VIRGO

Gemini	Virgo
Changeable	Conscientious
Unpredictable	Responsible
Interested	Painstaking
Must know	Must perfect
Moody	Critical
Seeks to communicate	Seeks order
Likes change	Likes efficiency
Versatile	Dutiful

Gemini Sun Parent/Virgo Sun Child

Geminis have no trouble in creating a stimulating environment in which any child can flourish. Little Virgo has a bright, responsive mind, quick to grasp new ideas and put them to practical use. This ease of learning soon makes this relationship strong in terms of communication. Although mentally a perfect match for this intelligent parent, young Virgo's drive takes a different route. Establishing modest but efficient patterns and routines gives this youngster self-confidence and security. Often painfully shy, little Virgos can take unlimited praise for effort without becoming in the least big-headed. Don't make the mistake of thinking that it isn't necessary though. That matter of fact manner belies the need for a fair share of Gemini hugs and kisses. This child's respect for reason and authority makes clashes almost non-existent. However, Gemini's sometimes scattered and unpredictable enthusiasms can put too much on Junior's plate for comfort. If you don't want a supercritical nervous wreck, let little Virgo finish one job before starting the next.

Best activities to share: word games (Lexicon, Scrabble), quizzes and puzzles; small household responsibilities (sorting out Dad's nailbox, shopping lists, bookshelves etc.); toy typewriter, cooker, vacuum cleaner (all expertly used); anything creative but useful.

Virgo Sun Parent/Gemini Sun Child

Keeping up with little Gemini's quick talking, fast moving, dazzle of curiosity and experiment can get most parents puffing with exhaustion. The Virgoan, however, is made of sterner stuff. Modestly, and with little fuss, Junior's needs will be met, satisfied and supported by this patient perfectionist. The Virgoan's own well-organized life allows ample time to be devoted to the responsibility of looking after even a whirlwind Gemini. Little Gemini's love of words and incessant chatter will always find quick response, wit, and useful information from this bright-thinking parent. But, and there is a but, Virgo has to finish completely and satisfactorily, every job that is tackled. Gemini, on the other hand, can jump from project to project and finish nothing. Strict discipline and calls to duty will only develop this youngster's natural ability for evasion and will achieve little. However superficial it may seem, this scattered energy approach has method when applied to young Gemini's multi-talented, all-round potential. Skilfully managed compromise can get the necessities dealt with, while leaving this fertile mind free as a bird for all else.

Best activities to share: games and gadgets for quick fingers and faster minds; musical instruments; calculators; chemistry sets; word games galore; table tennis (must have been invented by a Gemini); encyclopedias (Gemini reads bits rather than whole books) and nearly always two things at the same time.

GEMINI / LIBRA

Gemini	Libra
Changeable	Amenable
Unpredictable	Easy-going
Interested	Cooperative
Must know	Must relate
Moody	Diplomatic
Seeks to communicate	Seeks company
Likes change	Likes harmony
Versatile	Just

Gemini Sun Parent/Libra Sun Child

The quick-thinking Gemini parent thrives on good communications and will encourage wholeheartedly little Libra's potential for self-expression. The sooner this youngster gets to the chattering stage the better Gemini likes it. Right from the cradle little Librans are easy-going, anxious to please, charmers. That is, until you leave them on their own. 'People who need people' must have been written with these company-seekers in mind. In this need to always be with someone else lies the Libran strength, and the Gemini parent will delight in Junior's quick development of diplomacy, logic, and ability to see the other side. This parent will produce a constant flow of stimulating information and knowledge to keep the relationship friendly and formative. There may be times when Gemini's broad, scattered, schooling will be too much, and too fast, for this youngster's compulsion to weigh every pro and con. The Libran desire to come to the perfect conclusion can result in exasperating indecision when faced with too many Gemini options. Constant pressure to give quick answers will be met with 'anything to please', 'whatever you think best' negativity. Both Gemini and Libra are good 'mind' signs, Gemini's faster but Libra's more thorough. Cut down the alternatives when helping Junior decide and you'll encourage balanced judgement rather than weak-kneed 'giving in'.

Best activities to share: word games; artistic pursuits (especially things to decorate and enhance the home); social trips, and continuous conversation.

Libra Sun Parent/Gemini Sun Child

Little Gemini's inquisitive, non-stop, nervous energy will find an open-mind, ready answer, and easy companionship in the loving Libra parent. Reason is the Libran strongpoint, and parental responsibility produces few pompous, dogmatic or authoritarian figures from this sign. Little Gemini will respond well and grow confidently in a tolerant, friendly atmosphere. Keeping up with the speed at which Junior exhausts interest in games, materials, and books can be a Herculean task. Often happiest doing more than one thing at a time, this 'live wire' can be double the trouble with twice the rewards. Geminis learn fast despite this scattered and seemingly superficial lack of concentration. Their unique view of the world becomes coherent through a natural talent for organizing unrelated snippets into a comprehensible whole. The Libran parent's good sense will know how to keep Junior's interest alive long enough to get the basic essentials firmly established. The only real snag for this relationship can come from Libra's sometimes exaggerated desire for harmony and peace at all costs. 'Anything to keep the little one happy' will encourage a whirlwind of over-indulged whims, to the point of spoilt, bad-tempered, nervous exhaustion. A little Libran balance saves the headaches.

114

Best activities to share: long conversations; storytelling; crafts for adept little fingers; gadget toys and working models; quizzes and puzzles; short trips everywhere.

GEMINI / SCORPIO

Gemini	Scorpio
Changeable	Intense
Unpredictable	Powerful
Interested	Passionate
Must know	Must defeat
Moody	Penetrating
Seeks to communicate	Seeks power
Likes change	Likes challenge
Versatile	Magnetic

Gemini Sun Parent/Scorpio Sun Child

The Gemini's natural curiosity will delight in studying the probing, penetrating mind of little Scorpio. Though often difficult to understand and rarely as freely expressive as this chatty parent, the little Scorpion will learn quickly from Gemini's stimulating company. Scorpios' 'knowing' minds easily grasp ideas and methods with an ability sometimes far beyond their years. Few secrets are safe from the piercing intuition of this child, who often gives the disconcerting impression of knowing what you are thinking before you have said it. The Gemini parent's fund of knowledge and broad interests will expand and help develop Scorpio's strong self-reliance. Challenge is difficult to refuse for Scorpio, and the extreme nature of this child will find the 'forbidden' almost impossible to resist. The little girl with the curl who 'when she was good was very, very good, but when she was bad she was horrid' typifies this potential. Black or white, but never grey,

Scorpio's 'need' to try *everything* out, is not unlike Gemini's own, but some subtle help from this quick-thinking parent can modify the attractions of the undesirable. Sounds like a handful, but the loyalty, strength of character and determination that grows with imaginative and caring companionship, makes the adventure worthwhile.

Best activities to share: puzzles galore; chess (quite early); conjuring sets; chemistry sets; microscope and telescope; stories with superheroes (they can even take the nasty bits in Grimms); anything difficult.

Scorpio Sun Parent/Gemini Sun Child

If any parent can take the non-stop, hustle, bustle, and fidgety energy of little Gemini, without batting an eyelid, it's Scorpio. Proud and devoted parents, the Scorpions root out, nurture, and boost their little one's talents to full, confident expression. Ideally, Scorpio's great strength is in being constantly supportive without being so obstrusive as to hamper the child's self-reliance. Rarely finishing any activity before moving on to the next, young Gemini can exasperate parents with a more conscientious approach. Scorpio's intuition, however, soon senses the Geminean need for the maximum input of information in the minimum time. The application of a little subtle parental help can convert this potential 'jack of all trades, and master of none' into a positive successful 'all-rounder'. Negatively, the domineering side of the Scorpio nature may result in developing young Gemini's skilful art of evasion. A quick back-answer and swift side step can bring out the worst of this relationship. Scatter the crumbs for your cheeky little sparrow, enjoy the antics and throw the cage in the dustbin.

Best activities to share: picture books and story books; encyclopedias; arts and crafts; playing musical instruments (at least two); puzzles (the old-fashioned metal ones are loved); board games (as complex as you like); travelling by bus, train, bike and foot everywhere.

Gemini	Sagittarius
Changeable	Tolerant
Unpredictable	Honest
Interested	Interested
Must know	Must understand
Moody	Outgoing
Seeks to communicate	Seeks to know
Likes change	Likes adventure
Versatile	Philosophic

Gemini Sun Parent/Sagittarius Sun Child

The enthusiastic quest for knowledge and experience is shared by this perpetual-motion duo. The rest of the household may find the pace and action of this high-spirited youngster and 'Peter Pan' parent a trial, but this couple will love it. Sagittarians need freedom and the open road and even Gemini can be amazed at how quickly, after learning to crawl, this little Archer can reach supersonic speeds. A door left ajar sees Junior disappearing down the corridor in seconds. This adventurous dash sums up the young Sagittarian's approach to learning and Gemini will find a close affinity to such an optimistic child. This parent's talent for invention will easily provide plenty of shared projects to develop confidence and understanding in the young Sagittarian. The little Archer's love of truth demands and respects straight answers to all questions and gives the same in return. Such honesty may often cause alarm in its blunt, unabashed frankness and some gentle but reasonable guidance may be necessary to avoid Junior continually opening his mouth and putting his foot in it. Petty restriction and pomposity will produce an explosion of righteous indignation. Give trust and this youngster will never abuse that precious freedom.

Best activities to share: rambling; fishing; camping; biking; museum-visiting; finding out 'why?' and 'why not?'.

The open-minded Sagittarian takes parenthood as it comes. The Archer has few fixed ideas, is ready for anything, and has a great interest in understanding little Gemini's needs. Once this little one can walk and talk – which is earlier than most – the real action starts. Memories of the Sagittarian's own inquisitive, adventure-seeking childhood will be awakened by this hyperactive ever-questioning child. Small Geminis' love of words turn them quickly into companionable little chatterers picking up snippets of information and generously sharing it around. These busy quicksilver minds move swiftly from activity to activity just to let you know that variety is the spice of Geminean life. A little Sagittarian wisdom judiciously applied can extend Junior's staying powers where it matters. An increasing trail of unfinished games, drawings, and discarded projects are, nevertheless, inevitable. The Sagittarian parent respects freedom too highly to be restrictive but taken to extremes this easy-going manner can cause little Gemini problems. 'No limits' can set this youngster aimlessly rushing in every direction at once, burning up energy with no tangible results, and fizzling out in nervous exhaustion. A few well-reasoned guidelines keep Junior happily on the right track.

Best activities to share: good conversation; reading; old clocks to take apart; boxes of bits and pieces to make things; sewing (both sexes love work for nimble fingers); cat's cradle; two-ball juggling; puppetry; visiting.

Gemini	Capricorn
Changeable	Cautious
Unpredictable	Persistent
Interested	Ambitious
Must know	Must improve
Moody	Dutiful
Seeks to communicate	Seeks achievement
Likes change	Likes authority
Versatile	Responsible

Gemini Sun Parent/Capricorn Sun Child

This parent may well find the untiring concentration and dogged devotion to learning of little Capricorn conflicts strongly with Geminean ideas of carefree childhood. Often seeming older and more serious than their tender years would suggest, little Goats never falter in their slow sure steps to independence. From quite early on, responsible little Capricornians begin to inisist, in no uncertain terms, that their lives be run to a good predictable routine. Variety loving Geminis may feel this a bit of a drag but, to Junior, order spells happiness. The bonus is, that if Gemini adapts with a little more system than usual, the resulting independence of Capricorn makes life much easier for both. Gemini's wit and imagination can work wonders in softening this little worker's sometimes too serious outlook. A little below the surface of this no-nonsense prodigy lies the zaniest sense of fun. Help release it now and again; it's a good safety valve. Disconcerted by lack of system and unexpected let-downs, Junior will become a crusty critic, nagging disapproval of all and sundry. Keep to the pattern and you'll have a delightful paragon of helpfulness.

Best activities to share: any creative work with a useful result (Christmas calendar for grannie, papier mâché flower-pot holders); helping mum and dad (*real* jobs for this responsible child); playing grown-up (teachers, doctors, etc.); simple cooking.

Capricorns are calm, patient, and well organized. Little Geminis are hyperactive, impatient, and scatterbrained. At least that's how it could seem to a conscientious Capricornian. They're also sharp as a tack, friendly, precocious and inquisitive. With seemingly little application and no sustained effort, these will-o'-the-wisp youngsters learn with a speed and ease that breaks all the rules in the Goat's book. The temptation to keep the small Gemini concentrating sensibly on one task at a time, may often be hard to resist. The need to spread widely (however thin) and take in more experience is a vital part of the versatile Gemini nature. Half-read books, half-finished projects, won't produce a one-track specialist but later Junior's intelligent views on anything and everything will make clear how well it works. Good Capricornian common sense can help maintain interest long enough to finish the necessities. Incessant nagging sends the sparkling energy inwards to produce evasion and twitchy nervous tension (the frustrated Gemini

'You just don't realize how restricting kids can be!'

malaise). Talk to, gently guide, but never rigidly channel this delightful little companion.

Best activities to share: reading, writing and word games; toy typewriter and telephone; musical instruments (not *too* serious on the practising); trips to science museums etc.; plenty of friends to tea.

GEMINI / AQUARIUS

Gemini	Aquarius
Changeable	Unpredictable
Unpredictable	Spontaneous
Interested	Humanitarian
Must know	Must be different
Moody	Changing
Seeks to communicate	Seeks causes
Likes change	Likes the unusual
Versatile	Rebellious

Gemini Sun Parent/Aquarius Sun Child

Always open to new ideas, even bright Gemini may have to open wider for nutty little Aquarius. Unpredictable, amusing, and often unashamedly eccentric, the little Aquarian flouts convention and questions everything. Born inventors, small Water Carriers insist on discovering for themselves and doing everything their own way. This unusual and independent approach should stimulate and delight the sharp-minded Gemini. A fine recipe for a close, friendly, talkative relationship with a good measure of argument. Healthy debate is a must. These youngsters need a good constant to push against in order to establish their own unique ideas and successful self-confidence. Like sociable Gemini, little Aquarians are easy 'mixers', taking quickly to kindergarten and school life with few problems and no tearful partings. Clashes between these 'good communications' experts should be few, and probably the only danger is Gemini's open mind allowing *too* much freedom. Aquarians, with nothing to kick against, will go to extremes of outrageous behaviour, using shock tactics in order to find the limits. No prison bars, but a few strategically placed fences help.

Best activities to share: masses of odds and ends; bits and bobs to invent things with; reference books; space-age toys; calculators (it could be computers later); open house to little friends (they'll be a strange mixture too); pets.

Aquarius Sun Parent/Gemini Sun Child

The stuffy traditional approach to parenthood has no appeal to the freedom-loving Aquarians. Often avant-garde in the eyes of others, their free exploration of new ideas makes a stimulating bond with inquisitive little Gemineans. These fast-talking, quick-walking, infants thrive on just the kind of 'big kid' open interest that typifies the Aquarian. Neither parent nor child is comfortable with clinging displays of affection, but close friendship and mutual respect gives Junior a better basis for security. Keeping up with the way in which little Gemini's quick enthusiasms cool off in favour of the next, can be tiring to say the least. The accumulation of scattered playthings and unfinished projects can become an insurmountable problem without help in sustaining interest. Little Gemini's drive is to gain as much diverse information and experience in as short a time as possible. This may seem facile and scatterbrained at first, but it's their way of building early confidence and understanding of the world as a whole. These two both thrive on freedom, but with no limits, little Gemini can overextend in all directions at once, eventually fizzling out like a spent squib. Nervous twitches are a good warning.

Best activities to share: endless conversations; gadget-making; encyclopedia delving; museum visits; word games; fun-recording on cassette; plenty of group activity.

Gemini	Pisces
Changeable	Sympathetic
Unpredictable	Helpful
Interested	Selfless
Must know	Must give
Moody	Imaginative
Seeks to communicate	Seeks ideals
Likes change	Likes fantasy
Versatile	Poetic

Gemini Sun Parent/Pisces Sun Child

Gentle little Pisceans seem as elusive as the elves and sprites in the stories they'll love Gemini to read to them. How do you make contact with these soft, sensitive dreamers ? In one word, imagination. Gemineans are blessed with more than a fair share of this useful commodity, and love nothing more than to share it with others. Little Pisces' love for the world of fantasy will soon show in early play. Imaginary 'friends,' day-dreaming, and being 'lost to the world' are typical pastimes. Highly intuitive, and deeply sensitive, this little one may need more sympathetic encouragement than most to put firm feet on the ground. Gemini will be quick to realize that sharing this child's imaginings and giving them concrete expression in creative outlets is the way to build confidence. Though in some ways impractical, the little Piscean is almost psychically 'in touch' with the needs and feelings of others. Quick to sympathize and selflessly offer real help to any lame duck, hurt friend and tired parent, they can positively sparkle with efficiency. Occasional impatience giving way to outbursts of the sharp critical Gemini tongue may well cause much deeper hurt than intended. The resulting escape into 'never never' land can take enormous time and trouble to reverse. Let Junior share that 'vision' with the rest of us.

Best activities to share: reading and telling stories, of course; music and dance (you may have another Piscean Nijinsky);

painting; drawing; looking after hamsters, tadpoles, and baby brother, all interspersed with plenty of reassuring hugs.

Pisces Sun Parent/Gemini Sun Child

Warm, loving Piscean parents can be the softest 'touch' in the Zodiac. They understand the shyness and vulnerability of their little charges and supply oceans of love and reassurance when and where it's needed. The quick, bright-eyed little Gemini is rarely shy, and less vulnerable than most but loves attention. The 'giving in' nature of the Piscean parent may have to suffer reappraisal in the first few helter-skelter years of Junior's progress. Bustling with the need for things to do, scarcely starting one before looking for the next, 'spoilt' little Geminis can be a nightmare of demands. Soft pedalling the ever-ready Piscean helping hand gives this little one chance to develop the real Gemini talents. This child's self-reliance, confidence and ease of expression, can grow early if imaginatively supported and encouraged. Parent and child share a vivid imagination and sense of fun that should keep the relationship bright and happy. There is little danger of clashes but 'peace at all costs' Pisces may sense the need for good healthy argument in little Gemini's make up. Keep it friendly but keep it going.

Best activities to share: Piscean tall stories; long and short trips to museums, exhibitions and zoos; puzzles, quizzes and conjuring tricks; books galore.

CANCER / CANCER

Cancer
Sensitive
Reliable
Devoted
Must care
Responsive
Seeks to protect
Likes the familiar
Caring

Blessed with the longest memories in the Zodiac, Cancer parents have no difficulty in recalling vividly the emotions and impressions of their own childhood. Well-behaved, sensitive little Cancer will find the dream parent in this caring 'home bird' adult. The need to love and cherish is so strong in both that they may find themselves later swapping roles. 'I'll be mummy and you be me' is a favourite Cancer game. Little Crabs learn steadily, though more through feelings and experience than text-book information. They laugh and cry easily with close friends but are cautiously shy in making new ones until they feel *really* secure. This impressionable youngster may hide a wealth of sensitivity and imagination if not given sufficient encouragement to express these creatively. Often artistically talented, warm appreciation of early efforts builds good self-confidence that may eventually develop an exceptional ability. It would be hard to visualize a quarrel at all in this all-feeling, all-caring relationship. Overprotection, that's the snag. If the Cancer home becomes too much of a cosy, warm cocoon Junior may never be brave enough to leave. Show this little Crab the big, tough world outside. His tough outer shell can take it.

Best activities to share: collecting things (shells, picture cards, ornaments, stamps); doll's houses (not just for girls); painting, drawing; making music; acting (they're great little mimics).

CANCER / LEO

Cancer	Leo
Sensitive	Impulsive
Reliable	Generous
Devoted	Spontaneous
Must care	Must lead
Responsive	Expansive
Seeks to protect	Seeks admiration
Likes the familiar	Likes big ideas
Caring	Dramatic

Cancer will be a receptive audience, prompt, scriptwriter and stage-dresser to this sunny little performer. Leo is a natural leader and thrives on encouragement. Lion cubs can be bossy and overbearing with other children but their happy, playful disposition can rarely give offence. The Cancer parent will be aware that 'putting down' Leo's abilities for taking over anyone or anything is bound to produce a roar of hurt pride. An appeal to Leo's natural generosity will ensure that the others get a look in. The Cancer parent is a great home-maker and will need to keep open house for the string of buddies that little Leo will have to entertain. At least Junior will keep them amused. Overindulge the luxury loving Leo and you'll have a tyrannical monster on your hands, spoilt, snappy and ungrateful. Do the opposite and you'll be met with, not a dignified lion, but a whining, approval-seeking pussycat. Cancer's feeling and sensitivity are a good guide for hitting the middle road.

Best activities to share: organizing and putting on a show; play acting, model theatre and puppetry; painting and drawing (the bigger the scale, the better); entertaining friends, and board games galore.

Leo Sun Parent/Cancer Sun Child

The Leo parent is generous, amiable, big-thinking and takes a great pride in the family. The Cancer child's every achievement will be noticed, appreciated and applauded with warm pleasure. Leo's love of showmanship and creative self-expression will prove good encouragement for little Cancer's sensitivity to be expressed in positive ways. For Leo understands the importance of creative activity in giving confidence to this potentially talented child. Cancereans learn by experiencing the feelings and actions of others, trying things out with their superb talent for mimicry. This will be a source of delight for the Leo parent who will hope for a superstar but generously settle for a good companion if the bright lights aren't achieved. Negatively, big-acting Leos can be crushingly overdramatic, always centre stage, leaving their little Cancers with minor walking-on parts, swamped and hiding nervously in the wings. Little crabby ones with this treatment can spend a lifetime in their shells. You'll be appreciated if you let the understudy take the leading role sometimes.

Best activities to share: play acting; painting; drawing; music; dressing up.

CANCER / VIRGO

Cancer	Virgo
Sensitive	Conscientious
Reliable	Responsible
Devoted	Painstaking
Must care	Must perfect
Responsive	Critical
Seeks to protect	Seeks order
Likes the familiar	Likes efficiency
Caring	Dutiful

Cancer Sun Parent/Virgo Sun Child

The Virgo child is a quick learner and has the innate ability to work hard at things in order to get them right. Cancer parents never forget their own childhood pleasures and difficulties and are able to sense when and when not to help. Little Virgos are seldom troublesome, enjoy being given small responsibilities, and take pride in doing their best. The Cancer parent will not be critical (the Virgo love of perfection hates mistakes) but will quietly help when things go wrong. Virgos can be constant worriers if made to feel they are not coming up to scratch.

Cancer can dish out large helpings of encouragement and admiration and it won't go to the head of this modest little one. Big dangers with this parent-child relationship is that over-emphasis on perfection and order by Virgo may produce a supercritical nature that finds fault with everything and everybody. People can stand just so many 'you shoulds'. Cancer's gentle humour and ability to send-up without malice may help. The serious Virgoan is made even more perfect with a good measure of laughter added.

Best activities to share: books, story and information (even old timetables will delight Junior); collecting and putting in order sets of things; work; pets (they love the responsibility and won't neglect them); mind games; quizzes.

Virgo Sun Parent/Cancer Sun Child

The Virgo parent runs an efficient, clean, practical home and tends to the needs of others with great care and modesty. The sensitive Cancer child will be supported conscientiously at every stage of development. With a Virgo parent nothing is too much trouble. The child will be read to, washed, fed an intelligent diet, played with, entertained and educated, all with a quiet efficiency that typifies the Virgo. In this atmosphere little Cancer will develop self-assurance and a good knowledge of how to deal with the material world. Sounds too perfect to be true, and of course there are snags that even Virgo's good critical faculties don't always notice. In fact all that good common sense may overlook the highly imaginative, creative side of little Cancer. No room for the unusual, unexpected and doing things when one feels like it rather than when it's time, can leave Junior emotionally denied and a slave to routine. It's not always a crime to break the rules – that's how we find our own originality and uniqueness.

Best activities to share: you make out your own list, but add a little zany irresponsibility, a few unexpecteds and one or two mistakes.

CANCER / LIBRA

Cancer	Libra
Sensitive	Amenable
Reliable	Easy-going
Devoted	Cooperative
Must care	Must relate
Responsive	Diplomatic
Seeks to protect	Seeks company
Likes the familiar	Likes harmony
Caring	Just

Cancer Sun Parent/Libra Sun Child

The Libran child thrives best on shared activities, and the Cancer parent, a natural home-lover, will not leave this child to 'go it alone'. It is not that Librans cannot stand on their own two feet, but they learn best through teamwork. Because of their natural charm and desire to get on with others, they learn quickly to see the other person's point of view. The Cancerean parent is imaginative and sensitive enough to provide good stimulation for developing the intellectual powers of the young Libran. The Cancerean home will become open house to the many friends this child makes, providing the company in which the Libran diplomatic leadership potential grows. The ability to see all sides of a question is young Libra's biggest advantage and conversely the biggest problem. The Cancer parent's overwhelming desire to give of the best may produce too many options, making decisions for the small Libran impossible. With Libra the 'set meal' is preferable to the 'à la carte' menu, at least some of the time.

Best activities to share: conversation; friendly debates; art; music; socializing, etc.

Librans create beautiful homes, have an easy charming manner that rarely gets ruffled, and love good company. Cancers are delightful company. This is a relationship of beauty, love, sensitivity and sparkling conversation. Both respond well to others and young Cancer's self-expression can grow in the confidence that nothing disharmonious will disrupt this household. Not if Libra has anything to do with it. Libra can always see the other side and Cancer can always feel for the other person. What a combination for peace and goodwill. Works a treat on one level but like any other relationship it has occasional snags if not confrontations. Libra's desire to please both sides on an issue at the same time can lead to frustrating indecision and often acute embarrassment for Junior.

Best activities to share: anything artistic; museum visits with friends; helping with home decoration; collecting (anything); keeping a diary.

'Don't be silly dear, of course guardian angels haven't got claws and big black teeth!'

CANCER / SCORPIO

Cancer	Scorpio
Sensitive	Intense
Reliable	Powerful
Devoted	Passionate
Must care	Must defeat
Responsive	Penetrating
Seeks to protect	Seeks power
Likes the familiar	Likes challenge
Caring	Magnetic

Cancer Sun Parent/Scorpio Sun Child

The Scorpio child will respond well to the demonstrative, caring ways of the Cancerean parent. Young Scorpio senses immediately the genuine feelings of others and reacts accordingly. Like Aries children, Scorpios need a worthwhile challenge to bring out their best, they seem almost to turn the simplest task into a near disaster in order to surmount the difficulty. Cancer will quickly sense this need, understanding that by always testing their extreme potential, Scorpios learn to handle their powerful emotions with confidence. Cancer will realize that a heavy authoritative manner achieves little with young Scorpio whose inclination for self-discipline is marked. The obvious clash for this couple is when Cancer's overprotective instincts leave no room for Scorpio's strong sense of self. This can result in open rebellion but is far more likely to manifest as secretive withdrawal, all communications being broken off. Don't protect Scorpios, admire their undoubted talent for survival and let them protect you.

Best activities to share: impossible jigsaws; problem solving; chess (quite early – there are lots of Scorpio chess masters); mending things; breaking up old things.

The Scorpio parent has a strong self-will, deep feelings, and builds a home that is invulnerable. Cancer needs a secure emotional and physical environment in which to grow and finds it in this relationship. Scorpios sense potential in people, situations and things and are compelled to transform raw material into positive achievement. This quality in its best form, is subtle, selfless and loving and young Cancer will grow in confidence and self-reliance, enthusiastically supported in any activity or talent needing to be expressed. Although powerful in the defence of loved ones, Scorpio knows that developing the child's own inner strength is better protection against the knocks of life than stepping in to interfere at every opportunity. Negatively Scorpio is manipulative and domineering, pushing little Cancer further than is comfortable and producing a fear of failure out of all proportion to the facts. Cancer's care and Scorpio's disappointment can produce a lifetime of guilt. Cancereans' aims are always modest but their achievements can be great if they are emotionally stable.

Best activities to share: collecting; shopping for junk and jumble sale scavenging; photography (filling albums full); looking after pets; keeping a diary.

CANCER / SAGITTARIUS

Cancer	Sagittarius
Sensitive	Tolerant
Reliable	Honest
Devoted	Interested
Must care	Must understand
Responsive	Outgoing
Seeks to protect	Seeks to know
Likes the familiar	Likes adventure
Caring	Philosophic

Cancer Sun Parent/Sagittarius Sun Child

The Cancer parent is imaginative, understanding, and will feel intuitively the Sagittarian's need to be free to try out things for himself. It may be disconcerting at first to find Junior fighting shy of material hugs and disappearing into the middle distance on supermarket trips, but that's the adventurous Archer. With this child's need to understand the truth of anything the Cancer parent should not lay down rules and regulations without first explaining why, in good logical terms. And the reasons had better be selfless, for Sagittarius can detect dishonesty quickly with a couple of well-aimed questions and the blunt frankness of the answer back will set you on your heels. Although Junior will probably find out sooner than most that Father Christmas is only dad tripping over the Scalextric, this is no down to earth, dreary, realist. Cancer and Sagittarius will share impossible dreams romantic adventures and hilarious revels (usually as a result of one of Sagittarius's naively frank '*faux pas*'). Troubles escalate if Cancer's protectiveness and need to be close, requires constant reassurance from Sagittarius about elusive behaviour. Love and independence go together for the Archer, but love with strings just brings on claustrophobia. Sagittarians are to be shared.

Best activities to share: almost anything energetic as long as it's somewhere else.

Sagittarius Sun Parent/Cancer Sun Child

Sagittarian parents are optimistic and freedom-loving with a broad understanding of life and people. Discipline is liable to be lax but that's because the Sagittarian parent will seem more like a jovial friend. Little Cancerean's horizons will be expanded by this free-ranging parent. Travelling with mum or dad Sagittarius will open up new vistas that will not be found within the family circle, and prepare young Cancereans for the big world outside. The Sagittarian will show by example that the honest expression of what one thinks and feels is not only permissible but essential for true individual development. The clashpoint in this relationship is obviously the Sagittarian desire to be unshackled and the Cancerean need to hold on. In this situation the Archer can use frank honesty and blunt hurtful home truths, and the Crab as usual is back in the shell, but not without getting that big claw firmly on the ankle of the parent, in the form of perpetual guilt. The best way to gain independence is to share it.

Best activities to share: games from other cultures; adventure stories; outdoor activities with groups; clowning around.

CANCER / CAPRICORN

Cancer	Capricorn
Sensitive	Cautious
Reliable	Persistent
Devoted	Ambitious
Must care	Must improve
Responsive	Dutiful
Seeks to protect	Seeks achievement
Likes the familiar	Likes authority
Caring	Responsible

Cancer Sun Parent/Capricorn Sun Child

Capricorns need to go at their own pace within a well-defined set of guidelines. The Cancerean parent will respond to this need, showing clearly what is acceptable behaviour and what is not. Although easy-going with children, Cancer understands that the Capricorn respect for authority provides an example for their own ambitions. Little Goats watch and learn from people they admire in order to climb the heights safely. Both parent and child share a love of the past, well established tradition and proven methods. If the Cancerean sensitive imagination combines with Capricorn's patient determination they will each benefit. Given no limits young Capricorns will push farther and farther in order to find out just where to stop. Amenable Cancer may, out of misguided 'kindness', adjust to each new stage without ever putting on the brakes. Frustrated Goats get bossy, critical and overbearing. Agree on the rules before you start playing; and stick to them.

Best activities to share: creative projects with a useful end product; games of patience and achievement (chess, Monopoly); helping around the home.

Capricorn Sun Parent/Cancer Sun Child

The Capricorn parent has an unassuming authority, love of order, and respect for the tradition of the family, building the secure home background that little Cancer needs. For Capricorn relationships work best when there is a clearly defined but reasonable set of guidelines to keep to. The ever-changing and sometimes confusing 'feelings' of the small Cancerean soon gain confidence of expression within this secure, firm but fair arrangement. No shocks of sudden revelation will be allowed to disrupt the Capricornian home but Junior will be assisted with great care and unlimited patience in the art of never putting a foot wrong. In this safe environment, this naturally fearful child will feel no threats and be able to channel the full Cancerean imaginative talents into concrete achievement. Capricornians are as appreciative of others' abilities as they are ambitious with their own. Negatively the socially conscious Capricorn can be continuously worrying about what the neighbours think, to such a degree that Cancer will clam up against the rain of dos and don'ts. If you don't want your little Crab to develop a thicker shell and use all that soft-centre imagination in predicting the next disaster (a favourite time-wasting Cancer talent) then inject the rules with a little rubber and stretch 'em.

Best activities to share: educational, but fun, toys and games.

Cancer	Aquarius
Sensitive	Unpredictable
Reliable	Spontaneous
Devoted	Humanitarian
Must care	Must be different
Responsive	Changing
Seeks to protect	Seeks causes
Likes the familiar	Likes the unusual
Caring	Rebellious

Cancer Sun Parent/Aquarius Sun Child

The warm, caring, and humour-loving Cancer parent will delight in the antics of this inscrutable little Aquarian eccentric. Bubbling with curiosity, outrageously nonconformist, but far too sociable to be unruly, this freedom-fighter will bring out the best of Cancer's imaginative abilities. Cancer will respond to, and encourage, young Aquarius's love of group activity, though with perhaps just a twinge of remorse when Junior rushes into play-school on the very first day without even a backward glance. Parent and child in this inventive and imaginative relationship will easily find ways to make dull and necessary routine a new adventure every day. Aquarians, no matter how young, can often seem like absent-minded professors with a detachment and aloofness that is almost a challenge to Cancer's need for closeness. Excessive emotional demands will only widen the gap; Aquarians react explosively to undue restriction of their freedom. This one's a delightful friend but never a treasured possession.

Best activities to share: things to take to pieces, convert, and assemble; scientific games and toys to enjoy; join goups, good causes (Save the Whale, Wildlife Fund etc.).

Aquarius Sun Parent/Cancer Sun Child

Aquarians are sociable, unusual, forward-looking, detached and tolerant. Highly imaginative, young Cancereans need a strong emotional rapport to bring out their exceptional caring, artistic and creative abilities. Aquarius will rarely be the dogmatic, heavy parent, but rather the helpful friend. The ability to take an unpredjudiced view of any situation can be invaluable in reassuring little Cancer's biased, self-protective fears. There will be few set rules in this relationship, each situation being resolved when it arises with an open mind and little fuss. Although Cancer's desire to give and receive demonstrative affection may not be totally satisfied by the sometimes detached manner of the Aquarian parent, the child will never feel neglected. A genuine interest and insatiable curiosity in this sensitive child will give closeness combined with an opening up of the normally inward looking Cancer. The biggest factor causing rifts in this relationship is the contrast between Aquarius's future-orientated outlook and Cancer's need to live on past experience. A strange twist of parent/child behaviour. The Water Carrier will open the doors to new, unusual, and sometimes bewildering, experience leaving little Cancer with a host of past experience which now seems irrelevant. Utopian Aquarians may need to take Cancer's hand a bit more convincingly into the 'Brave New World'.

Best activities to share: ideas won't be short but new ones do not always please, as your little one learns by experiencing and reliving each experience so 'Play it again Sam'.

CANCER / PISCES

Cancer	Pisces
Sensitive	Sympathetic
Reliable	Helpful
Devoted	Selfless
Must care	Must give
Responsive	Imaginative
Seeks to protect	Seeks ideals
Likes the familiar	Likes fantasy
Caring	Poetic

Cancer Sun Parent/Pisces Sun Child

This couple share a love of imaginative, creative ideas and activity. Cancer will be sensitive to young Pisces' need to express in physical ways the rich sense of fantasy and highly inventive imagination this child possesses. Cancer will understand that the young Piscean comes to terms with the reality of life through the realization of ideas rather than through accumulating facts and figures. Pisceans are sensitive to the moods and feelings of others, and adapt easily to each situation. This natural ease at falling in with what others want may, however, become so comfortable for family relations that the Cancer parent fails to notice that Junior's individual needs are not being met. Unfulfilled ideas and individuality in the Piscean child are thrown inwards and reflect in daydreaming, and fantasizing. Sharing and appreciating these abilities will develop a gentle giant of confident creativity.

Best activities to share: music; dance; storytelling and writing; imaginative games (Buccaneer, etc.); pets; water activities (swimming, boats); imaginary 'friends'.

Pisces Sun Parent/Cancer Sun Child

Piscean parents are artistic, creative, and highly imaginative. Snap! So are Cancereans. The difference is that Junior may just have the edge when it comes to down-to-earth things. This won't hurt a bit in this loving, warm, and always close relationship. The Piscean spontaneous sense of whimsy and fantasy will encourage young Cancer to experience the full range of feelings, yet never overpower Junior's own contribution to the fun, laughter and tears. The eternal child in Pisces is totally at one with little Cancer, intuitively sensing and removing fears, or recognizing and supporting signs of independence. The rose-tinted spectacles can get a little cloudy if Pisces sets Junior up on too high a pedestal. The tough Crab shell can take a few hard knocks but won't enjoy falling from a great height. Cancers hate to let their loved ones down and yet are a little more modest than Piscean dreams sometimes allow.

Best activities to share: beach walking; fairy tales.

LEO / LEO

Leo
Impulsive
Generous
Spontaneous
Must lead
Expansive
Seeks admiration
Likes big ideas
Dramatic

Leo Sun Parent/Leo Sun Child

For a Leo parent who has a good honest self-knowledge, this child should present no problems. There will be differences of course, but the similar desire for recognition and need to think big will strike a familiar note. When you criticize Junior's arrogance, and extravagance, you may first have to take the splinter from your own eye. Big Leo's ambitions for the child coupled with little Leo's ample self-confidence could conquer the world, and probably will. Along the way the Leo parent can help this youngster get that great leadership potential into perspective. All that coming out on top at the expense of little playmates can lead to rejection and hurt pride. However, generous to a fault, little Leos will share all possessions with their friends, and if this can extend to letting the others have a turn at being 'boss' so much the better. As Leo Junior gets older there could be a little conflict as to who's king of the castle and without a liberal dose of good humour this could be a power struggle. A friendly joint-directorship wins every time.

Best activities to share: plenty of games (to try and top each other); dressing up and play acting; puppetry; hoards of materials for big creative activity.

LEO / VIRGO

Leo	Virgo
Impulsive	Conscientious
Generous	Responsible
Spontaneous	Painstaking
Must lead	Must perfect
Expansive	Critical
Seeks admiration	Seeks order
Likes big ideas	Likes efficiency
Dramatic	Dutiful

Leo Sun Parent/Virgo Sun Child

The Leo parent, whose motto is 'big is beautiful', and who always operates on a large scale, may find it hard at first to understand the Virgo child's preoccupation with accuracy and detail. Little Virgo likes to get a thing right even if it takes a lifetime to do so. This child's critical faculties are unparalleled, finding the proverbial needle in the haystack at a speed which can stagger the *laissez-faire* attitude of the easy-going Lion. Young Virgos carry out their tasks conscientiously and precisely. That's where their particular talents lie. Accuracy to them is far more important than success, recognition, or applause, and they work more happily behind the scenes than in the spotlight. Leo, who needs a pat on the back to get by in life, may puzzle over shy young Virgo's humility, but it is this very modesty, this willingness to work and serve without recognition that represents real strength. If Leo's enthusiasm manifests in a domineering, pushing way this youngster's critical tendency may sharply point out faults that are a little hard to swallow. The best of warm-hearted Leo's nature can, with tolerant affection, develop young Virgo's discriminating rather than nit-picking nature.

Best activities to share: jigsaw puzzles; colouring; Meccano and other construction kits; sewing (boys and girls); helping with the housework (don't rush 'em).

Virgo Sun Parent/Leo Sun Child

The Virgo parent of a Leo child will soon learn one fact of life: these two sun signs operate on entirely different planes and mutual understanding and tolerance are essential for happy coexistence. The Virgo mother or father is a stickler for accuracy whereas the Leo child can be hopelessly inept when it comes to the details. Virgo senior is sparing with praise and despises any form of arrogance or ostentation, whilst the young Lion simply can't exist without appreciation and approval. Virgo believes in modesty in all things including shows of affection, but little Leo needs plenty of loving hugs and cuddles for reassurance. As usual it befalls the parent to adapt, and seeing things through Junior's eyes can achieve a great deal. Young Leo, never a perfectionist in the same way as the Virgo parent, makes an inspired leader, excellent organizer, and admired performer. This little one's warm enthusiastic approach will add plenty of good-natured fun to Virgo's life. Encouragement rather than nagging, constructive help in preference to sharp criticism, can unobtrusively rectify the 'weaknesses', with both parties kept happy.

Best activities to share: play acting (Virgoans make good actors, too); painting (you'll need to help tidy up); board games of all kinds (a good introduction to detail).

LEO / LIBRA

Leo	Libra
Impulsive	Amenable
Generous	Easy-going
Spontaneous	Cooperative
Must lead	Must relate
Expansive	Diplomatic
Seeks admiration	Seeks company
Likes big ideas	Likes harmony
Dramatic	Just

Leo Sun Parent/Libra Sun Child

Libra children are reputed to be a delight to rear – friendly, affable, charming, anxious to please, well-mannered, the list is endless. To the Leo who feels burning pride in all offspring, they are probably a dream come true. Young Libra has a deep need for company and will probably spend as much time as possible with indulgent Leo. This is flattery indeed for the Lion who loves so much to be needed. The Libran desire to please others and willingness to comply, can sometimes develop into an inability to assert themselves when it comes to making decisions. Here Leos can instil a little of their own self-confidence, making the point that you can't please all of the people all of the time. Friction between this parent and child is rare, but should Leo feel like getting angry, bear in mind that rows and aggressive arguments are poison to little Libra. The gentle make up of the Balance just can't tolerate them. A just and well-reasoned reproach fits in much better with this youngster's sense of fairness. The Libran love of harmony extends to their immediate surroundings and they will respond well to a restful and pleasantly decorated room of their own. Allowing them to use their good taste in these matters can go a long way in developing the ability to make decisions.

Best activities to share: quiet chats, later learning the art of debate; entertaining close friends; and almost anything with a partner (not at their best in their own company).

Libra Sun Parent/Leo Sun Child

The Libra parent's strong desire for peace and harmony can lead them to spoil their children. The 'anything for a quiet life' attitude can result in Leo junior getting away with murder. Not that Leo children are particularly difficult to bring up. Self-confident and extroverted, they are affectionate by nature and anxious to please their parents. However, unless shown from an early age that they can't always play king pin and that the world does not revolve round them alone, Lion cubs can become bombastic, self-centred animals. Librans are extremely considerate of others and can teach little Leo that even 'stars' sometimes have to share the bill. The close friendship of the Libran parent, only too ready to lend an ear to Leo junior's

'Of course he's going to kiss his nice kind auntie, he knows that silly shy boys don't get special treats, EVER AGAIN!'

exploits, provides the willing audience this youngster needs. Leo children demand respect and give theirs wholeheartedly to a parent they can look up to. Libra will need to overcome the natural tendency to take the easy path of non-commitment, coming down firmly on the side of right or wrong. Young Leos are powerful stuff in the making and are helped with strong guidelines. The Libran parent nevertheless is scrupulously fair, and by meting out justice (without fail), can easily gain the devotion and respect of the little Lion.

Best activities to share: anything creative and competitive; entering painting competitions; junior drama workshops; giving parties; games to develop the art of being a fair and friendly 'boss'.

LEO / SCORPIO

Leo	Scorpio
Impulsive	Intense
Generous	Powerful
Spontaneous	Passionate
Must lead	Must defeat
Expansive	Penetrating
Seeks admiration	Seeks power
Likes big ideas	Likes challenge
Dramatic	Magnetic

Leo Sun Parent/Scorpio Sun Child

When the Leo parent, who loves to rule the roost (usually making an excellent job of it), is confronted with the iron will of a little Scorpio, sparks can fly. Head on confrontations must be avoided at all costs in this relationship. Both have fixed opinions, like their own way, and tend to dig their heels in, but Leo will realize sooner or later that when it comes to sheer grit, tiny Scorpio may surprisingly have the edge. Leos' natural tendency to direct their children can help the intense little Scorpio to channel the great willpower that can lead to strength or downfall. In understanding the Scorpio child's uncanny talent for psychology (having one's weaker motives 'sussed' is an occupational hazard with parents of little Scorpios) Leo will do well to behave with scrupulous honesty and candour. Nevertheless these two signs have a great deal in common. Both are loyal and warm-hearted, both have sticking power when it comes to achieving a goal. The Leo parent loves a winner and should derive great satisfaction from young Scorpio's determination to make a success of life. By introducing a little fun and laughter into the 'winning game' to which Scorpio is compulsively drawn, Leo can lighten the intensity of the little water sign, teaching leadership rather than conquest.

Best activities to share: mending things (broken toys, etc.); solving puzzles and problems (Cluedo is a favourite game); collecting; indulging passionate crazes.

Scorpio Sun Parent/Leo Sun Child

The great Scorpio temptation is that in the desire to bring out the best in their youngsters they will forcefully manipulate them. Not so with little Leo. The Leo child is ambitious, confident and anxious to succeed. Backed by the sheer determination of a Scorpio parent, with the knack of 'making things happen' there's nothing this enthusiastic little one can't achieve. Scorpio can quite literally be the 'power' behind the Leo 'throne'. These two signs working together will be a formidable partnership. The Scorpio's inherent psychological understanding will recognize little Leo's need for appreciation and be quick to give sincere support. Building self-confidence without excessive self-importance will be a task worthy of this intelligent parent. Little Leo's sense of fun and love of life is irrepressibly catching and Scorpio's natural wit will find easy response with this young partner. Negatively, power struggles with ensuing tests of will can produce nothing but noisy dramatics and sullen showing off with no credit to either party. Win together but not against each other.

Best activities to share: stories with strong heroes; charades; painting and music; regenerate the power with long outdoor walks.

LEO / SAGITTARIUS

Leo	Sagittarius
Impulsive	Tolerant
Generous	Honest
Spontaneous	Interested
Must lead	Must understand
Expansive	Outgoing
Seeks admiration	Seeks to know
Likes big ideas	Likes adventure
Dramatic	Philosophic

Leo Sun Parent/Sagittarius Sun Child

This is a very agreeable blend of signs, and parent and child should have no trouble in striking up a relaxed harmonious relationship. The happy-go-lucky Sagittarius child will find an appreciative audience in the Leo parent. Good-humoured Leo will revel in the young Archer's sense of fun, joining in with the horseplay, laughing at the jokes and soon becoming a good friend rather than just a parent. When Junior pops out for 'five minutes' and doesn't turn up till three hours later, Leo mum or dad won't resist a smile when giving a cursory dressing down, understanding fully the little Sagittarian's wanderlust. These free-ranging youngsters often give their parents red faces by coming out with blunt comments in public; the saying that 'many a truth is spoken from the mouth of a child' was surely coined with such 'Honest Johns' in mind. Although this is normally good entertainment to fun-loving Leo, the Lion's phenomenal pride may occasionally suffer a blow through an ill-timed Sagittarian *faux pas*. The Leo mum or dad can encourage this youngster's sense of humour but provide a few guidelines, pointing out that sometimes the truth hurts and that, quite simply, some people can't take a joke. Discipline should present no problems provided the Leo parent uses reason rather than dogmatic 'bossiness'. Fair play gets this little one's respect.

Best activities to share: hide and seek games; mystery tours; horse play (plenty of energy to expend); all open-air activities; games of chance (teach Junior the odds, a good message for this born gambler!); anything adventurous.

Sagittarius Sun Parent/Leo Sun Child

Sagittarians can best be described as extremely just friends but no-nonsense parents. Their fair-minded attitude to children makes them popular but in no way doting mums and dads. Fresh air and exercise tends to be the Sagittarian answer to their youngster's problems. That, with a good sense of fun, can keep most things on an even keel. The Leo child, though soon self-reliant, has a sensitive side that may react over-dramatically to Sagittarius's sometimes blunt, matter-of-fact manner. Fun is shared with enthusiasm, but if it's at his own expense the proud Lion may show little amusement. There is a deep need for reassurance, though Junior's self-confident showmanship may keep it hidden. By praising successes and consoling failures, Sagittarius can be a constant support for this young one's creative self-expression. Blessed with an excellent sense of proportion, the Archer can teach little Leo the difference between being a shining light and a boring 'show off'. Potentially a lasting, good fun relationship.

Best activities to share: sports (watching and playing); putting on shows for friends; visits to the circus; outdoor sketching; anything for a laugh.

LEO / CAPRICORN

Leo	Capricorn
Impulsive	Cautious
Generous	Persistent
Spontaneous	Ambitious
Must lead	Must improve
Expansive	Dutiful
Seeks admiration	Seeks achievement
Likes big ideas	Likes authority
Dramatic	Responsible

Leo Sun Parent/Capricorn Sun Child

The Capricorn child, responsive to good discipline, thrives on a well ordered upbringing. Leo parents, enjoying great pride in their offspring, will delight in the young Goat's perfect manners, and sense of responsibility. Parent and child seek achievement in life, but whereas Leo tends rather to take the world by storm, young Capricorn will work slowly but surely towards a goal. The Leo parent, preferring quick action, may feel that this reserved, plodding youngster needs winding up. This rarely works, and hustling can only produce insecurity. The need to prove themselves by steady achievement conquers the common Capricorn trait, self-doubt. Praise is an important morale booster and no one delivers it as effectively as the confident Leo parent. Although ambitious, little Capricornians never push themselves to the fore, shying away from all forms of show. Often appearing grown up almost before they are out of rompers, it's all too easy for Leo parents – who love a willing slave – to place too much responsibility, too soon, on these able small shoulders. A little extra help with the fun side of life – easy for playful Leos – can give a better balance to the somewhat serious 'all work and no play' Capricorn.

Best activities to share: jigsaws (a good test of Capricornian patience); playing at schools; planning things in advance (they love organizing); making useful objects from card, paper and paints; visits to places of tradition and ceremony.

Capricorn Sun Parent/Leo Sun Child

Capricornian parents offer their children great security, and firm but fair discipline. Praise will be given when it is deserved and not otherwise. The Leo child develops early confidence and self-reliance in a good atmosphere, but without constant reasurance can languish and become withdrawn. Here a fair balance should be struck. In the understanding that Leo needs a certain amount of recognition and applause, Capricorn can teach the young Lion the difference between true pride in achievement and sheer vanity. Cautious by nature the Capricornian parent is thrifty, responsible and slow to venture on untrodden ground. In contrast the Leo child is a born spender in all senses. Small Lions throw themselves enthusiastically into untried but attractive projects with little thought to the necessary details that ensure success. No parent has more patience than the Capricorn for the task of familiarizing Junior with the 'nuts and bolts' side of life. Keep it subtle though. Over-discipline and excessive restriction of young Leo's exuberance will drive this little one to retaliate with 'putting on an act' and dramatic tantrums. Common ambition is the key to this relationship and respect for each other's different ways can build lasting friendship.

Best activities to share: competitions, talent contests and play acting; artistic activities with a good end product; board games; entertaining friends.

149

Leo	Aquarius
Impulsive	Unpredictable
Generous	Spontaneous
Spontaneous	Humanitarian
Must lead	Must be different
Expansive	Changing
Seeks admiration	Seeks causes
Likes big ideas	Likes the unusual
Dramatic	Rebellious

Leo Sun Parent/Aquarius Sun Child

The fact that this parent and child are opposite in terms of their Zodiac signs can be both a help and a hindrance. Leos make generous, loving parents who will do everything in their power to give their children the best things in life, and as such expect a certain amount of recognition, if not adulation, from their offspring. Aquarius junior, a human rights supporter from the cradle, is reluctant to bow down to anyone, and that includes Leo ma and pa! Water Carriers give great respect though – where it's due – and to just about anyone that they consider deserves it. Thus friends and acquaintances (which will be staggeringly large in number) will comprise every conceivable variety of the species. The Leo parent, host par excellence, will be given ample opportunity to keep open house for this motley entourage. Effusive and demonstrative, Leo loves the physical contact of bear hugs, piggy backs, tickling etc., and may find it hard to accept little Aquarius's detachment and independence. The name of the game is to treat this youngster as an equal: from an early age discussion of the world at large will produce quick understanding and unique Aquarian views. Leo must realize that the autocratic approach is out; any attempt to lay down the law without explaining the whys and wherefores to the intellectually orientated little one will only arouse the rebel at the heart of every Aquarian and spoil what could be a beautiful friendship.

Best activities to share: lots of parties; dropping in on friends and relatives (the more bizarre the better); visits to museums; reading (particularly encylopedias and non-fiction); intellectual games such as chess, and draughts; a visit to the House of Commons; belonging to clubs or societies.

Aquarius Sun Parent/Leo Sun Child

Gregarious Aquarius thrives on company and has a home that is usually filled with interesting, unusual visitors of every description. To the Leo child, born to be a star, if only a minor one, this provides a ready-made audience. Young Leo should flourish in the social activity that is part and parcel of the Aquarius parent's lifestyle. Both parent and child share a love of people, but whereas Aquarius prefers to mingle with the crowd, and be part of the group, little Leo needs to come to the fore and take a special bow. A natural leader and performer, herein lies Leo's talent and also the main contrast with the Aquarian. This parent will need to accept young Leo's desire to stand out from the crowd and encourage self-expressive activities, at the same time spelling out the Aquarian truth that all human beings deserve respect and no man is superior to any other. If successful in treading the tightrope of developing modesty without squashing Leo's sense of uniqueness, the Aquarian will be well rewarded. One should also bear in mind that Leo children need to express their warm feelings; the young fire sign hasn't the detachment of this parent and will indulge in the occasional over-dramatic tearful outbursts; calm reasoning may help a little, but not as much as a big cuddle.

Best activities to share: going to the theatre, acting games in which each gets a turn at playing the lead (charades); almost all board games (developing the ability to lose gracefully); anything artistic and creative.

Leo	Pisces
Impulsive	Sympathetic
Generous	Helpful
Spontaneous	Selfless
Must lead	Must give
Expansive	Imaginative
Seeks admiration	Seeks ideals
Likes big ideas	Likes fantasy
Dramatic	Poetic

Leo Sun Parent/Pisces Sun Child

Leos have a natural sense of family pride that requires the best of recognition for their children, wanting them to shine like the rays of Leo's ruling planet, the sun. Although gentle little Pisces doesn't yearn for a name in lights, preferring to take a back seat, this child can be just cause for Leo pride. Gifted with vivid imagination, often with artistic and musical ability, and not least, a compassionate sympathy for all living creatures, young Pisces can certainly make this loving parent's breast swell. However, unlike the Lion, a young Pisces doesn't crave the applause. True, both signs share a love of play acting, but whereas Leo is up there for the cheers, Pisces enjoys the sheer delight of make-believe. Nevertheless, sharing this world of fantasy can build a close loving relationship with oceans of fun. Big-hearted Leo, understanding the value of praise, can boost the sometimes fragile Piscean confidence, giving Junior a firm foot in the world of reality. Given security, the great imaginative powers of this child can often develop into an exceptional talent. Leo's ambitions are lofty, and pushing this child into the spotlight, though possible, is rarely desirable. Little Pisces, with loving devotion and a desire to please, may try hard to fit the bill, but the strain of this uncharacteristic role may prove too much. Let little Pisceans shine with their own light and not yours.

Best activities to share: acting; storytelling; dressing up; painting; drawing; music; a pet to care for (even a tadpole will do).

Pisces Sun Parent/Leo Sun Child

To the ever-loving Pisces parent, young Leo can be a constant ray of sunshine embodying the very self-confidence that Fishes often lack, and a potential for making real the fantasies of this imaginative parent. Little Leos take advantage of willing service more than any other, and positively lap up maternal or paternal doting. However, the Piscean's selfless attitude and ever-ready helping hand can change the proud Lion into a purring 'lazy cat' if over-indulged. This natural tendency may be difficult to restrain but well worth the effort. Highly creative and energetic, young Leo responds well to an appreciative audience. Shared projects with plenty of imagination and vision that allow Junior to take the fore will build experience in handling the natural talent for leadership. Sensitive Pisces can teach the understanding of other people's feelings; preventing Leo's well meant exuberance from riding roughshod over less powerful playmates. Learning to give the others a 'turn' can be an important lesson in helping to produce a just ruler rather than a bossy tyrant. Once this is sorted out the unchanging warm affection and grand achievements of big-hearted Leo will more than repay this parent's loving self-sacrifice.

Best activities to share: acting; stories with a strong dramatic note; puppet shows; plenty of make-believe games with good Piscean inspiration.

Virgo
Conscientious
Responsible
Painstaking
Must perfect
Critical
Seeks order
Likes efficiency
Dutiful

Virgo Sun Parent/Virgo Sun Child

This is a happy, orderly, bright-minded duo, and the conversations, once Junior's mastered the language (and that's usually pretty quickly), will be sparkling. Little Virgo is just bubbling with insatiable curiosity to know every fact and figure about the world around. What can't be stored in the mind will later fill neat notebooks and files. Just like the Virgo parent this youngster is here to get some semblance of order and system out of this messy old world. A perfect relationship between two perfectionists! Well we may just find that too much of a good thing may leave Junior with the idea that the rest of the world are inefficient slobs. Mum or dad Virgo have learnt that it takes all sorts to keep the wheels turning and it could be well worth passing that on to little Virgo before beautiful friendships are broken with the jab of a supercritical tongue. However modesty usually prevails, to the extent that these little ones can become self-effacing and painfully shy. A few well selected friends round to tea on a fairly regular basis can do much to develop confidence in this area. Parent and child show love and affection in practical ways and encouraging Junior to help you will expand feelings of closeness.

Best activities to share: puzzles, quizzes and mind games; collecting things; keeping catalogues, notes and diaries; modelmaking; sewing dolls' clothes; helping in the home.

VIRGO / LIBRA

Virgo	Libra
Conscientious	Amenable
Responsible	Easy-going
Painstaking	Cooperative
Must perfect	Must relate
Critical	Diplomatic
Seeks order	Seeks company
Likes efficiency	Likes harmony
Dutiful	Just

Virgo Sun Parent/Libra Sun Child

Little Libra's love of harmony and pleasant surroundings will find comfort in the neat efficiency of the Virgo home. Junior's need of good company and Virgo's fertile mind make for long conversations and a close relationship. Born charmers, little Librans develop early the social graces, and a natural desire to please others can make life easy for the Virgoan parent. This ease, however, though enjoyably undemanding, may not always be in the best interests of the child. Continually fitting in with the ideas of others, may prevent the development of the necessary self-confidence to make a personal decision. The Virgoan parent's ability to sift the facts and draw an accurate conclusion can be of invaluable help in rationalizing Junior's dilemma. Encouragement to express opinions – even asking advice on small matters, will slowly build this little diplomat's self assertion. If this vital point is missed, Virgo's sense of punctuality, order, and desire to get things done can unwittingly put on enough pressure to hopelessly confuse little Libra. Perfection you may seek but try not to make it beyond Junior's reach.

Best activities to share: painting and decorating anything; visiting and entertaining friends; [board games for two; helping in the home (not dirty jobs just yet though); making clothes for doll or Action Man; masses of chatter.

Virgo and Libra are both mentally active and communicative and parent and child should have plenty to say to each other. Often reserved and shy little Virgo, in this sociable parent's company, will soon develop the confidence to feel comfortable with others. The easy-going Libran will find Junior's preference for regular routines and predictable patterns of behaviour somewhat limiting but worth adapting to for the self-reliance that follows. Little Virgo's careful attention to details makes for quick learning and once school is started the end of term reports can be a delight. Discipline is never a big problem with these conscientious youngsters as they are prepared to provide most of it themselves. This relieves the Libran parent of having to become a firm authority figure, a role that doesn't fit too well on the shoulders of such a peace lover. Rarely comfortable with showy displays of affection, and often undemanding in this area, Junior prefers to show love in practical ways. Being allowed to help mum and dad has double the meaning to this little one. The other side of the Virgo coin is not so pretty a picture. Without positive help and encouragement to learn the Libran art of relaxing and taking it easy, this child can become obsessively fussy, finickey, supercritical and a constant nag. All work and no play, you know the rest.

Best activities to share: dress-making; model-making; music-making (it's easy with their quick fingers and minds); discussions, quizzes, and word games (Lexicon and Scrabble); helping.

VIRGO / SCORPIO

Virgo	Scorpio
Conscientious	Intense
Responsible	Powerful
Painstaking	Passionate
Must perfect	Must defeat
Critical	Penetrating
Seeks order	Seeks power
Likes efficiency	Likes challenge
Dutiful	Magnetic

Virgo Sun Parent/Scorpio Sun Child

Mentally bright and verbally expansive, Virgoan parents may find little Scorpio's sometimes impenetrable intensity more than a mystery. Virgos put all the facts on the table, add them up, and come to a correct and well reasoned conclusion. Little Scorpios rarely put the facts on the table. Secretive but not deceptive, these tiny psychologists intuitively probe surroundings, relationships, experiences, other people, and you, revealing nothing until the appropriate moment. In this way the little Scorpion builds the self-confidence and strength to tackle life's biggest challenges. The orderly Virgoan needs things to run efficiently and is firm in adhering to a good well-proved system. This is just the kind of strength that young Scorpio respects, the natural instinct to occasionally knock against authority is usually a need to assess the strength and prove that respect is justified. Standing firm, backed with good friendly Virgoan logic, makes the point. The Scorpio drive to put everything to the test applies equally to themselves at both extremes. Working with phenomenal passion on impossible projects on the one hand and lounging around for days in self-indulgent lethargy on the other; they try the lot. If the calm Virgo parent can accept the extremes, and put up more worthy challenges when the 'experiments' look unproductive, Junior's achievements will be a just reward.

157

Best activities to share: talking about other people; mind games, puzzles, quizzes; treasure hunting (with a metal detector?); painting and drawing; scientific toys.

Scorpio Sun Parent/Virgo Sun Child

The perceptive Scorpio parent will soon discover little Virgo's delightful mental agility. Sharp as tacks, quick to learn and even precocious in their skilful orderliness. With this little one, Scorpio can lock away the powerful discipline (Junior's own is perfectly adequate) and bring out the love and affection. Small Virgos read, question and talk, filing away the information in the tidy pigeon holes of their bright minds. A place for everything and everything in its place builds Junior's self-confidence. Scorpio's almost psychic understanding of other people's strengths and weaknesses will be invaluable support for this modest Virgo. The expression of feelings in a child that dislikes show and pretension, will need gentle coaxing, but never smothering affection. Though happy in play, little Virgos are happiest when applying themselves to projects with good tangible end results. Helping mum and dad with 'real' jobs will be enjoyably constructive, for in this practical way they can easiest express their love. Family clashes should be minor in this relationship, with little to arouse Scorpio's sometimes quick temper. However, breaks of routine for Junior are not always taken easily and may cause a sharp critical response. Help this little one to learn that occasionally bending and even breaking the rules adds a little fun to life.

Best activities to share: collecting and filing things (recipes or LPs listed in notebooks); microscope and slides; books galore, especially encyclopedias, dictionaries, etc.

Virgo	Sagittarius
Conscientious	Tolerant
Responsible	Honest
Painstaking	Interested
Must perfect	Must understand
Critical	Outgoing
Seeks order	Seeks to know
Likes efficiency	Likes adventure
Dutiful	Philosophic

Virgo Sun Parent/Sagittarius Sun Child

The Virgo parent will have both hands full looking after this lively little enthusiast. Small Sagittarians have bags of fun-loving energy and a spirit of adventure that keeps them constantly on the move. In no way clinging vines, these little wanderers need a long, long, rein and if they had a say in the matter, none at all. Even the explorer needs a home base and the Virgoan's good organization and well proved systems provide a more than adequate support for Junior's free-ranging exploits. The Virgo's attention to detail and down to earth practicality can equip Junior with a good grounding in common sense. This commodity, the Virgoan parent may equate with intelligence, but this youngster, whilst sometimes lacking the former, has more than a fair share of the latter. The search for truth is Sagittarius's basic drive and if throwing a little caution to the wind gets the desired result, then so be it. The best way to get through to Junior is straight talk and good logic handed out as friend to friend, and you'll receive the same honest treatment in return. Nagging and nit-picking will only guarantee a clean pair of heels moving quickly into the middle distance, mentally if not physically. Keep it friendly and fun and the wanderer will return.

Best activities to share: outdoor sports and games; shopping expeditions; exploring countryside and town (with camera and notebook in darkest Ealing); information books for quieter moments.

Sagittarius Sun Parent/Virgo Sun Child

Parent and child, though widely different in temperament, have a mutual respect for the truth that should make for close companionship. Sagittarius's friendly, straight from the shoulder honesty, and kindly tolerance, fits well with little Virgo's love of the plain unvarnished facts. Now for the differences. Fun-loving Sagittarian mums and dads like to be free as birds, hate ties and are rarely happy with routine. Small Virgos have their feet on the ground, like to know the limits and thrive on routine. A big contrast, but in no way inconsolable once recognized. Junior's need for firm guidelines and familiar patterns will, if supported, develop into an early self-reliance that makes few demands on this freedom-loving parent. Little Virgo's insatiable interest in getting the facts and Sagittarius's mine of information make good conversation the mainstay of this relationship. The Sagittarian impulse to propel themselves

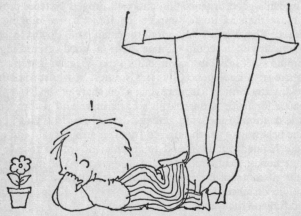

'I've got more important things to do than to answer your stupid questions. How the hell do I know who made God!'

recklessly into new experiences will not be shared by this cautious child. If Junior's coming along for the ride, make plans and make sense. Little Virgos are great organizers, and this talent can be given a boost if Sagittarius encourages help in drawing up the itinerary and mapping the route. The reward is high if the risks are kept low.

Best activities to share: constant friendly discussion; model-making; sewing; a junk shop typewriter will be much loved; nature walks (with notes); little, but real, jobs around the house.

VIRGO / CAPRICORN

Virgo	Capricorn
Conscientious	Cautious
Responsible	Persistent
Painstaking	Ambitious
Must perfect	Must improve
Critical	Dutiful
Seeks order	Seeks achievement
Likes efficiency	Likes authority
Dutiful	Responsible

Virgo Sun Parent/Capricorn Sun Child

This is a good harmonious combination of down-to-earth, capable characters with a strong sense of security. The Virgo parent is devoted to the needs of home and family, understanding easily the little Capricornian's love of a good disciplined routine. The small Goat's respect for authority and Virgo's consistency in this area, are well matched, giving little cause for clashes. However, as in all combinations of like minds there is a tendency to over-emphasize certain aspects of the respective natures. With this couple, life could get just a little too serious for Junior's own good. This blend of perfectionist and hard-working achiever may become so insular and supercritical as to make relationships outside the family circle difficult. The introduction of good measures of fun into the routine can build a more tolerant attitude when dealing with less conscientious souls. Rarely 'pushy' by nature, little Capricorns can move easily into popularity amongst their small playmates with their exceptional organizing abilities. At school too, this talent could result in responsibilities such as monitor, form captain, etc., and it is easy to see here the importance of good humour and tolerance in softening any 'bossiness' that may occur.

Best activities to share: plenty of friends to tea; helping mum and dad; building and construction kits; patience games: dressing up and playing the fool.

Capricorn Sun Parent/Virgo Sun Child

Capricorn and Virgo will get a great deal of enjoyment from each other's company, having in common a healthy respect for the practical, material aspects of life. In the secure support of this parent the little Virgo's bright inquisitive mind will develop quickly and confidently. Always ambitious for their children the Capricornian parents spend unlimited time and patience on their little charges. However perfect they may seem to this parent, the extreme modesty of small Virgos will need plenty of enthusiastic encouragement to boost a sense of self-worth. It's all too easy to overlook this necessity when Junior's self-discipline works so well. Often finding it difficult to express affection in other than helpful practical terms (doing little jobs for mum and dad) the desire to receive hugs, kisses, and compliments is powerful, but if you don't give them, they won't ask. Little Virgo's a talker, and from the earliest days good conversation will be an important key to this relationship. Overindulged in their perfectionist natures these little ones can be infuriating fusspots, picky eaters, and harsh critics. Soften yours up with large doses of love and tomfoolery.

Best activities to share: books; encyclopedias; notebooks; scrapbooks, and diaries; collecting sea shells, wild flowers, stamps, etc.; making artistic but useful objects; 'helping'.

Virgo	Aquarius
Conscientious	Unpredictable
Responsible	Spontaneous
Painstaking	Humanitarian
Must perfect	Must be different
Critical	Changing
Seeks order	Seeks causes
Likes efficiency	Likes the unusual
Dutiful	Rebellious

Virgo Sun Parent/Aquarius Sun Child

Little Aquarians thrive on the unexpected, the unpredictable, the untried and the new. Virgo parents like order, system and efficiency, set up good routines and stick to them. This may seem an incompatible duo but in fact it can work very well for both. Though Junior needs to kick against rules and regulations, Virgo's well-reasoned ones will more than stand the test, which was all that little Aquarius wanted to find out anyway. These small rebels question everything, accepting nothing at face value. In this way they develop their own individual approach and early self-confidence. Virgo's good down-to-earth answers to this little one's probing arguments should provide a healthy dialogue and stimulating relationship. Providing a good balance between reasonable guidelines and a fair share of freedom may be a touch like walking a tightrope but the rewards are great. These little Water Carriers are amongst us to knock down the fuddy-duddy outmoded ideas replacing them with more workable ones to take us into the future. As soon as Junior discovers the world outside family life the friends start to roll in. Face the fact, the parent of a small Aquarian that keeps open house, keeps a happy Aquarian.

Best activities to share: entertaining friends of all kinds (including stray dogs and cats etc.); joining groups, especially for good causes (Junior RSPCA, Save the Whale); inventing and making things.

Aquarius Sun Parent/Virgo Sun Child

The Aquarian parent provides plenty of stimulation and excitement to keep the zippy little Virgo's intellect busy. The infectious spontaneity and amusing originality of Aquarius can contribute much towards easing the sometimes excessive modesty and caution of this little perfectionist. However, the Virgoan desire for order and system may not react so favourably to the constant change of routine that is second nature to the free-thinking Aquarian. Much as this parent loves complete freedom, disliking ties of any kind, little Virgo's self-assured independence will more than repay sticking to repeat patterns of family behaviour. Within such a good predictable structure Junior can get on, unhampered, with the business of becoming better and better (at everything). The need to be helpful and turn their talents to practical use makes young Virgos take on responsibilities far in advance of their years. As they usually prefer to express their love in the same practical way, helping mum and dad takes on extra meaning for them. Plenty of praise for jobs well done is essential to build self-confidence and there is no chance of modest little Virgo getting big-headed. Negatively, if these orderly youngsters are thrown into confusion by Aquarius's unpredictability they can become the most nagging nit-pickers in the Zodiac.

Best activities to share: crafts for deft fingers; modelmaking; sewing; drawing; quizzes and word games; keeping a diary; making notes and lists for mum and dad.

VIRGO / PISCES

Virgo	Pisces
Conscientious	Sympathetic
Responsible	Helpful
Painstaking	Selfless
Must perfect	Must give
Critical	Imaginative
Seeks order	Seeks ideals
Likes efficiency	Likes fantasy
Dutiful	Poetic

Virgo Sun Parent/Pisces Sun Child

Like all opposite signs of the Zodiac Virgo and Pisces have the basic ingredients for a good balanced relationship. With open minds each has so much to learn from the other. Virgo's practical, down-to-earth realism contrasts widely with little Pisces' highly imaginative, impressionable and almost mystical idealism. For the little Fishes the borderline between vivid imagination and reality is undefined and it will take patient and sensitive guidance to separate the two. Junior's day-dreaming, far from being useless for practical day-to-day living, can, if given full expression, become a positive talent and source of tangible achievement. Virgo's routine approach can be enhanced by sharing this youngster's world of fantasy, and by giving encouragement to write, draw, and act out these imaginings so as to develop little Pisces' self-confidence. Both parent and child share a love of caring for others, and helping around the home. Particularly when the parent is ill or tired the efficient side of Junior's sympathetic nature comes out. Looking after pets is another good bet for this character. This loving child will give all in order to live up to the parent's expectations, and plenty of warm demonstrative affection is the only reward necessary.

Best activities to share: dressing up and acting; painting, drawing and music-making; keeping little pets (why not goldfish ?); a personal patch in the garden to dig and plant; reading and writing stories.

Pisces Sun Parent/Virgo Sun Child

Piscean parents are gentle, loving, and devoted to the care of their children. Though rarely sticklers for routine their intuitive feelings tell them when and where the needs are. Pisceans play things according to the feel of the moment. This can make for sloppy schedules with any but a Virgoan child, who, as soon as the communicative arts are mastered, will take over with the stop watch. Thriving on regular routines and familiar habit patterns this is one you don't have to spend half an hour calling in for lunch. Little Virgo probably laid table and hinted that the fish fingers should be under the grill. OK, Junior quickly gets the nuts and bolts side of this practical little life sorted out and with this parent, the bonus of all that creative Piscean imagination can go a long way towards expanding the sometimes narrow Virgoan vision. Virgos, though born realists, are often artistically talented and encouragement to indulge in some form of self-expression can sometimes develop exceptional talent. Good conversation, story-telling and writing will help to stimulate young Virgo's love of words and at the same time forge a close bond between parent and child. Clashes will nearly all be about disrupted routine and bad timing but Pisces' giving nature is too demonstrably affectionate not to work wonders at smoothing Junior's frustrations.

Best activities to share: playing house (watch this little one's efficiency) or hospitals; keeping scrapbooks, notebooks, and diaries; modelmaking, music-making, dressmaking (these busy little hands will make anything useful); long, long conversations.

Libra
Amenable
Easy-going
Cooperative
Must relate
Diplomatic
Seeks company
Likes harmony
Just

Libra Sun Parent/Libra Sun Child

This must be the easiest relationship in the Zodiac. Relating to others is so important to this couple that they just can't help getting on. You'd think there couldn't be a snag, well there is but they may just not notice it. Big and little Libra can always see the other fellow's point of view, get a great kick out of pleasing people and 'fitting in' harmoniously. What's wrong with that? Nothing if one of the partners knows exactly what she or he's going to do. Two Librans, however, each desperately trying to please the other can debate interminably in a plethora of indecision. The Libran desire for justice demands that every angle is explored before final judgement, but there are times when the need for quick action makes this impossible. This is where Junior needs real help from this intelligent parent. Cutting down the options to manageable proportions, for example 'would you like blue or red?' is less demanding than 'which colour would you like?'. Little points but they work well in building the confidence of this bright but sometimes too amenable youngster. Close companionship, good conversation (from the earliest days) and friendly, but never heated, argument, will keep this duet in perfect harmony.

Best activities to share: long talks; quiet walks; best friends to tea (never a noisy crowd); making the home look better (pictures etc. by Junior; looking at paintings at the gallery.

Libra	Scorpio
Amenable	Intense
Easy-going	Powerful
Cooperative	Passionate
Must relate	Must defeat
Diplomatic	Penetrating
Seeks company	Seeks power
Likes harmony	Likes challenge
Just	Magnetic

Libra Sun Parent/Scorpio Sun Child

Whereas the Libran parent likes the balance of the middle road in all things, the young Scorpio experiments with extremes. Working with passion, lazing lethargically; warm and loving, cold and cruel; a paragon of good behaviour or positively delinquent, Junior uncontrolled will try them all on for size. These powerful little characters almost demand a strong parent to look up to. Though rarely seeing themselves in this role the easy-going Libran parent has a fair-mindedness which, coupled with a few strong guidelines, will soon gain the respect of little Scorpio. The Scorpion's penetrating mind grasps things quickly and given sufficient challenge will tackle the most difficult tasks with unbounded enthusiasm. Deeply emotional, although often outwardly calm, the little Scorpion responds warmly to Libran shows of affection. Though Libran households rarely indulge in battles or clashes, troubles can occur through the very diplomacy that keeps the peace. If this amenable parent fails to establish good definite limits on behaviour the challenge in finding just how far it is possible to go may be irresistible.

Best activities to share: treasure hunts, puzzles and problem solving; microscope and slides; collecting things; drawing, painting, and making music.

Life is a grand challenge to the powerul Scorpio and great enthusiasm is thrown into the responsibility of being a parent. Ambitious for their children, they nurture their talents and support and strengthen their weaknesses. Little Librans are charming, sociable, adaptable, and love company. Both parent and child have a strong feeling for artistic pursuits and Scorpio will encourage little Libra's natural good taste and positive talents. The easy-going nature of this youngster will do almost anything to keep their nearest and dearest happy. The dangers in this all too comfortable situation will be obvious to the perceptive Scorpio. In trying to please all of the people all of the time, Junior may not get a look in where personal desires are concerned. Though often content to carry on pleasing, it does little to produce and develop self-confidence. Libran indecisiveness comes from their great sense of balance in all things, and in order to reach a judgement everything has to be taken into consideration. Discussion and debate can do much to familiarize little Libra with the more assertive side of his or her nature. Plenty of visits from young friends will continue the good work.

Best activities to share: painting and drawing; decorating little Libra's room; *tête-à-tête* conversations; dressing up dolls or action men.

LIBRA / SAGITTARIUS

Libra	Sagittarius
Amenable	Tolerant
Easy-going	Honest
Cooperative	Interested
Must relate	Must understand
Diplomatic	Outgoing
Seeks company	Seeks to know
Likes harmony	Likes adventure
Just	Philosophic

Libra Sun Parent/Sagittarius Sun Child

The companionable and caring Libran parent will delight in this little fun-loving, energetic, adventurer. Life for the little Sagittarian is a series of doors to be opened and roads to be explored both physically and mentally. The close friendly attitude of the Libran will bring out the best of this youngster's natural honesty and warm affection. Keep it close but never cloying and possessive for Junior likes freedom above all things. Neither parent nor child is excessively ambitious so pressure in these areas will be minimal. Little Sagittarius doesn't learn in order to compete, but purely to find out the truth. Junior lays all the cards on the table and expects everyone else to. Straight answers to frank questions and this little one's happy. This blunt honesty, though always well meant, may get some adverse reactions from the outside world if not aided with a large helping of the Libran's diplomacy. There is little chance of serious clashes with this duo, as the combination of Libra's easy-going nature and Sagittarious's ability to see the funny side of everything, makes flare-ups short, sharp and minimal.

Best activities to share: lots of outdoor fun and games; sports both played and watched; a good lolloping mongrel to romp with; visits all over the place.

Sagittarius Sun Parent/Libra Sun Child

Sagittarian parents are warm, impulsive, fun-loving friends to their children. No lack of stimulation and excitement in the Archer's household. Little Libra, never a loner, looks for close loving companionship and gets plenty of that with this parent. Rarely sticking to strict routines, the Sagittarian prefers, much to the joy of little Libra, to take each day as a new and exciting adventure. Whilst giving honest adult answers to all the child's probing questions, loving truth above all things, this parent will support the delightful make-believe necessary in the child's early life. Little Libra's charming manner and desire to please should make for little or no clashes in this good relationship.

Though Sagittarius's ideas and enthusiasms will always be amenable to this easy-going youngster, care will have to be taken that Junior isn't just giving in to keep everything harmonious. These little diplomats are all too happy to lose their entire identity in keeping other's lives running smoothly. Encouragement to make decisions, and praise when they're made, will help, but don't give in to the Libran trick of throwing back the statement 'I'll do whatever you want to do'. Stand firm and Junior's confidence will grow.

Best activities to share: long discussions; visits to and from friends; painting and drawing (easier areas for Junior to make decisions); helping choose things for the home.

LIBRA / CAPRICORN

Libra	Capricorn
Amenable	Cautious
Easy-going	Persistent
Cooperative	Ambitious
Must relate	Must improve
Diplomatic	Dutiful
Seeks company	Seeks achievement
Likes harmony	Likes authority
Just	Responsible

Libra Sun Parent/Capricorn Sun Child

Good relationships mean a lot to the easy-going Librans and they'll work hard to keep their children happy and companionable. Little Capricornians like to know where they stand and what is expected of them and do their very best to come up to scratch. This cut and dried approach has great meaning in the life of the ambitious little Goat but may pose a few problems for the Libran parent. Always seeing the other person's point of view rarely makes for hard and fast rules and throwing the decisions back at Junior with 'Whatever you'd like best, dear' may leave a little to be desired in this one's mind. The Capricornian respect for authority is their way of learning how to deal with their own future potential as organizers. So the egalitarian harmonious Libran will have to be boss to suit the little Goat's needs. Within a regular, familiar, and well organized routine these little workers flourish and grow in confidence. However a modicum of Libran balance will be necessary to keep Junior from becoming lopsidedly materialistic and too serious. Art, pleasure and good fun (Libran affinities) can be inserted into the routine to advantage.

Best activities to share: helping in the home (decorating and painting would be adventurous); dressing up and acting; organizing parties, visits and family schedules; trips to historic places.

Capricorn Sun Parent/Libran Sun Child

With loving care and attention the well-ordered Capricorn home runs smoothly and efficiently. With little to ruffle the young Libran's love of harmony this environment will be ideal. Capricorn parents let their children know just what is expected of them with clearly drawn guidelines for each stage of development. Little Librans, wanting to be close and pleasing to their parents though rarely needing strong discipline or authority, will find great security in knowing where they stand. These helpful, charming little diplomats will fit in with just about everybody's plans without thought for their own preferences. Fine for family peace but not so hot for developing Junior's individuality. Librans have good logical minds with an unbiased approach that can see all sides of any question; a talent that makes for good arbitrators in later life. However, a great deal of help and encouragement will be necessary in order to get Junior to make decisions. Weighing the pros and cons interminably can drive all but the patient Capricornian to distraction. Artistic choices are the most helpful starters; colours, fabrics, clothes etc. bring out the best of Libran good taste. Keep the options minimal though and you'll win in time.

Best activities to share: cosy conversations; games for two; painting and drawing (tell them what to draw if they can't make up their minds); dressing up.

LIBRA / AQUARIUS

Libra	Aquarius
Amenable	Unpredictable
Easy-going	Spontaneous
Cooperative	Humanitarian
Must relate	Must be different
Diplomatic	Changing
Seeks company	Seeks causes
Likes harmony	Likes the unusual
Just	Rebellious

Libra Sun Parent/Aquarius Sun Child

With good, but not like, minds this couple share a love of sociability and excellent company that should make them the best of pals. The Libran's need for close relationships makes for sensitivity to the wishes of others, and they'll bend over backwards to please and keep their children happy. Little Aquarians have no desire to live up to anybody's expectations; take them or leave them they don't mind. These nonconformists set up their own way of life from the earliest years, seeming to have none of the usual child's insecurity about looking or acting different from the rest. Their role in life is to explore the ultimate in possibilities, and rules and regulations are never going to be accepted without question. Easy-going Libra sets up few rules, hopefully providing a good diplomatic balance as and when each situation occurs. However Junior will need a few brick walls to scale and the 'anything for a quiet life' Libran attitude can leave this little one a rebel without a cause. Balance the giving in with a little firm resistance and little Aquarius will be happy.

Best activities to share: anything unusual – scientific, space-age, electronic, computerized, or outrageous.

Aquarius Sun Parent/Libra Sun Child

The Aquarian approach to parenthood is original, unusual, and always interesting for themselves and their children. Plenty of stimulation, a busy social whirl and a constant flux of activity will be a fitting and exciting environment for the companionable little Libran. Good *tête-à-tête* conversations are the keynote to happiness in this excellent relationship. Little Librans' desire to please, get on, and keep everything running smoothly make them the most charming, amenable and sociable of children. Aquarius's many friends and visitors will be delighted at the manners and confidence displayed by this little diplomat. Libra's good reasoning power makes for steady learning at school though friendships will be of more importance than schoolwork. This need will be easy for Aquarius to understand. However, Junior's propensity for 'giving in' to keep others happy, may need a little watching if it is not to develop into a wishy-washy characteristic. So happy to please, these little peace-keepers can be oblivious to their own needs and opinions to such an extent, that they may lack confidence in making decisions in the future. A difficult one to solve, but encouragement to express judgements in family situations, getting Junior's view, acting on it, and praising the results, can be a help.

Best activities to share: long discussions and friendly arguments; all artistic pursuits; decorating (with Junior deciding the colours and wallpapers).

Libra	Pisces
Amenable	Sympathetic
Easy-going	Helpful
Cooperative	Selfless
Must relate	Must give
Diplomatic	Imaginative
Seeks company	Seeks ideals
Likes harmony	Likes fantasy
Just	Poetic

Libra Sun Parent/Pisces Sun Child

The companionable Libran parent has just the brand of friendliness that can bring dreamy little Pisces out of the land of make-believe and into the world of reality. Without a bump! Vulnerable little Pisceans have a wealth of intuition and imagination that enables them to live utopian dreams inside their heads when the going gets tough. When they are 'far away' you can bet that they're in a better place than we are. The Libra parent, however, can encourage this small Fish to confidently express and share these talents with all. Parent and child have a sympathetic and sensitive approach in relating to others that precludes any real disagreement. In fact it would be difficult to say whether parent or child would be most horrified in the unlikely event of a battle. Smoothly as this team will run, little Pisces will quickly become overdependent if the Libra parent adapts too willingly to every whim. Share the fantasy and fun but encourage self-reliance in allowing Junior to do things for you. Through helping others little Pisceans find their real vocation in this world.

Best activities to share: making up fantastic stories (later junior Sci-Fi may appeal); playing nurse to dolls, teddies, pets, and mum and dad; dressing up and acting (they will lose themselves in the character); anything artistic or imaginative.

Highly intuitive Pisces can tune in to the thoughts and feelings of others almost before they have them. Little Libra's need for constant company will find sensitive support with this loving and giving parent. Both parent and child have a natural talent for artistic expression and will share a love of beauty and harmony. This combination of Piscean idealist and Libran diplomat is a certain recipe for everything in the garden being lovely; not a cloud in the sky. Little Librans learn, because of their companionable nature, to understand the other person's point of view. Weighing up the pros and cons, examining every angle, Junior gains a wealth of broad knowledge. However, in order to be absolutely fair in making a decision the process can become interminable. There lies the potential snag to this otherwise perfect relationship. Pisces' ever ready helping hand may be there just a little too soon and too often for young Libra ever to acquire the confidence to make a judgement. Get Junior to help you with decisions, encourage and admire them when they are made, and the self-reliance will grow. Judgement on colours, house decoration and clothes are less of a problem to this little expert in good taste.

Best activities to share: decorating anything; long, long conversations; board games for two (too many options in chess though!); best friends round to tea (encourage company outside the home quite early); music; dance; all artistic pursuits.

Scorpio
Intense
Powerful
Passionate
Must defeat
Penetrating
Seeks power
Likes challenge
Magnetic

Scorpio Sun Parent/Scorpio Sun Child

Young Scorpios can learn easily from this parent how to develop and deal with the great power this sign manifests. Big Scorpio can give loving support, understanding the intense feelings that lie hidden beneath the deceptively calm surface of this little volcano. All or nothing is the watchword of this couple and as comrades in arms they are invincible. This sounds like a militaristic duo but in truth the love of battle and challenge is Scorpio's driving force. Intelligent, perceptive, little Scorpio learns quickly and easily, though he or she may often neglect the more mundane necessities in favour of more demanding projects. Both highly intuitive, born psychologists, parent and child will enjoy discussing others about them, discovering their strengths and their weaknesses. This understanding makes them the most loyal of friends and the most devastating enemies. Mutual respect should keep the power struggles to a minimum, but confrontation of two Scorpios can seem like a fight to the death, each capable of inflicting unhealable hurt on the other. Campaign on the same side and you can conquer the world.

Best activities to share: treasure hunting (metal detectors); quizzes and puzzles; chess; Mastermind (even for younger Scorpios); chemistry sets; keeping secrets.

Scorpio	Sagittarius
Intense	Tolerant
Powerful	Honest
Passionate	Interested
Must defeat	Must understand
Penetrating	Outgoing
Seeks power	Seeks to know
Likes challenge	Likes adventure
Magnetic	Philosophic

Scorpio Sun Parent/Sagittarius Sun Child

The free-ranging, fun-loving Sagittarian child will find a good supportive home base in the Scorpio parent. This understanding parent will admire and encourage Junior's early self-confident wanderings in search of adventure, knowledge and above all truth. Taking little at face value this youngster must know why, where, and how, and if it doesn't make sense, forget it. To this end nothing is sacred to the blunt questions of the little Archer. This honest approach will sometimes appear exasperatingly thoughtless and naive to the ever aware Scorpio but the task of smoothing a few of the rough edges will be irresistible. The Scorpio who reasons 'You'll do it because I said so!' and is met with Junior's 'Is that because you're bigger than me?' may feel more than a twinge of guilt. No hurt intended, the little Archer just wanted to know! With patient discussion, and a few more crushed egos later, Scorpio can help young Sagittarius resist dispensing freely the more devastating 'home truths'. The startling knowledge that others sometimes have to bend the facts a little to keep their dignity, will, when proved, make for easier Sagittarian public relations. All this aside, Junior's one of the most entertaining fun-loving characters in the book.

Best activities to share: plenty of travel; lots of outdoor activity, exploring beach, countryside and town; discussion; a scruffy mongrel friend.

Sagittarius Sun Parent/Scorpio Sun Child

Sagittarian parents admire independence and treat their children with frank honesty and respect. Little Scorpio's strong will and positive manner offers no threats to the Archer's great love of freedom. The powerful young Scorpion needs a strong parental figure to live up to and Sagittarius's friendly straight-talking nature fits the bill well. No sticklers for dull routine, these parents take life as a continuing adventure, and the resulting day to day surprises and challenges are the stuff of life to little Scorpio. Between the two of them, a few necessities may get overlooked but the ensuing good 'hits' are worth a few misses. Young Scorpios learn quickly and with passionate enthusiasm from this knowledgeable parent. Often indifferent to anything they consider trivial this little one's love of worthwhile challenge will even provoke near disasters in order to conquer them. Behind this battling 'superchild' feelings run deep. More vulnerable to be hurt than most, they can harbour resentment, showing little on the outside of what is going on within. If Sagittarius's honesty hits this youngster too savagely in a soft spot the violent retaliation, however long delayed, can be disastrous. Play rough but pull the punches.

Best activities to share: outdoor sports of all kinds; puzzles and detective work (finding dad's cufflinks); a microscope and slides; entertaining friends (Scorpio's a leader and needs practice); anything creative.

Scorpio	Capricorn
Intense	Cautious
Powerful	Persistent
Passionate	Ambitious
Must defeat	Must improve
Penetrating	Dutiful
Seeks power	Seeks achievement
Likes challenge	Likes authority
Magnetic	Responsible

Scorpio Sun Parent/Capricorn Sun Child

Little Capricorns are quietly ambitious, respect authority and are usually paragons of orderliness and good manners. The firm, but caring Scorpio parent is a tower of strength, in the shadow of which this little one can confidently blossom. Not quickly though. Strong-willed and positive, earthy little Goats, like their namesakes, tread each step up the mountain with steady precision, erring on the side of caution, but never making a slip. That's why a good set of house rules is invaluable and even demanded by these conscientious little workers. You may wonder, with the serious little Capricornian, whatever happened to carefree mischievous childhood. Don't worry, this one has it later, probably in the 'teens, and certainly in maturity. Work first, play later for these chaps. Scorpio's good understanding of psychology, enables this parent to pick the right time to loosen up and develop the little one's sense of humour. Little and often is the best receipe. This balance, well maintained, will avoid Junior becoming a holier-than-thou, bossy prude, and featuring low in the popularity stakes. Brought safely through initial shyness, little Capricornians' good organizing abilities can make them much in demand amongst more scatterbrained playmates.

Best activities to share: board games with complex rules (Monopoly etc.); swapping roles (you be the children and I'll be teacher); visits to Buckingham Palace, Changing of the Guard etc.; helping mum and dad.

Capricorn Sun Parent/Scorpio Sun Child

Powerful little Scorpios won't have to go to extremes with this parent to establish just how far they can go. Good, firm but fair guidelines will be set and adhered to, long before Junior remembers. Capricorn, as with everything else, steps into the responsibility of parenthood with eyes wide open and plans well made. Ambitious for their children, they know that a good predictable pattern makes family life run smoothly and builds confidence in their young ones. Though with little Scorpios one must expect a few battles, these will be more for the experiment of testing their own strong wills than an attack on authority. Potentially the most powerful sign in the Zodiac, Scorpio admires strength and will need great help and reassurance in dealing with this explosive energy. Extreme by nature; black/white; saint/sinner; a powerhouse of enthusiasm or a plethora of self-indulgent laziness. Take your pick. Good firm guidance and plenty of affection can put this born winner on the right road. Play strong and fair with Junior and the loyalty will be unbounded, but unbending stingy nitpicking can cause a resentful rift in the relationship that may never be bridged.

Best activities to share: visits to museums (science, natural history etc.); chemistry sets; collecting (stamps, badges, etc.); puzzles and mind games (chess, Mastermind).

SCORPIO / AQUARIUS

Scorpio	Aquarius
Intense	Unpredictable
Powerful	Spontaneous
Passionate	Humanitarian
Must defeat	Must be different
Penetrating	Changing
Seeks power	Seeks causes
Likes challenge	Likes the unusual
Magnetic	Rebellious

Scorpio Sun Parent/Aquarius Sun Child

Scorpios rarely let the talents of their children gather dust. Quick to sense their strengths and weaknesses, they are a constant support if not a driving force in their offspring's early years. The Aquarian child, however, is a very different kettle of fish. Inventive, impulsive, unusual, original and almost impossible to pin down. The heavy dogmatic side of Scorpio will find an argumentative rebel, the ever-loving hug may get an indifferent shrug, and attempts to get some order into Junior's life will be met with an absent-minded attitude. Once these angles have been sorted out Scorpio can put in some good work towards developing the individualist that is already there. Little Aquarius questions everything and Scorpio probably has all the answers to keep this relationship happily sizzling. Not overly affectionate, young Aquarians share their love equally with all and sundry, friends, parents, other kids' parents, dogs, cats, you name it, they love it. There's no room for Scorpio possessiveness with this social mixer; this one's looking to you as a friend, not as a boss. Little Aquarius hates rules, but taking them away could leave a lot of energy with nowhere to go. Keep the rules but keep them fair.

Best activities to share: electronic toys and games; metal detector exploring; boxes of bits and pieces for making world-shattering inventions; science fiction books and games, and anything space-age or brand spanking NEW.

Aquarius Sun Parent/Scorpio Sun Child

The Aquarian is bound to have a few original or avant-garde tricks up the sleeve when it comes to bringing up children. 'What was good enough for my parents is good enough for me' may suit some, but the Aquarian, never! Open to anything extreme or challenging little Scorpio will find great stimulation and fun with this unusual parent. Both find enormous interest in other people, Junior through a natural intuitive under-standing of what others are thinking and feeling, while the parent just loves people for themselves. The dialogue and succession of visitors can be perpetual. Scorpios' extreme nature, without some limitations in the form of well adhered to guidelines, will lead them to experiment at both ends of any

'If I come up there and find it, you're in trouble my girl. And don't make that room in a mess!'

scale. Doing nothing by halves, they can be saints or sinners; with no limits they'll try the lot. Much as rules and regulations go against the grain with Aquarians they are a positive must if you want Junior to hit the peaks rather than the depths. The penetrating mind of this intense and enthusiastic youngster will respond well to the individual theories and ideals of the Aquarian parent. Strong and often extremely self-possessed outwardly, Scorpions needs plenty of demonstrative affection to feel really secure, they're tough enough to do without it but why should they ? Give them a hug as often as you can.

Best activities to share: exploring and detective work (treasure hunting with metal detector etc.); a telescope or microscope (or both); mind games, chess, Mastermind etc.; learning first aid (they often become doctors).

SCORPIO / PISCES

Scorpio	Pisces
Intense	Sympathetic
Powerful	Helpful
Passionate	Selfless
Must defeat	Must give
Penetrating	Imaginative
Seeks power	Seeks ideals
Likes challenge	Likes fantasy
Magnetic	Poetic

Scorpio Sun Parent/Pisces Sun Child

This can be one of the most loving and sensitive relationships in the book. Scorpio parents, intense and devoted, can be positive entrepreneurs where their children are concerned; gently guiding and encouraging their particular talents to fulfilment. The intuitive and highly imaginative little Pisces has much to offer in the way of artistic ability, and an almost psychic awareness gives this child a sympathetic insight into other people's thoughts and feelings. The extraordinary vividness of Junior's imagination will be loved and allowed full expression by the admiring Scorpio parent. By coaxing these fantasies out of the head and into drawings, stories, and little acted-out scenes, Junior can be encouraged to distinguish the borderline between make-believe and reality. As long as Scorpio's support remains unobtrusive, the little Piscean poet can build real self-confidence with this powerful parent. However, over-protectiveness will guarantee a clinging vine, with Pisces readily escaping into day-dreams when the going gets tough. These youngsters need to give and it is in helping others that they find real fulfilment. If Junior can help you in really practical ways self-assurance and efficiency will positively grow.

Best activities to share: drawing; painting; dressing-up and play acting; playing nurse; caring for little pets (hamsters, fish, frogs and tadpoles); and a good deal of storytelling.

Pisces Sun Parent/Scorpio Sun Child

Gentle Pisceans rarely forget the strong images of their own childhood, and sympathetically and sensitively understand the hopes, fears, strengths, and weaknesses of their little charges. Young Scorpio's strong feeling nature will find warmth and security with this caring parent. Though highly sensitive, the concentrated power that emanates from these little Scorpions can be bewildering. Extremes of action seem to be the rule: overwork or laziness; saint or sinner; black or white, but never grey. A great deal of help from the Piscean imagination will go a long way in putting up more worthwhile challenges for this youngster to defeat. Though seeming quite confident and self-possessed from an early age, the little Scorpio is quite prepared to hide any deep hurts and emotional insecurities with hardly a clue given. Pisces' almost psychic awareness will sense these and give constant caring support. This will go a long way towards helping but will never stop this youngster from needing to experience and internalize the extremes of emotion. Little Scorpios need to live life intensely and to the full, and this will include the worst temptations you can imagine, so some pretty good guidelines will have to be drawn. You set the challenge and Junior will live up to it.

Best activities to share: detective games like Cluedo; puzzles and mind games (chess, Mastermind); telescope and microscope (both ends of the scale for Scorpio).

SAGITTARIUS / SAGITTARIUS

Sagittarius
Tolerant
Honest
Interested
Must understand
Outgoing
Seeks to know
Likes adventure
Philosophic

Sagittarius Sun Parent/Sagittarius Sun Child

Both parent and child are intuitive, creative, exuberant and continuously on the move. As long as they are both travelling in the same direction this relationship has all the potential for a long-lasting, fun-loving, energetic friendship. There'll be no subterfuge, humbug or even 'white lies' with these two; little Sagittarius will get all the answers straight from the shoulder and be expected to respond likewise. The search for truth dominates both big and little Sagittarius, and Junior's life quest for more and more knowledge will be well supported here.

Developing early self-confidence, the little Archer soon gets itchy feet for the outside world. Quickly taking to kindergarten, school and visits anywhere, this little wanderer has no need to cling to the confines of home. The love of the great outdoors and adventure will see parent and child energetically sharing much physical activity (horses and large dogs are often invited to join in). Though ideal company for each other Junior may never discover, in this straight honest relationship, that other people do not behave in the same open manner. This vital piece of information will take some learning as the Sagittarian art of wielding truth like a blunt instrument is compulsive. A trail of crushed egos does not make friends and influence people.

Best activities to share: anything outdoors and risky or adventurous; sports – playing and watching them; a large pet (horse, if possible); long philosophical discussions (usually whilst out walking).

SAGITTARIUS / CAPRICORN

Sagittarius	Capricorn
Tolerant	Cautious
Honest	Persistent
Interested	Ambitious
Must understand	Must improve
Outgoing	Dutiful
Seeks to know	Seeks achievement
Likes adventure	Likes authority
Philosophic	Responsible

Sagittarius Sun Parent/Capricorn Sun Child

The sheer exuberant energy generated by the Sagittarian parent will be accepted but rarely emulated by the cautious

Capricorn child. Little Goats, with their love and respect for authority, respond to this parental honesty and openness and learn much, but they continue to hold back their own feelings and ideas until really sure of them. This relationship has the potential for an unusual reversal of roles, with Junior seeming to take life more seriously than this enthusiastic parent. 'Old head on young shoulders' rings true for the little Goats. Junior's precocious self-discipline and conscientiousness relieves Sagittarius from 'heavy parent' duties but will demand in return a strict adherence to good routine. Take away familiar order and system and little Capricorn gets edgy. The Sagittarian parent's fund of knowledge and great sense of fun will do much to loosen up the over-serious nature of this youngster. Although Capricorn, always ambitious, needs little encouragement to 'get on', small, tangible rewards are more appreciated than a wealth of praise. Their own expression of love is more likely to manifest in the same practical way, showing in helpfulness rather than big demonstrations of affection.

Best activities to share: making and mending things; helping in the house, garage and garden; outdoor fun but nothing risky; visits to historical places (Capricorn loves the traditional, and Sagittarius loves going anywhere).

Capricorn Sun Parent/Sagittarius Sun Child

The Capricorn parent is a realist, and a strong authority figure, conscientiously attending to the material needs of the family. In fact, the traditional firm but fair parent. Little Sagittarians are extrovert, fun-loving, expenders of unlimited energy in every direction at once. The traditional child. The Capricorn love of good manners and behaviour may suffer a few setbacks when faced with little Sagittarius's outspoken openness. These youngsters are great seekers of truth, and saying exactly what they feel when they feel it is second nature to them. They can take, without offence, exactly the same treatment from others so why should people get so upset about it?. You'll have to explain, patiently, and with exceptional reasoning, that other people are less secure, and home truths can be hurtful, a concept that may take a wealth of blunders to learn. However, it bodes well for a good relationship that this child puts all his cards on the table. Though little will be necessary in order to support this small Archer's natural self-confidence, Capricorn can go a long way in teaching the more practical essentials that take the risk out of Junior's enthusiastic exploits. Young Sagittarius loves freedom, so allow just a few well chosen open doors out of all that Capricorn system, and you'll both stay friends.

Best activities to share: anything to do with the great outdoors; active sports with plenty of chance to run around; pony riding; a big dog will be much loved; long discussions of their broad views.

SAGITTARIUS / AQUARIUS

Sagittarius	Aquarius
Tolerant	Unpredictable
Honest	Spontaneous
Interested	Humanitarian
Must understand	Must be different
Outgoing	Changing
Seeks to know	Seeks causes
Likes adventure	Likes the unusual
Philosophic	Rebellious

Sagittarius Sun Parent/Aquarius Sun Child

This is a meeting of the Zodiac's two freedom-lovers. Sagittarians: warm, adventurous, energetic, always looking for new paths to tread, and Aquarians questioning every rule and regulation in the book in order to establish their own individual and uniquely original ideas. Different manifestations of basically the same idea – the search for knowledge and truth. The tolerant Sagittarian will put few limitations on Junior's actions however unusual or nonconformist they are, but will give the right kind of straight-talking information that little Aquarius respects. This parent's logic, good sense, and open-mindedness will give little cause for young Aquarius to go to anarchistic extremes in the home. However, Junior's drive to knock against something will be hard to conquer and if it can manifest as shared work for good causes, well and good. The clashes, if any, will be shortlived as these two rarely hold grudges, but knife-edged Sagittarian 'home truths' will be well met with Aquarian shock tactics in short sharp encounters. You make better friends than enemies.

Best activities to share: plenty of visiting and visitors, joining Junior clubs and organizations; broken gadgets from which to make new super-inventions.

Aquarius Sun Parent/Sagittarius Sun Child

The free-thinking Aquarian parent is bound to have a few theories on childcare. They won't be traditional and there's a fair chance they'll be flexible. Little Sagittarius, as long as there's plenty of room for movement, will fit in with the wildest avant-garde methods. Fun-loving freedom-seeking little Archers will explore happily any new territory with this original inventive parent. Aquarius will love and respect Junior's honest enthusiasm, encouraging the adventurous spirit and sharpening up the youngster's understanding with argument and debates. Good lengthy conversations are the keynote to closeness in this good relationship, though they may have to take place on the move; talking while walking is a Sagittarian favourite. Aquarians enjoy ideas for their own sake whilst Sagittarians see ideas as leading to action, and this may cause a few setbacks if promises don't get fulfilled. With this little one trust and respect allows no room for double-dealing, and no amount of further promises can make up for that. Small Sagittarians will always tell the truth as they see it even if it's to their disadvantage and this parent has the same high ideals. A close friendly relationship with few clashes.

Best activities to share: outdoor games and sports; travel anywhere (where you go Junior goes happily); adventure stories and films; bikes, skateboards and go-carts (to keep on the move).

SAGITTARIUS / PISCES

Sagittarius	Pisces
Tolerant	Sympathetic
Honest	Helpful
Interested	Selfless
Must understand	Must give
Outgoing	Imaginative
Seeks to know	Seeks ideals
Likes adventure	Likes fantasy
Philosophic	Poetic

Sagittarius Sun Parent/Pisces Sun Child

The warm, active extrovert Sagittarian parent can be a perfect balance to the warm, loving, introvert little Piscean. This combination of outward-looking and inward-looking individuals have much to teach each other. They share a love of peace and truth, and although their expressions of these ideals may differ they provide this couple's closest link. Little Pisceans have exceptional imaginative and intuitive talents that often make it difficult to define the borderline between make-believe and reality. Sagittarius's philosophical nature and long-term vision will see the potential and encourage the physical expression of the small Fish's ideas. The 'if you feel it say it' attitude will go an enormous way towards developing self-confidence and above all a supremely trusting relationship.

191

This impressionable and undemanding child will adapt easily to any role the parent suggests in a desire to please. With insensitive handling Junior's great talent for selfless devotion to others can be wasted in living up to a phoney character instead of sharing that imagination and sensitivity with the world at large. We need artists.

Best activities to share: all artistic pursuits; dressing up; play acting; talks about far distant lands and ideas: storyreading and telling; and fun Sagittarian romps.

Pisces Sun Parent/Sagittarius Sun Child

Piscean parents are gentle, loving, and sensitive to the needs of their children. Rarely strong on authority or sticklers for rigid routine they handle things imaginatively according to the feel of the moment. This will suit little Sagittarius down to the ground. Adventurous, energetic, fun-loving and above all demanding freedom to range far and wide Junior will find flexibility and masses of stimulation in the fantasy mind of this parent. Both express themselves through feelings, but little Sagittarius's may be more blunt than this sensitive Piscean's. Honest as the day is long Junior's road to understanding is questions, questions: 'Why is that lady so fat? Does she eat too much? Is she having a baby? How do you make babies? Why?' No poetic waffling; this one wants a straight answer. The patience of the long-suffering Piscean may be stretched to the limits by the business of trying to soften the impact of such a child's sharp and sometimes unknowingly hurtful arrows. But frank openness and sheer warmth of character more than compensates for the public blunders that may have to be endured. Junior's love of adventure and sometimes oblivious attitude towards risk may cause the Piscean protectiveness to overwork, but keep it subtle for any hint of 'reins' will send Junior to further extremes, defeating the purpose.

Best activities to share: storytelling (far-distant places and adventures); lots of shared outdoor fun; visits to safari parks (neither approve of zoos with all those cages); pets to care for (the bigger the better for young Sagittarius – big dogs, and at least a try at riding a pony).

CAPRICORN / CAPRICORN

Capricorn
Cautious
Persistent
Ambitious
Must improve
Dutiful
Seeks achievement
Likes authority
Responsible

Capricorn Sun Parent/Capricorn Sun Child

The Capricorn child will find great support and understanding in the Capricorn parent. These youngsters take life very seriously in the early years, often not letting up on rigid self-discipline until reaching maturity. With this relationship we may find almost a reversal of roles, with the parent youthful and relaxed and the child dutiful and conscientious. The need to, and indeed the love of patiently applying themselves to the business of learning, will be understood by this parent, and although encouraged, never allowed to become obsessive. The little Capricornian's confidence thrives on order and system, so it will help in relating to other children if you add a little tomfoolery to the schedule. Keep it regular and it'll be more acceptable, for cautious little Goats will find it hard to take unpredictable and unprecedented 'madness' from mum or dad. Well-mannered and respectful of authority, these children rarely show their strong ambition in 'pushy' or more aggressive ways. Quietly confident, they pick the right time and the right place to shine. There'll be few clashes, but with all that comfortable obedience, parent Goat may overlook the lighter side of this youngster, producing a perfect prig instead of a precious paragon.

Best activities to share: games concerned with money and time (two Capricorn favourites!) such as Monopoly, chess etc.; making useful objects; keeping a diary; patience games (jigsaws, crosswords) and visits to historical places.

CAPRICORN / AQUARIUS

Capricorn	Aquarius
Cautious	Unpredictable
Persistent	Spontaneous
Ambitious	Humanitarian
Must improve	Must be different
Dutiful	Changing
Seeks achievement	Seeks causes
Likes authority	Likes the unusual
Responsible	Rebellious

Capricorn Sun Parent/Aquarius Sun Child

It might well be said that Capricorn's motto is 'discipline' whilst that of the Aquarian child is 'freedom'. This doesn't mean that all young Aquarians are anarchists, but accepting rules and regulations without question just doesn't figure in their way of doing things. Aquarius is the nonconformist of the Zodiac, and children born under this sign feel a strong urge to revolt against existing structures, and bring in new ideas. However, give them a good logical reason for doing something and it will find easy acceptance. It's often difficult for a parent to come to terms with a child on a totally different wavelength, but if Capricorn can tune in to young Aquarius the possibilities are unlimited. Aquarian children often have inventive, original, scientific minds and will be responsive to encouragement and assistance from Capricorn senior – the supreme realist – in putting their novel ideas into practice. Though little Aquarians need to knock against authority it is the balance between reasonable rules and reasonable freedom that will keep this relationship challenging, friendly and productive.

Best activities to share: visits to museums, exhibitions, to the Royal Society's children's lectures; electronic games, electrical construction kits, chemistry sets; boxes of odds and ends for 'inventions'; science fiction books and films.

Aquarius Sun Parent/Capricorn Sun Child

Aquarians may well qualify as the most easy-going parents around. They like to give their children free-rein and encourage their independence and ability to think for themselves. As a rule they're pretty unshockable, though they may very well be surprised that little Capricorn doesn't rush off to take advantage of all that liberty with much enthusiasm. Small Goats actually thrive on a bit of discipline, and can feel utterly lost if their parents don't provide a few firm guidelines. All's well if the Aquarian parent understands that this youngster prefers the well-beaten track, only exploring new ground with the utmost caution. However, the freethinking Aquarian parent can do much to widen the horizons of the sometimes 'blinkered' little Capricorn. Aquarius is in fact fundamentally concerned with the future, whereas Capricorn clings faithfully to tradition. A meeting of old and new can be enlightening to both parent and child. The stimulating Aquarian household is likely to have much coming and going of interesting and unusual visitors, giving the sometimes shy little Capricornian ample opportunity to gain confidence in dealing with others socially. There are bound to be clashes with such a contrasting couple but the little Goat's respect for authority will make this child less severe, especially if just occasionally the Water Carrier can slip into a 'traditional' role.

Best activities to share: patience games, jigsaws etc.; history visits (castles, museums, etc.); exhibitions of modern and space-age technology; and useful jobs around the house.

'Big boys don't take silly old Teddies to school'

CAPRICORN / PISCES

Capricorn	Pisces
Cautious	Sympathetic
Persistent	Helpful
Ambitious	Selfless
Must improve	Must give
Dutiful	Imaginative
Seeks achievement	Seeks ideals
Likes authority	Likes fantasy
Responsible	Poetic

Capricorn Sun Parent /Pisces Sun Child

The main requirement of a Capricorn parent is that a child should be well-mannered, obedient and dutiful, and should generally prove to be a credit to the family. Unlike many other signs, the Piscean child complies almost too readily with this parent's demands. Little Pisceans are pliable – they lend themselves readily to suggestions, and will attempt to fit the mould their guardians have prepared for them. Though comfortable for the parent this may be less helpful to the child whose impressionable young personality can easily be swamped by an upbringing that is too rigid, too defined. Although Pisces children will often go to the limits to live up to their parent's expectations, basically little Fishes resent restriction. They are gifted with a glorious imagination which needs plenty of freedom of expression to achieve real, practical results. The practical nature of Capricorn, if sensitive to young Pisces' abilities, can be invaluable in helping to bring intangible ideas into reality. Encouragement to express their own intuitions and feelings in storytelling, creative projects, and views on everyday things will contribute greatly to the development of Piscean self-confidence. Too much emphasis on the no-nonsense mundane world will get compliance but will lose Junior's real talent in self-indulgent daydreams.

Best activities to share: learning to play a musical instrument; drawing and painting; storytelling (you listen to Junior's); caring for pets.

Pisces Sun Parent/Capricorn Sun Child

The Pisces parent, to whom the world of the imagination is a very real thing, may be gently brought down to earth by the practical nature of the Capricorn child. Tales of pixies and fairies with 'happy ever after' endings so beloved by Pisces in their own childhood may be resisted by the supremely 'sensible' little Goat in favour of Tommy the Tractor and Billy the Bulldozer. To Capricorn the world of reality is what it's all about. For imaginative Pisces, coming to terms with this youngster will be no chore. The job is to commend the common sense and expand the breadth of vision at the same time. Capricorn children are distinguished by their serious approach, and outstanding self-discipline. The phrase 'an old head on young shoulders' was coined about a little Goat. However, those talents aside, Junior may need more than a little help with the fun aspects of living. Piscean whimsy can go a long way in achieving a balance for this youngster, though spontaneity may have to give way to a regular fun routine. Tom-foolery from four to four-thirty each day could make more sense to this Capricorn super-organizer. Clashes will be minimal as long as good guidelines are maintained, and if allowed full expression this little one's need to be helpful around the house will make for close and busy companionship.

Best activities to share: playing 'grown up' – nurse, teacher, etc.; artistic projects with tangible end products (useful things made out of egg-boxes, detergent bottles etc.); jobs to help mum and dad; a little 'loosening up' fun.

AQUARIUS / AQUARIUS

Aquarius
Unpredictable
Spontaneous
Humanitarian
Must be different
Changing
Seeks causes
Likes the unusual
Rebellious

Aquarius Sun Parent/Aquarius Sun Child

When parent and child are born under the same sun sign they usually enjoy a natural empathy, and questions of conflict do not normally arise. It can, however, produce extremes of their particular qualities without a little deliberate counterbalancing. As Aquarians are, anyhow, nonconformists often taking things to the limits, this can present a problem. Mutual independence, freedom and tolerance will be demanded and granted in this relationship. Aquarian parents will let their children have their head from an early age and in return will expect to lead a life of their own, free of the excessive demands of an overdependent child. That's fine, but though Junior will knock against authority it's nevertheless important for this little one to have some firm structure or guidelines to avoid becoming a rebel without a cause. Through healthy challenge and argument the little Aquarian forms his or her own unique ideas and sense of justice. Setting up a strict but reasonable routine, though out of character for the Aquarian parent, will develop more effectively Junior's independence and self-confidence.

Best activities to share: science fiction games, books and films; joining clubs and groups; a share of dad's workshop for building incredible inventions; space-age games (electronic wizardry).

AQUARIUS / PISCES

Aquarius	Pisces
Unpredictable	Sympathetic
Spontaneous	Helpful
Humanitarian	Selfless
Must be different	Must give
Changing	Imaginative
Seeks causes	Seeks ideals
Likes the unusual	Likes fantasy
Rebellious	Poetic

Aquarius Sun Parent/Pisces Sun Child

Aquarian parents are often universal aunts or uncles; never displaying favouritism, their affection is distributed equally between all children in their care. This includes nephews, nieces, friend's offspring, waifs and strays alike. In their eyes every living creature deserves an equal share of love. Little Piscean, however, needs a slightly more equal share than most. Super-sensitive, highly imaginative, small Fishes give everything when they love someone and so require an extra large measure of affection in return. Both parent and child are idealists but the expression of this differs. Aquarians take a logical reasoned approach, with Pisces the intuitive visionary takes over. Caring for others can be a shared meeting point. This parent's love of the new, unusual and the unexpected will relate well to the unlimited imagination of the little Piscean. Encouragement to express ideas inventively in music, dance, writing, and painting may uncover a wealth of talent, and will certainly develop independence and self-assurance. The Piscean vision is better shared than thrown inwards, better another poet for the world than a drop-out dreamer.

Best activities to share: caring for pets and people; joining good causes (Junior RSPCA, Friends of the Earth, etc.); painting, drawing and story writing.

Pisces Sun Parent/Aquarius Sun Child

Whereas devoted Piscean parents would go to any lengths to keep their children happy (even overdoing it occasionally with a spot of smother love), Aquarian children just don't like being wrapped in a cosy cocoon and feel the urge to make their own way in the world from a surprisingly early age. Little Aquarians do not need the same amount of protection as the more vulnerable sun signs, and if not granted freedom will demand it as their right. The Piscean's natural anxiety may have to be somewhat compromised. These free-ranging youngsters respond better to logic and reasoning, than to pleading; present them with a reasonable argument in favour of something and they'll usually comply. However, do expect little Aquarius to be sometimes outrageously nonconformist, for in this way these little innovators develop their talent for bringing in the new.

Although cooler in their affections than emotional Pisces could ever be, they delight in the company of as many friends and playmates as possible. The way to keep these children happy is to throw open the doors to all and sundry. Little Aquarians are totally unprejudiced and get on with grown ups as easily as with children. Pisces' delightful sense of fantasy will forge close links with this little one's love of the bizarre and expand the imaginative faculties. Few clashes for this relationship, but give Junior a few things to knock against – rebels without a cause get very insecure.

Best activities to share: science fiction and plenty of space-age toys; boxes of junk for 'inventions'; chemistry sets and electronic games; and start saving for a mini-computer.

PISCES / PISCES

Pisces
Sympathetic
Helpful
Selfless
Must give
Imaginative
Seeks ideals
Likes fantasy
Poetic

Pisces Sun Parent/Pisces Sun Child

This is one of the most mutually loving parent/child relationships, the Piscean need to care for others is often taken to the point of self-sacrifice. Pisces senior will understand the dreamy nature of highly imaginative little Pisces, sharing and developing the creative potential that is so strong in this sign. With such an inventive mind Junior can live more easily in the rosy world of make-believe when the reality of living gets tough. Plenty of encouragement to express these thoughts through easy conversations, storytelling, and imaginative games will result in exceptional self-expressive abilities. Though often thought to be impractical, little Pisceans, like the parents, give of their best and show great efficiency when helping others. Through being allowed to assist mum and dad as often as possible, confidence in handling the 'nuts and bolts' side of life will grow. The biggest snag in this otherwise perfect relationship is not in clashes or argument, but in excessive 'giving in', each wishing to please the other. Taken to extremes this natural Piscean quality can leave Junior with no real awareness of self or identity. The Piscean dreams are better out than in, as the world can't afford to lose another creative idealist or artist.

Best activities to share: storytelling and writing; acting and dressing-up; music playing and listening; painting; small pets to care for.

MOON SIGN RELATIONSHIPS

MOON COMBINATIONS

ARIES / ARIES

	Aries
expresses feelings	Immediately
needs	Challenges
threatened by	Uniformity
values	Directness

Aries Moon Parent/Aries Moon Child

At least these two fiery types will know exactly where they stand with each other. Aries Moons express their emotions immediately and put their cards on the table with charming honesty. 'Good or bad, take me as you find me', they say to each other – 'let's have a quick hug or reprimand, and no sulking afterwards'. They may not feel the same thing at the same time, but life's too short to worry anyway – and really can be a lot of fun for these two. As long as Aries Moon parents realize that when they say 'my feelings first' so do their little ones.

ARIES / TAURUS

expresses feelings	Immediately	Slowly
needs	Challenges	Stability
threatened by	Uniformity	Changes
values	Directness	Tangibility

Aries Moon Parent/Taurus Moon Child

Spontaneous Aries Lunar parents must wait for their Taurus Moon child to show his or her feelings. Taureans are not slow, they just need to feel sure, which takes time. One thing Aries parents can rely on is that their Lunar Bulls are loyal – they don't back down once they have placed their affections.

Loving Taurus Moon parents can give their Aries Moon children a solid emotional background. Young Lunar Rams can rush into friendships without a second thought, reaping all the joys and sorrows along the way. Cautious mums and dads can provide security for their fiery-hearted little ones to come home to after a day in the fray.

ARIES / GEMINI

expresses feelings	Immediately	Excitably
needs	Challenges	Novelty
threatened by	Uniformity	Regulation
values	Directness	Everything

Aries Moon Parent/Gemini Moon Child

Aries Moon mums and dads have the happy knack of firing their little Gemini Moons off into new emotional pathways. Although they have a large number of friends, little Lunar Twins think about everyone's feelings all the time – Lunar Rams can be forgiven for not remembering their names. Gemini Moons don't mind – they don't dwell on details – life's too full and exciting.

Gemini Moon Parent/Aries Moon Child

Light, airy Gemini Moon parents provide a stimulating emotional climate in which young Lunar Arietians flourish. Being Peter Pans themselves, Lunar Twins understand the 'now' feelings of their Lunar Rams. Similarly, as Moon Geminis are surrounded by lots of friends themselves, they always have room for a couple of dozen more and will love their little Ram's friends as if they were their own.

expresses feelings	Immediately	Sentimentally
needs	Challenges	Cherishing
threatened by	Uniformity	Withdrawal
values	Directness	Familarity

Aries Moon Parents/Cancer Moon Child

Cancer Moon children care about everyone, and everything they do and say is based on how they feel. Aries Moon parents approach life from a different angle and may have to stand still to consider how their children function. This can open up endless possibilities for both – Aries Moon parents will realize that other people feel things too, and Cancer Moon children will begin to appreciate that sticking to the familiar can sometimes be boring.

Cancer Moon Parent/Aries Moon Child

Young Aries Moons are turned on by the new – their Cancer Moon parents are turned on by the familiar. Lunar Rams need to find new friends and experiences 'to boldly feel what no one has felt before' – understanding Lunar Crabs know all about tears of rage and joy, and will happily nurture their little Rams' feelings to revitalize them for the next great onslaught.

ARIES / LEO

expresses feelings	Immediately	Generously
needs	Challenges	Appreciation
threatened by	Uniformity	Indifference
values	Directness	Respect

Leo Moon children respond to their Aries Moon parents' spontaneity with Lion-sized portions of love and warmth. These two signs are Fire signs, meaning that both parent and child have tremendous energy to express their feelings; no matter what they feel, much force and power will be put into their responses. Lunar Aries mums and dads must treat their Lion like a King occasionally, or the Fire could get out of hand.

Leo Moon Parent/Aries Moon Child

Leo Moon parents are full of self-confidence about their feelings – of course what they feel is right, how could it be otherwise, they ask. But little Rams feel that they are right too, and never being able to put down a challenge, may react with full emotional fire. Leo mums and dads have so much pride in their Lunar Rams that they can defuse them with affectionate humour.

ARIES / VIRGO

expresses feelings	Immediately	Selectively
needs	Challenges	To be needed
threatened by	Uniformity	Coarseness
values	Directness	Delicacy

Virgo Moon Parent/Aries Moon Child

Virgo parents show their feelings with careful consideration and may wish their little Lunar Ram to do the same. However, Arietians announce their feelings loudly for all to hear, expecting an immediate response. Take me or leave me, is their motto – it never occurs to them that others don't feel the same.

Moon in Virgo children are not as ready to make the spontaneous gestures that Aries Moon parents are. These children make certain that the recipients of their emotions are worthy first, which takes careful selection. They may even select which emotions to show, for as in everything else, Virgos like to be efficient.

ARIES / LIBRA

expresses feelings	Immediately	Pleasantly
needs	Challenges	Unity
threatened by	Uniformity	Discrimination
values	Directness	Peace

Aries Moon Parent/Libra Moon Child

Warm-hearted Aries Moon parents express their feelings with great fervour whatever those feelings are. Compromising Lunar Librans may go into great emotional contortions to be in harmony with their parents, with the result that these young Lunar Balancers may not express themselves fully for fear of rocking the boat. However, when they do express themselves it is with great consideration towards others.

Libra Moon Parent/Aries Moon Child

Libra Moon parents try to keep everyone happy – and can deal calmly with young Lunar Rams who show all their emotions energetically no matter what. They may be totally unaware of the effect they are having on everyone else, and could thank their lucky stars that they have a Lunar Libran parent around to show them diplomacy and tact. In turn, they demonstrate that sometimes to express what they feel NOW can work out to be a virtue, as no one is ever left in any doubt.

ARIES / SCORPIO

expresses feelings	Immediately	Profoundly
needs	Challenges	To feel
threatened by	Uniformity	Discovery
values	Directness	Privacy

Aries Moon Parent/Scorpio Moon Child

Lunar Aries parents react spontaneously, and flare-ups are soon over and forgotten. Not so with young Lunar Scorpions – no emotional situation is ever forgotten: motives are turned over and examined from every angle for a long time. Lunar Aries parents may be risking all-out war if they approach their Moon Scorpio children too directly, but by doing so might also encourage them to learn to cope with their feelings.

Scorpio Moon Parent/Aries Moon Child

The feelings of Moon in Scorpio parents run deep and are extremely powerful. They are sensitive to the weaknesses of others and so can easily help their little Lunar Rams to handle their own insecurities in times of stress. The strength of these parents provides an absolute rock for their Aries Moon children to emulate and challenge.

expresses feelings	Immediately	Openly
needs	Challenges	Warmth
threatened by	Uniformity	Ties
values	Directness	Freedom

Aries Moon Parent/Sagittarius Moon Child

For Sagittarius Moon children the world is a warm, loving place and they respond in a like manner. Aries Moon parents are ready to fire their little Lunar Archers off saying loving words when the mood takes them. When the mood doesn't take them little Lunar Sagittarians are unruffled and hold no grudges at all. A fun relationship all round.

Sagittarius Moon Parent/Aries Moon Child

Sagittarius Moon parents are as spontaneous as their Aries Moon children – no moods, no brooding – everything is in the open, dealt with, and over. Little Lunar Rams always know that they can bring their friends home at the drop of a hat.

ARIES / CAPRICORN

expresses feelings	Immediately	Sensibly
needs	Challenges	Order
threatened by	Uniformity	Over-enthusiasm
values	Directness	Standards

Spontaneous little Lunar Rams flood with tears of anger or happiness whenever the mood strikes, regardless of where they

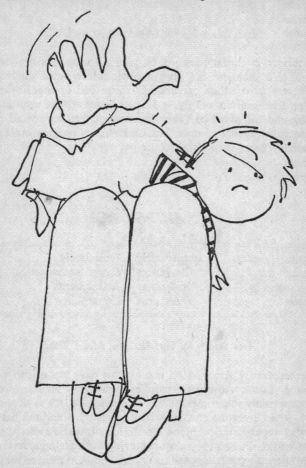

'I don't know where you pick up that bloody language you rude little bastard!'

are and who they are with. Capricorn Moon parents may wish that their Aries Moon children would control themselves – but they might take a leaf out of these children's books. Better to show feelings than bottle them up.

Aries Moon Parent/Capricorn Moon Child

Propriety is the watchword of young Lunar Capricorns – emotional manners are always observed by such children. Whereas Aries Moon parents may voice their opinions openly anywhere – often noisily – Lunar Goats dislike emotional show and will avoid it. Taken to extremes they may avoid any kind of emotional contact, but Lunar Aries parents can help them by being direct and to the point.

ARIES / AQUARIUS

expresses feelings	Immediately	Objectively
needs	Challenges	Experimentation
threatened by	Uniformity	Attachments
values	Directness	Impartiality

Aries Moon Parent/Aquarius Moon Child

Demonstrative Aries Moon parents can have lots of fun with young Lunar Aquarians who express their feelings quite unexpectedly sometimes. When everyone else laughs they can cry, when everyone else cries, they can laugh – and not bat an eyelid about what everyone else thinks. Lunar Aries are unabashed too, when it comes to showing their feelings, so these two share a basic fellow feeling, which will help them to understand each other.

Lunar Aries' motto is 'if you feel it, show it' – Lunar Aquarius' motto is 'if you feel it, discuss it' (preferably with lots of other people). Aquarius Moon parents are nearly unshockable – good at shocking others, though – and they will encourage their spontaneous Lunar Rams to let it all hang out. Lunar Aquarians are great theorists when it comes to emotional behaviour, and will love to put their theories into practice at home.

ARIES / PISCES

expresses feelings	Immediately	Poetically
needs	Challenges	Devotion
threatened by	Uniformity	Criticism
values	Directness	Love

Aries Moon Parent/Pisces Moon Child

Little Lunar Fishes take everyone's feelings into account and will be hurt if theirs are overlooked by enthusiastic Aries parents. Pisceans, as all water signs, need time to assimilate new emotional experiences, such as moving house, school, etc., and may take a long time to adjust. Aries parents know it's all right to cry if the need arises and won't be impatient with their little Fishes if they burst into tears.

Pisces Moon Parent/Aries Moon Child

Little Rams are even active emotionally – they rush into every friendship, enjoying the ups and downs, winning and losing. Sensitive Pisceans prefer feelings to flow over them like water and will be quite stimulated by this obvious open expression of emotion by their little Arietian Moon child.

TAURUS / TAURUS

expresses feelings	Slowly	
needs	Stability	
threatened by	Changes	
values	Tangibility	

Taurus Moon Parent/Taurus Moon Child

Two earthy emotional people together are able to express their feelings for each other through touch and bodily expressions. Although both parent and child may show their feelings slowly with other people, they know each other well enough to respond quicker and more openly. Possessiveness could turn earth into concrete, however, so parents should watch for signs early on in their children's lives.

TAURUS / GEMINI

expresses feelings	Slowly	Excitably
needs	Stability	Novelty
threatened by	Changes	Regulation
values	Tangibility	Everything

Taurus Moon Parent/Gemini Moon Child

Gemini Moon children have many friends – here today, but never gone tomorrow: socially it's an expanding universe for Lunar Twins. Taurus Moon parents may feel that their children should stick to one friend at a time, but they won't, of course – they operate on the 'more the merrier' level.

Taurus Moon children have a steady best friend, who may come to be regarded as an actual possession – Gemini Moon parents can help their Lunar Bull realize that no one belongs to anyone else, and that sharing a friend with a third person can bring in a lot more fun.

TAURUS / CANCER

expresses feelings	Slowly	Sentimentally
needs	Stability	Cherishing
threatened by	Changes	Withdrawal
values	Tangibility	Familiarity

Taurus Moon Parent/Cancer Moon Child

Taurus Moon parents can give their little Lunar Crabs lots of rock solid emotional backing. Cancer Moon children love to be cared for and Taurus Moon parents do this willingly – always happily supplying little treats and physical affection. Cancer Moon temperaments fluctuate, turning children crabby and ready to nip the first person who comes near. Stubborn Lunar Bulls may withhold affection until the phase passes.

Cancer Moon Parent/Taurus Moon Child

Lunar Taurean children can be persistent if they feel they need something – so can their Cancer Moon parents, only with them it's called tenacity. The result being that both may hold on to their emotional position with neither giving way. This won't happen often because Lunar Crabs are natural parents from the age of 0 – and know instinctively what is right for their children. Warm, sensual Lunar Bulls respond with physical affection and all is well again.

TAURUS / LEO

expresses feelings	Slowly	Generously
needs	Stability	Appreciation
threatened by	Changes	Indifference
values	Tangibility	Respect

Taurus Moon Parent/Leo Moon Child

Leo Moon children give as much as they take and that's a lot – 'the Lion's share' applies to feelings as well as anything else. Taurus Moon parents have warm hearts and can fan the flames of their Lunar Lion's emotions, while Bull-like steadiness can help balance an overbearing Moon Leo when his pride is hurt.

Leo Moon Parent/Taurus Moon Child

Both Leo and Taurus are fixed signs so feelings between parent and child will be stable. Leo Moon parents can give out huge shares of loving affection to these beauty-loving little ones. The Lion's roar can only be heard when the little Bull retreats into stubborn silence – a sweet Taurean smile can soon have the parent Lion purring again.

expresses feelings	Slowly	Selectively
needs	Stability	To be needed
threatened by	Changes	Coarseness
values	Tangibility	Delicacy

Taurus Moon Parent/Virgo Moon Child

Taurus Moon parents can be depended upon – being responsive and steady emotionally. Not given to making sudden changes they can give their Virgo Moon children security to build on. As both these signs are Earth signs, these two like to see tangible expressions of feelings, i.e. physical affection, a gift or a task shared.

'Thousands of children are starving in the world today and you won't eat up your crispy cod fries!'

Virgo Moon parents are quite mutable in their attitudes and can change quite readily. Lunar Taureans, however, can sustain a feeling – be it love or hate – for a long time. If young Lunar Bulls feel insecure they may run riot over the rest of the family – Virgo Moons can more easily handle Taurean tantrums with close affection, rather than sharp criticism.

TAURUS / LIBRA

expresses feelings	Slowly	Pleasantly
needs	Stability	Unity
threatened by	Changes	Discrimination
values	Tangibility	Peace

Taurus Moon Parent/Libra Moon Child

These two signs are ruled by Venus, the planet of harmony, beauty and love. Both parent and child thus have a fair share of Venusian influence in their emotional make-up, and are warm, needing others around them. Libra children need close friends and share their emotions readily. Taurean Moon parents will need to keep a rein on natural possesiveness with this sociable child.

Libra Moon Parent/Taurus Moon Child

Libra Moon parents have a gift for pleasing others and will be only too happy to lavish affection on their little Lunar Taureans – such children answer this affection with open arms. Prone towards possessiveness, young Lunar Bulls may take it hard having to share Mum and Dad if a new baby comes along –

diplomatic Lunar Balancers can ensure that no one is left out, and everyone gets their fair share.

TAURUS / SCORPIO

expresses feelings	Slowly	Profoundly
needs	Stability	To feel
threatened by	Changes	Discovery
values	Tangibility	Privacy

Taurus Moon Parent/Scorpio Moon Child

Taurus Moon parents show their feelings physically once they are sure how they feel. Touch is very important to them and is useful in bringing out the hidden feelings of their young Lunar Scorpions. However much Scorpio Moons like to keep *their* emotions secret, they always enjoy being shown affection by others – especially when done with such Taurean warmth and tenderness.

Scorpio Moon Parent/Taurus Moon Child

Scorpio Moon parents will be charmed by the obvious pleasure that their young Taurus Moons derive from expressing their feelings physically – by hugs and hand holding. Taurus Moon children love the real world and know very little about the hidden undercurrents so loved by their Lunar Scorpio parents. These two can open up new realms for each other and learn to use a whole range of emotional expression – a good thing for these two fixed signs.

TAURUS / SAGITTARIUS

expresses feelings	Slowly	Openly
needs	Stability	Warmth
threatened by	Changes	Ties
values	Tangibility	Freedom

Taurus Moon Parent/Sagittarius Moon Child

Taurus Moon parents love to spoil their Moon Sagittarius children and Lunar Archer's social circle will be well fed when they come to tea. These children are quite ready early on in their lives to go stay overnight with their friends – Lunar Taurean parents need to encourage their children in this and learn not to hold on to them too hard.

Sagittarius Moon Parent/Taurus Moon Child

Sagittarius Moon parents welcome all children who come to their home. Lunar Taurus children may respond with 'but they're *my* friends' if Lunar Archer parents get too involved with the newcomers, 'and you're *my* parent'. Sagittarian Moon parents can help their little Lunar Bulls to relax and just enjoy the fun that comes from a lot of people sharing life together.

TAURUS / CAPRICORN

expresses feelings	Slowly	Sensibly
needs	Stability	Order
threatened by	Changes	Over-enthusiasm
values	Tangibility	Standards

Taurus Moon Parent/Capricorn Moon Child

The emotional background which Taurus Moon parents provide is steady, prudent and warm. Young Lunar Capricorns thrive in this environment and neither parent nor child show feelings which shock or disturb. Little Lunar Goats want to improve themselves all the time, which Taurus Moon parents understand, and they give them all the emotional encouragement to do so.

Capricorn Moon Parent/Taurus Moon Child

Sensible Lunar Capricorns provide a good home for their children, but may equate 'having the best' with 'feeling the best'. This can encourage young Lunar Bulls only to have friendships with the 'best' children, rather than the nicest children. Affectionate little Lunar Taureans need down-to-earth emotional expressions from their basically down-to-earth Capricorn parents to bring out the 'best' in themselves.

TAURUS / AQUARIUS

expresses feelings	Slowly	Objectively
needs	Stability	Experimentation
threatened by	Changes	Attachments
values	Tangibility	Impartiality

Taurus Moon Parent/Aquarius Moon Child

Lunar Taurus parents show their feelings conservatively, whereas young Lunar Aquarians love to shock – in fact sometimes they react emotionally in a way designed to do just that. Little Lunar Water Carriers appreciate it if their Taurean

Moon parents talk to them about their feelings rather than reacting in a stubborn way.

Aquarius Moon Parent/Taurus Moon Child

Progressive Aquarian Moon parents shock their little Lunar Bulls without realizing it, for Taurean Moon children can be remarkably strait-laced and not appreciate the unconventional expression of feelings used by their parents. Such children need routine and an ordered life, with hugs and kisses at the *right* time, not the wrong time. Of course, to erratic Aquarian Moon parents there is no such thing as the wrong time and they will open their Taurean Moon child to a more easy-going attitude.

TAURUS / PISCES

expresses feelings	Slowly	Poetically
needs	Stability	Devotion
threatened by	Changes	Criticism
values	Tangibility	Love

Taurus Moon Parent/Pisces Moon Child

Taurus Moon parents can share a great many emotional situations with their little Lunar Fishes. Loving to dream of far-away people and places Moon Pisces children can seem to lose touch with the physical world so easily. But not so Taurean Moon parents – they encourage their dreamy little ones to express their feelings and fantasies in the material world by helping them to paint, write or sing about them.

Pisces Moon parents will dote on their Lunar Taurus children and they both love it! Lunar Fishes readily understand their little Lunar Bull's need to express feelings tangibly, and readily acquire pets for the child to care for. Piscean sensitivity will help the possessive Taurean Moon child to share rather than bottle up their own emotions. It takes a lot to stir calm Taurean feelings, so never take them lightly.

GEMINI / GEMINI

expresses feelings	Excitably
needs	Novelty
threatened by	Regulation
values	Everything

Gemini Moon Parent/Gemini Moon Child

Busy, busy, busy Gemini Moons filter all their feelings through their heads first – their urge is to communicate their emotions. They can actually say exactly what it is they are feeling. Gemini Moon parents realize how necessary and how important it is for their little Lunar Twins to have more than one friend to relate to – the more the merrier in fact. Moon Geminis can accept the best and completely ignore the worst in their friends. Everyone seems 'great' – and everyone is 'great' in response.

expresses feelings	Excitably	Sentimentally
needs	Novelty	Cherishing
threatened by	Regulation	Withdrawal
values	Everything	Familiarity

Gemini Moon Parent/Cancer Moon Child

Gemini Moon parents need to communicate their feelings and they do it verbally – Cancer Moon children on the other hand don't need to talk about theirs. They love the familiarity of the same old faces around them and may go into their shells if their Gemini Moon parents introduce too many new faces too quickly. Gemini Moon parents can open up a whole new exciting world for their Lunar Cancerean children – as long as old Teddy can come along too.

Cancer Moon Parent/Gemini Moon Child

Protective Cancer Moon parents may hold young Lunar Geminis in when it's the last thing they need. These lively, friendly little ones need to experience the world by going out to meet it – and bringing all the people they meet home again. Intuitive Lunar Cancer parents feel instinctively that their Lunar Twins can spread themselves too thinly by keeping more friendships going than is good for them, and will offer a calming home background for them.

GEMINI / LEO

expresses feelings	Excitably	Generously
needs	Novelty	Appreciation
threatened by	Regulation	Indifference
values	Everything	Respect

Gemini Moon Parent/Leo Moon Child

Big-hearted Leo Moon children will dramatize their feelings to the hilt – Gemini Moon parents can quite easily switch their feelings off if there is something more interesting to do. Lunar Lions then roar – acting out the whole melodrama in which they play *all* the parts – until they gain the attention they need. Good-humoured Lunar Gemini parents know the exact moment when it's time for the funny remark designed to make young Leos smile again.

Leo Moon Parent/Gemini Moon Child

Zippy little Gemini Moon children chop and change their feelings, wearing their nervous energy quite thin. Leo is a fixed sign and therefore Moon Leo parents don't change their feelings once they are made up. Demonstrative Lunar Lions can give a great deal of emotional support and help the Lunar Twins recharge their batteries ready for another day.

GEMINI / VIRGO

expresses feelings	Excitably	Selectively
needs	Novelty	To be needed
threatened by	Regulation	Coarseness
values	Everything	Delicacy

Gemini Moon parents may not feel that it is important for anyone to have a routine, but Lunar Virgos emotionally depend on one. They won't want friends around all the time either – they like efficient use of time and may feel that chatting to others all day is not an efficient way of using it. They need to choose relationships carefully and consider how to relate to their friends – whereas Gemini Moons can get on with almost anybody.

Virgo Moon Parent/Gemini Moon Child

Moon Gemini children express their feelings verbally – friends will be plentiful and quickly made. Virgo Moon parents may wish to regulate their little Lunar Twins into some sort of order: at which point both of these Mercury-ruled Moon signs will become critical of each other, resulting in nervous tension in the home. The only people to channel Moon Geminis are themselves, and the only people whom Moon Virgos can regulate are themselves!

GEMINI / LIBRA

expresses feelings	Excitably	Pleasantly
needs	Novelty	Unity
threatened by	Regulation	Discrimination
values	Everything	Peace

Gemini Moon Parent/Libra Moon Child

Libra Moon children have an emotional need to avoid friction – Moon Gemini parents are too airy to let anything bother them for long. Consequently these two could avoid the darker side of their emotions by talking together about their feelings rather than just suffering them.

Libra Moon Parent/Gemini Moon Child

Harmonious Moon Libra parents can prove a calming influence on their dashing Lunar Gemini children. Endlessly curious, Moon Geminis know about everyone's emotional lives and loves and retell it all later. Lunar Balancers can introduce an element of discretion so that their little Moon Geminis don't end up spilling someone else's beans!

GEMINI / SCORPIO

expresses feelings	Excitably	Profoundly
needs	Novelty	To feel
threatened by	Regulation	Discovery
values	Everything	Privacy

Gemini Moon Parent/Scorpio Moon Child

Scorpio Moon children feel all the undercurrents surging around them – they know more about what everyone feels by not listening to the words. Gemini Moon parents need to talk their feelings out and could encourage their Lunar Scorpion to do the same, thus keeping the emotional atmosphere fresh and clear.

Scorpio Moon Parent/Gemini Moon Child

These energetic little Moon Geminis are busy expanding their social universe by collecting more and more friends – Moon

Scorpio parents may rarely let on what they feel about them. Young Lunar Geminis like to talk about their emotional lives and will gain deeper insight when Lunar Scorpio parents do open up and voice their acute impressions.

'Later dear, Daddy's very very busy just now'

GEMINI / SAGITTARIUS

expresses feelings	Excitably	Openly
needs	Novelty	Warmth
threatened by	Regulation	Ties
values	Everything	Freedom

Gemini Moon Parent/Sagittarius Moon Child

Spontaneous Sagittarius Moon Children are warm, open and generous, always seeing the best in everyone – Gemini Moon parents feel an affinity with these little ones and respond chattily to the ready affection they show. Of course, parents and child can be so turned on by the *idea* of feelings that they may miss the down-to-earth contact with the emotional world.

Sagittarius Moon Parent/Gemini Moon Child

The ease with which these two relate emotionally is a joy for them both. Gemini Moon's interest in the emotional lives of friends can be a constant source of discussion and speculation. Lunar Sagittarians recognize the need that their Lunar Twins have for more than one friend at the same time and are quite happy to organize outings for many rather than just one or two children.

GEMINI / CAPRICORN

expresses feelings	Excitably	Sensibly
needs	Novelty	Order
threatened by	Regulation	Over-enthusiasm
values	Everything	Standards

Gemini Moon Parent/Capricorn Moon Child

Little Lunar Goats are emotionally mature and may prefer friends from an older age group. They may only have a few relationships, but these will probably last for years. Gemini Moon parents can introduce a lighthearted attitude to emotional situations, which can help young Capricorns to talk about their feelings.

Little Gemini Moons feel everyone is interesting, regardless of background, race or creed. Emotional moods change as quickly as their interests. Capricorn Moon parents may over-emphasize to their Lunar Geminis that they should be 'sensible' about playground heartbreaks, but letting it all hang out works better for the Twins.

GEMINI / AQUARIUS

expresses feelings	Excitably	Objectively
needs	Novelty	Experimentation
threatened by	Regulation	Attachments
values	Everything	Impartiality

Gemini Moon Parent/Aquarius Moon Child

Gemini Moon parents will transmit their feelings by airing them to little Aquarian Moons. These parents are always ready with a quick quip, designed to convulse their children, thereby avoiding a potentially difficult emotional problem. If their Lunar Water Carriers are puzzled by other people's emotional reactions, then Gemini Moon parents can help out by explaining the situations perfectly with the right words.

Aquarius Moon Parent/Gemini Moon Child

Young Gemini Moons will never feeel stuck in a rut with an Aquarian Moon parent – mum or dad will constantly stimulate their little Lunar Twins with interesting friends and social interactions. They will not be likely to be tied down – Aquarius Moon can so quickly feel bogged down by other people's emotional demands. Little Lunar Geminis are hardly likely to do that – needing a great deal of open air around them too.

GEMINI / PISCES

expresses feelings	Excitably	Poetically
needs	Novelty	Devotion
threatened by	Regulation	Criticism
values	Everything	Love

Gemini Moon Parent/Pisces Moon Child

It's all right for Gemini Moon parents to talk to their little Piscean Moon children about emotions – but Piscean children also need to feel that they are loved, not just hear the words. Gregarious Gemini Moons need not worry that their little Fishes are lonely on their own – their wonderful imaginations can supply all the friendship they need – and a lot more besides.

Pisces Moon Parent/Gemini Moon Child

Gemini Moons like Gemini Suns are socially active – they have lots of friends. Piscean Moon parents may ask themselves if their little Gemineans really feel anything for these friends who seem to be 'here today, gone tomorrow'. Of course they do, it's just that airy little Lunar Twins can switch off their emotional needs quicker than their Fishy parents can.

expresses feelings	Sentimentally	
needs	Cherishing	
threatened by	Withdrawal	
values	Familiarity	

Cancer Moon Parent/Cancer Moon Child

Sentimental Lunar Cancerians give each other emotional care and support – the Moon is in its own sign in Cancer, so the best Lunar qualities are emphasized. Moon Cancer children need to nurture others as a natural course of events – Cancer parents are happy to supply pets, or arrange to have a friend's baby to take care of for the day – giving their young Crabs the opportunity to exercise emotional muscles. If they are not able to do this they may easily become crabby, cranky and will nag their parents, who will respond similarly.

CANCER / LEO

expresses feelings	Sentimentally	Generously
needs	Cherishing	Appreciation
threatened by	Withdrawal	Indifference
values	Familiarity	Respect

Cancer Moon Parent/Leo Moon Child

Caring Cancer Moon parents give their little Lunar Lions all the appreciation they need – they may retract into their shells if Lions roar too loud, but by and large they never ignore them consciously. If little Moon Leos aren't shining as brightly as usual, sympathetic Cancer Moon parents can stroke the clouds away and bring the Sun out again.

Leo Moon Parent/Cancer Moon Child

Leo Moon parents like their children to respect them and to treat them royally – Moon Cancer children do this, preferring the values of yesteryear. Young Lunar Crabs feel instinctively that Lunar Lions' roars are worse than their bites and happily nurture their parents by giving some little token of love, such as a cup of tea or a warm hug.

CANCER / VIRGO

expresses feelings	Sentimentally	Selectively
needs	Cherishing	To be needed
threatened by	Withdrawal	Coarseness
values	Familiarity	Delicacy

Cancer Moon Parent/Virgo Moon Child

Neat little Virgo Moons keep their feelings as tidy as the other aspects of their lives – Lunar Crabs don't care how tidy or untidy feelings are as long as they are *felt*. Sentimental parents can offer open emotional responses – after all, *they* rarely worry what anyone else will do with the response, so it is easily given – thus demonstrating to timid Virgo Moons that open emotions pay off each time.

Virgo Moon Parent/Cancer Moon Child

Dependent Lunar Crabs have a perfect rock to cling to in their Virgo Moon parents – one loves to need, the other loves to be needed. Virgo Moon parents can fuss over their Cancer Moon child who will turn the tables and fuss too, reversing the roles and having a whale of a time. Nothing brings a Virgo Moon out as easily as someone looking to *their* needs for a change.

CANCER / LIBRA

expresses feelings	Sentimentally	Pleasantly
needs	Cherishing	Unity
threatened by	Withdrawal	Discrimination
values	Familiarity	Peace

Cancer Moon Parent/Libra Moon Child

Little Libra Moon children need to keep the peace – never wanting any dark clouds in their lives at all. Cancer Moon parents can fluctuate emotionally and are as comfortable under a dark cloud as under a bright sun – it's all feelings to them. As long as they air their emotional states to their child, the emotional Balancer, then peace can be the order of the day. But let little Libras air their's first or you may never know what these adaptable youngsters really feel.

Libra Moon Parent/Cancer Moon Child

Harmonious Libra Moon parents may feel that what their Cancer Moon children are feeling is more important than their own feelings. Lunar Crabs' emotional responses are uncomplicated because this is the area in which these children are most relaxed. As long as little Lunar Cancers aren't washed over by the waves of conflicting emotions, as they sometimes can be, then Libra Moon parents know exactly where they stand.

expresses feelings	Sentimentally	Profoundly
needs	Cherishing	To feel
threatened by	Withdrawal	Discovery
values	Familiarity	Privacy

Cancer Moon Parent/Scorpio Moon Child

Emotional Cancer and Scorpio Moons relate purely on the nonverbal level – young Lunar Scorpions find out what their parents feel about life simply by their own observation, which is acute. Nothing is missed – so if Cancer Moon parents are feeling down, their little Scorpio Moons are there ready with sympathy and deep understanding. Similarly, Cancer Moons feel rightly that young Lunar Scorpions just need to be left alone when under stress.

Scorpio Moon Parent/Cancer Moon Child

Scorpio Moon parents love nothing more than the latest playground crisis to sort out – and little Cancer Moon children will always be in and out of friendship tussles. The relationship front is where they are happiest and where they experience the greatest satisfaction – as it is for Lunar Scorpions. Moon Scorpions are more ready to effect a change than are Cancers who tend to put up with things for a long time – so perhaps mum or dad can help them to move on more easily.

expresses feelings	Sentimentally	Openly
needs	Cherishing	Warmth
threatened by	Withdrawal	Ties
values	Familiarity	Freedom

Cancer Moon Parent/Sagittarius Moon Child

Lunar Sagittarians are ready to travel from an early age – even if it's only to stay with the kid next door. Lunar Cancer parents may feel homesick for their little ones, but it's lost on Lunar Archers. Their freedom is one thing that these children get emotional about, and Cancer Moons could sensitively construe this as withdrawal, but it isn't – it's just their urge to keep experiencing.

Sagittarius Moon Parent/Cancer Moon Child

When Sagittarian Moon parents get home, it's the little Lunar Cancer child who puts the kettle on. Cancer Moon children love to fuss over their parents and always notice when they are tired. These two signs can be expansive with each allowing the other emotional space to develop his or her own individuality and uniqueness.

CANCER / CAPRICORN

expresses feelings	Sentimentally	Sensibly
needs	Cherishing	Order
threatened by	Withdrawal	Over-enthusiasm
values	Familiarity	Standards

Cancer Moon Parent/Capricorn Moon Child

Cancer Moon parents care a great deal about how much loving affection they put into their home life. Little Lunar Goats, however, care a great deal how they appear to the outside world. 'Will I pass inspection?' they wonder – although who is inspecting they cannot say. Lunar Crab parents can do a lot to open up their Capricorn Moon children's attitudes towards demonstrative affection.

Capricorn Moon Parent/Cancer Moon Child

Capricorn Moon parents like their children to have all the right things, which could mean the emotions come at the bottom of the list – Cancer Moon children want to have affection at the moment they need it, not at some socially acceptable time 'later'. Capricorn Moon parents could find their little Crabs become cranky if they aren't on an emotionally rewarding diet.

CANCER / AQUARIUS

expresses feelings	Sentimentally	Objectively
needs	Cherishing	Experimentation
threatened by	Withdrawal	Attachments
values	Familiarity	Impartiality

Cancer Moon Parent/Aquarius Moon Child

Cancer Moon parents feel sympathy from the bottom of their emotional reserves. Aquarius Moon children also feel for others, but are not brought to the same point of exhaustion as their parents. Ultimately, young Lunar Water Carriers can carry water – emotions – to others without being drained themselves. Both parent and child can help one another to express emotions more effectively.

Aquarius Moon Parent/Cancer Moon Child

Aquarian Moon parents are detached in their emotional expression, filtering it through their heads first. Young Lunar Crabs flow and fluctuate in their expression – feeling the tides all around them – and will appreciate a more objective viewpoint when they become too introspective. Aquarian Moon parents can step in humanely with a coolly reached analysis, thus giving young Cancerians another framework to consider.

CANCER / PISCES

expresses feelings	Sentimentally	Poetically
needs	Cherishing	Devotion
threatened by	Withdrawal	Criticism
values	Familiarity	Love

Pisces Moon Parent/Cancer Moon Child

These two water signs understand each other's feelings very well. Little Cancerian Moons are natural nurturers and may take to 'mothering' their Piscean parents – even nagging them at times. Adoring Piscean Moon mums and dads freely express love for their children, giving them the strong emotional roots that Cancerians need so much.

Cancer Moon Parent/Pisces Moon Child

Cancerian Moon Parents express their feelings to their Piscean children non-verbally – every situation between them is approached on an emotional level. Allowances are made for tears – parent Crabs know instinctively which emotion has moved their child, because they, too, have a similar response.

LEO / LEO

expresses feelings	Generously
needs	Appreciation
threatened by	Indifference
values	Respect

Leo Moon Parent/Leo Moon Child

Two Kings of the Jungle in the house dramatizing every emotional response in the book sounds like fun for both parties – each has a built-in audience in the other. Leos are proud of their loved ones and these two can make each other feel appreciated and admired. They are then happy to bask lazily in each other's sunshine. If these two fiery ones try to pull rank on one another fire crackers will fly – the rest of the household will be distinctly fed up with this melodrama – so it's better to unite than divide.

'OK kids, egg and watercress sandwiches first!'

LEO / VIRGO

expresses feelings	Generously	Selectively
needs	Appreciation	To be needed
threateened by	Indifference	Coarseness
values	Respect	Delicacy

Leo Moon Parent/Virgo Moon Child

Little Virgo Moons are hoping for the perfect friend, while feeling that everyone is perhaps less than perfect. The pride that Leo Moon parents naturally feel for their Lunar Virgos can give a great deal of confidence – helping them to base their relationships on heart rather than on unrealistic hope.

Virgo Moon Parent/Leo Moon Child

Leo Moon children open their hearts to the world and love to bask in the admiration that this brings. Virgo Moon parents who prefer to ration emotions, could show their Lunar Lions how to reserve some of their emotional energy, so that they are not completely drained by it all.

LEO / LIBRA

expresses feelings	Generously	Pleasantly
needs	Appreciation	Unity
threateened by	Indifference	Discrimination
values	Respect	Peace

Leo Moon Parent/Libra Moon Child

With large gestures of kind-heartedness Leo Moon parents welcome the friends of their little Lunar Librans – everyone benefits from Leo Moon warmth. Young Lunar Balancers may find that they are as popular for their parents as for themselves. In fact, Leo Moon parents themselves have a great deal to be proud of in their beauty-loving little ones with their ability to find such beautiful friends.

Libra Moon Parent/Leo Moon Child

Little Leos, not only content with giving the Lion's share of affection, also want to take it too. Balancing Libra Moon parents may feel that this is not fair to everyone else, which could result in their Lion retreating into a royal sulk. Kings are Kings and need to be treated as such, Librans make good ambassadors and no court is ever without one. Now we know why!

LEO / SCORPIO

expresses feelings	Generously	Profoundly
needs	Appreciation	To feel
threatened by	Indifference	Discovery
values	Respect	Privacy

Leo Moon Parent/Scorpio Moon Child

Moon Leo parents who express their emotions spontaneously may be mystified by their quiet little Lunar Scorpions who keep their feelings to themselves. That's the idea! Young Scorpio Moons love a mystery, especially if they have the answer and no one else has. Both Leo and Scorpio are fixed signs and these two could have the usual head-on collisions, but Leo's generosity will go a long way to avert the famous Scorpio sting.

This is a powerhouse relationship – Leo Moons need to organize everyone into some kind of control, and Scorpio Moons are all about self-control. Moon in Scorpio parents need to recognize that young Lunar Lions are expansive in their emotional responses, and love to shower affection over everyone. Scorpio Moons may withdraw if they feel that they are not in control, leaving young Leo without an audience.

LEO / SAGITTARIUS

expresses feelings	Generously	Openly
needs	Appreciation	Warmth
threatened by	Indifference	Ties
values	Respect	Freedom

Leo Moon Parent/Sagittarius Moon Child

Sometimes young Sagittarius Moon children become very vague and forget how they felt half an hour ago – so the atmosphere is never chilly. Sunny Lunar Leos need, and make, warmth around them – so these two fiery people can have a fun-relationship together. Young Lunar Archers also have a dramatic streak in them and can respond to any Leo theatricals with great glee, turning everything into a huge comedy.

Sagittarius Moon Parent/Leo Moon Child

Fiery Lunar Leos need the Lion's share, and expansive Sagittarius Moon parents give just that. Fixed Leos may feel the Sagittarian Moons change their attitudes too quickly and are inconstant – and nothing makes Lions roar louder than feeling left out. Warm-hearted Lunar Archers are good humoured enough to be unruffled by this show of fury (and it is a show) and can steer their Leo Moons into another role.

LEO / CAPRICORN

expresses feelings	Generously	Sensibly
needs	Appreciation	Order
threatened by	Indifference	Over-enthusiasm
values	Respect	Standards

Leo Moon Parent/Capricorn Moon Child

Lunar Leo parents with their warmth and generosity can give their Moon Capricorn child an emotional background which will help to warm the cockles of the heart. Capricorn Moon children can give the impression that they don't feel – of course they do, they just don't dramatize every feeling that surges through them like their Leo parents. They are more reserved and can appreciate that Leo is the King of the Jungle, which pleases Leo parents greatly.

Capricorn Moon Parent/Leo Moon Child

Dramatic Leo Moon children may have to work hard to get a reaction from Moon Capricorn parents – they are prepared to do it, of course. Lions are the Kings of the Jungle by Divine right, whereas Lunar Capricorns expect to work up the ladder to eventual leadership. Young Leo Moons therefore expect to be treated royally and may create some great emotional scenes to get there – Capricorn Moon parents can learn to become appreciative audiences.

expresses feelings	Generously	Objectively
needs	Appreciation	Experimentation
threatened by	Indifference	Attachments
values	Respect	Impartiality

Leo Moon Parent/Aquarius Moon Child

Leo Moon parents are delighted that their sociable young Lunar Aquarians have a wide circle of friends – Leos love to have as large a court as possible. Lunar Aquarians may be forgiven for feeling that their parents are somewhat feudal in having a court in the first place, and may attempt to bring in a new democratic state of affairs. Lunar Lion parents can be as happy playing President as King – so the state can still be a peaceful one.

Aquarius Moon Parent/Leo Moon Child

Leo Moon children are kind towards everyone from their hearts – Aquarius Moon parents are as kind, but from their heads. Both love people, humanity, and have a common meeting ground in the groups of people they need around them. If young Lunar Lions feel that their cool Aquarius Moon parents are ignoring them in favour of someone else, the famous Lion's roar will announce their feelings amply.

LEO | PISCES

expresses feelings	Generously	Poetically
needs	Appreciation	Devotion
threatened by	Indifference	Criticism
values	Respect	Love

Leo Moon parents make huge gestures of affection, full of drama – Pisces Moon children respond with pathos. Both these signs are dramatic, each in their own way, and can have fun trying all the different emotional costumes out on each other. As long as Leo Moons don't roar too loudly, frightening their Piscean children, then this could be a fun relationship.

Pisces Moon Parent/Leo Moon Child

Little Lunar Lions need to feel special, and to Pisces Moon parents their children are exactly that. Little Leo Moons demand the Lion's share of everything including emotions, and will respond warmly to their Pisces Moon parents' adoration. If they notice their parents going off into a Piscean dream then they will roar louder until they have their attention again. Then all is quiet.

VIRGO / VIRGO

expresses feelings	Selectively
needs	To be needed
threatened by	Coarseness
values	Delicacy

Virgo Moon Parent/Virgo Moon Child

Lunar Virgo parents and children will express their feelings for each other very delicately and carefully. A small bunch of flowers from Junior, or a beautifully decorated cake both say 'I love you' as honestly as anything else. Virgo is an Earth sign and feelings are demonstrated best through physical responses – doing things that way is fine as long as both parents and children understand the code. To counteract materialism, the feelings behind the gifts and actions should be understood too.

VIRGO / LIBRA

expresses feelings	Selectively	Pleasantly
needs	To be needed	Unity
threatened by	Coarseness	Discrimination
values	Delicacy	Peace

Virgo Moon Parent/Libra Moon Child

Young Libra Moon children emotionally need friends, but they may have too high standards in terms of beauty and talent. While Virgo Moon parents can show their peaceful little Librans how to discriminate effectively, they must guard against compromising their children by criticizing their friends. Young Libra Moons, determined to keep a balance, may suffer from torn loyalties trying to harmonize their love for their friends on the one hand and their parents on the other.

Libra Moon Parent/Virgo Moon Child

Little Virgo Moon children express their emotions tentatively not certain what reaction to expect. Their Libra Moon parents are good at relating and can ease their less confident little ones into a friendship. They can also show observant Lunar Virgos that whatever one sees doesn't always have to be verbalized, so that they learn to avoid hurting others' feelings.

VIRGO / SCORPIO

expresses feelings	Selectively	Profoundly
needs	To be needed	To feel
threatened by	Coarseness	Discovery
values	Delicacy	Privacy

Virgo Moon Parent/Scorpio Moon Child

Young Lunar Scorpions observe their parents' reactions and will be able to see how carefully Moon Virgos approach emotional situations. The delicacy with which these parents handle their feelings should help passionate Scorpio Moons to rationalize some of their more volcanic reactions.

Scorpio Moon Parent/Virgo Moon Child

Scorpio Moon parents are protective towards their Virgo Moon children, feeling in their bones that their little ones have not the emotional power that they themselves have. Young Lunar Virgos, however, have a sweet, delicate, shy way of showing their affection which will please Scorpio Moon parents, who appreciate emotional contact of all kinds.

VIRGO / SAGITTARIUS

expresses feelings	Selectively	Openly
needs	To be needed	Warmth
threatened by	Coarseness	Ties
values	Delicacy	Freedom

Virgo Moon Parent/Sagittarius Moon Child

Sagittarius Moon children feel warm towards everyone, having a positive emotional outlook. Virgo Moon parents can point out to their broadminded little Archers that everyone in the world has a good and bad side, neither of which should be overlooked – or overemphasized, in order that they have a more complete understanding of their friends.

Lunar Sagittarius parents are cheerful and optimistic with their Virgo Moon children and all their friends – in fact, the whole world is welcome at home! Moon Virgos are selective and do not need a large number of friends around all the time: they have to fit in with their schedule, like other things.

VIRGO / CAPRICORN

expresses feelings	Selectively	Sensibly
needs	To be needed	Order
threatened by	Coarseness	Over-enthusiasm
values	Delicacy	Standards

Virgo Moon Parent/Capricorn Moon Child

Capricorn Moon children feel the rules laid down by their peer group are important, so they don't wish to break any barriers in their friendships. Virgo Moon parents can understand their Lunar Goat and will find little out of place to comment about their children's friends.

Capricorn Moon Parent/Virgo Moon Child

Little Virgo Moons get pleasure doing things for others in order to please them, rather than as a duty. Capricorn Moon parents can show their little Virgos they are pleased, putting value on emotional responses, rather than giving presents and unconsciously putting value on material goods.

'Complete freedom of expression, we believe, expands the individuality and allows the child to grow steadily into a whole human being. By the way has anyone seen him today?'

VIRGO / AQUARIUS

expresses feelings	Selectively	Objectively
needs	To be needed	Experimentation
threatened by	Coarseness	Attachments
values	Delicacy	Impartiality

Virgo Moon Parent/Aquarius Moon Child

Virgo Moon parents must be prepared for many wonderful people to be invited home by their Lunar Aquarian children. These parents can delicately tell their young Water Carriers how they feel about the friends – Lunar Aquarians are objective about their relationships and don't take constructive criticism personally. As long as it's constructive.

Aquarian Moon parents like friends who are out of the ordinary. Little Lunar Virgos tend to choose friends who are 'safe', whose reactions they can be sure about. These parents can open up a whole new world for their children by coolly inviting some untraditional types home for tea.

VIRGO / PISCES

expresses feelings	Selectively	Poetically
needs	To be needed	Devotion
threatened by	Coarseness	Criticism
values	Delicacy	Love

Virgo Moon Parent/Pisces Moon Child

Pisces Moon children are devoted to their parents, feeling that they are the most wonderful folk in the world. Virgo Moon parents respond to this need, while sensing that their children are perhaps over-idealizing them. Gently pointing this out to dreamy Pisces Moons does no harm – but it must be done gently.

Pisces Moon Parent/Virgo Moon Child

Virgo Moon children are lucky to have such adoring people as Lunar Pisces for parents. These children are made to feel perfect beings, and can respond like flowers in sunlight, growing strong and confident. Pisces Moon parents love to expand their children's emotional experiences by telling them fairy stories and myths, ensuring that little Lunar Virgoes' hearts are stretched to the full.

LIBRA / LIBRA

expresses feelings	Pleasantly	
needs	Unity	
threatened by	Discrimination	
values	Peace	

Libra Moon Parent/Libra Moon Child

The home of these two must be very peaceful indeed – both parent and child working hard to keep things on an even keel. It would help if Libra Moon parents let the negative things come to the surface, dealt with them in their usual unruffled way and then things would return to peace once more. If young Lunar Librans are encouraged to keep the peace at any price, they could be very shocked by their own darker feelings. Both these Lunar Librans are excellent company for each other and will always enjoy being together.

LIBRA / SCORPIO

expresses feelings	Pleasantly	Profoundly
needs	Unity	To feel
threatened by	Discrimination	Discovery
values	Peace	Privacy

Libra Moon Parent/Scorpio Moon Child

Libra Moon parents, happy in the harmony at home, may not realize that their apparently happy Scorpio Moon child is seething inside with some deeply felt emotion. Using Lunar Libran diplomacy and charm parents can bring the problem into the light of day – blatant questioning will put young Lunar Scorpions on the defensive and invite retaliation.

Scorpio Moon Parent/Libra Moon Child

Libra Moon children flourish in a harmonious atmosphere – any emotional undercurrents can upset them a great deal. It is therefore a good idea for Moon Scorpio parents to air their feelings rather than bottling them up. Little Lunar Balancers can find this parent handy to have around when friendships go wrong. Clean endings and new beginnings, especially emotional ones, are something Moon Scorpios excel at.

LIBRA / SAGITTARIUS

expresses feelings	Pleasantly	Openly
needs	Unity	Warmth
threatened by	Discrimination	Ties
values	Peace	Freedom

Libra Moon Parent/Sagittarius Moon Child

Blunt honest Moon in Sagittarius children can learn a lot from Libra Moon parents on how to express their feelings without putting their feet wrong – although Lunar Archers are so delightfully amusing that no one's feelings are hurt by their spontaneity. These two tend to express themselves in words and actions rather than at gut-level, so they can stimulate each other a lot.

Sagittarius Moon Parent/Libra Moon Child

Sagittarius Moon parents welcome everyone into their homes – and all are treated the same. Libra Moon children emotionally need to have friends, as well as to be friends with their parents. They also emotionally need everyone to get along – Sagittarian Moon parents are so optimistic and easy-going that they can't fail to get along with their young Libra Moons.

LIBRA / CAPRICORN

expresses feelings	Pleasantly	Sensibly
needs	Unity	Order
threatened by	Discrimination	Over-enthusiasm
values	Peace	Standards

Libra Moon Parent/Capricorn Moon Child

Both Lunar Libra and Lunar Capricorn need to fit in and be accepted – Lunar Libra because emotionally they need to get along with others, and Lunar Capricorn because they need to get along well in the social structure. Libra Moon parents can encourage their little ones to make friends with children they like, rather than with children who are significant – thus widening their social values and basic acceptance of others.

Capricorn Moon Parent/Libra Moon Child

Libra Moon children have a deep feeling for fairness and justice – they value their friends for their creative abilities and their looks, rather than their social standing. If they felt that any of their friendships were being given the cold shoulder by their parents, then they would feel distressed by the disharmony around them. Capricorn Moon parents can still prevent their children from courting social disaster by gently referring to their own standards.

expresses feelings	Pleasantly	Objectively
needs	Unity	Experimentation
threatened by	Discrimination	Attachments
values	Peace	Impartiality

Libra Moon Parent/Aquarius Moon Child

Libra Moon parents care what other people feel – they don't wish to cause any ill-feelings anywhere. Moon Aquarius children can act at times in the opposite way – they love to cause a stir by expressing their feelings in an unexpected manner. They don't worry at all what anyone feels – in that way they are detached from others. And yet, these two airy Moons can find harmony together in the verbal, creative, and artistic expression of emotional impulses.

Aquarius Moon Parent/Libra Moon Child

Aquarius Moon parents can learn a lot from the way their Libra Moon children behave with their young friends – they match their reactions to the feelings of those around them; never wishing to cause a ripple in the cordial seas of relationships. Moon Aquarius parents with their objective approach to other people can help their young Libra Moons to see where they may be sacrificing their individual feelings for the sake of 'peace at any price'.

LIBRA / PISCES

expresses feelings	Pleasantly	Poetically
needs	Unity	Devotion
threatened by	Discrimination	Criticism
values	Peace	Love

Libra Moon Parent/Pisces Moon Child

Piscean Moon children who don't assert themselves emotionally may hang back and miss out when affection is being handed out. Libra Moon parents, however, are always aware of 'fair shares for all' and will make certain that no one ignores their little Lunar Fishes, with the result that they are treated fairly and squarely by all.

Pisces Moon Parent/Libra Moon Child

Libra Moon Children have a deep feeling for fair play and justice – compassionate Pisces Moon parents feel the same although more subjectively. Nobody will be unloved, or loved more than anyone else, as far as this harmonious combination is concerned. Unpleasantness will be swept away – possibly even ignored – Libra Moon children don't want to see anything unlovely and Pisces Moon parents won't see anything that is.

SCORPIO / SCORPIO

expresses feelings	Profoundly
needs	To feel
threatened by	Discovery
values	Privacy

Two Moon Scorpios together sounds like a pretty dynamic combination. This watery relationship can work very well as both parents and children can feed each other's emotional diet. All playground traumas will be analysed – everyone's role and motive noted for future reference – and each will gain deeper understanding of the rest of the population's reasons for feeling the way they do. Sometimes parent and child can become secretive with their feelings, almost to the point of obsession, so parents will need to be objective enough to detach themselves slightly – something adult Scorpios can do, at times.

SCORPIO / SAGITTARIUS

expresses feelings	Profoundly	Openly
needs	To feel	Warmth
threatened by	Discovery	Ties
values	Privacy	Freedom

Scorpio Moon Parent/Sagittarius Moon Child

Scorpio Moon parents can use their keen understanding of other people's feelings and motives to help their Lunar Sagittarius children see their friends more realistically. Young Lunar Archers, who always see the best, could miss out on a vitally important aspect of relationships – Moon Scorpio insight could help them to be more aware.

Sagittarius Moon Parent/Scorpio Moon Child

Sagittarius Moon parents are warmly loving – their young Scorpio Moons are as loving – the difference being that they keep their feelings to themselves. When these children go into a Scorpion 'deep' phase, Sagittarian parents can lighten the atmosphere with their optimistic 'let's move on' attitude. Young Lunar Scorpions can take themselves very seriously and lose their sense of proportion about their feelings – Lunar Archers go straight to the heart of the matter and deal with it immediately.

SCORPIO / CAPRICORN

expresses feelings	Profoundly	Sensibly
needs	To feel	Order
threatened by	Discovery	Over-enthusiasm
values	Privacy	Standards

Scorpio Moon Parent/Capricorn Moon Child

Scorpio Moon parents pride themselves on being able to control their feelings – Capricorn Moon children pride themselves on being able to control everyone else. Young Lunar Goats are emotionally secure when everything is as it always has been. Although Scorpio is a fixed sign, resistant to change, Lunar Scorpions can effect drastic changes if they feel that life is becoming static and lifeless.

Capricorn Moon Parent/Scorpio Moon Child

Capricorn Moon parents gain emotional satisfaction from knowing their place – young Lunar Scorpions love to jump the queue. This can result in some emotional power struggles – leaving Lunar Goats confused when their little Scorpio Moons react happily to each show of parental strength.

expresses feelings	Profoundly	Objectively
needs	To feel	Experimentation
threatened by	Discovery	Attachments
values	Privacy	Impartiality

Scorpio Moon Parent/Aquarius Moon Child

Scorpio Moon parents keep their feelings hidden so well that their little Lunar Water Carriers can be forgiven for assuming their parents are as cool and detached as they are themselves. Nothing could be farther from the truth – Lunar Scorpios feel everything and analyse how and why they do so. This could be invaluable to Lunar Aquarians in helping them to understand emotions – their own and other people's.

'If you do that just *once* more. *OK*, just do it again that's all. *Right* the next time you do it there'll be trouble. *Now* you've done it. I shan't tell you again. *Right* . . .'

Young Lunar Scorpios don't appreciate having their feelings aired in public – they need to keep their emotions to themselves. Aquarian Moon parents can offer objectivity when young Lunar Scorpios get into an emotional vortex. These little ones are passionate about everything and love to 'agonize' over all their experiences – but alone, not in an Aquarian group.

SCORPIO / PISCES

expresses feelings	Profoundly	Poetically
needs	To feel	Devotion
threatened by	Discovery	Criticism
values	Privacy	Love

Scorpio Moon Parent/Pisces Moon Child

Water sign moons relate to each other easily – emotions are unspoken, being felt on a deeper level than the verbal. Moon Scorpio parents readily respond to the warm, dreamy nature of their Lunar Pisceans. Emotional experiences can be translated into artistic skills by Lunar Fishes when encouraged by acute Lunar Scorpio parents, who sense that their children are virtual reservoirs of emotional imagery.

Pisces Moon Parent/Scorpio Moon Child

Pisces Moon parents perceive easily that when their young Lunar Scorpios fall into deep reveries they are not being 'moody' but are chewing over all the feelings that have assailed them during the day – rather like cows chew the cud, and receive nourishment with each successive chew. When the famous sting is in evidence Pisces Moon parents can easily disarm their young Lunar Scorpios with gentle, affectionate support.

SAGITTARIUS / SAGITTARIUS

expresses feelings	Openly
needs	Warmth
threatened by	Ties
values	Freedom

Sagittarius Moon Parent/Sagittarius Moon Child

Two Moon Sagittarians together can be great pals – in fact the world is full of pals – fun friends to relate warmly to and then move on. Sagittarius Moon children need to experience relationships that don't tie them down – they may miss something exciting 'out there' if they hang around too long with one person. These two may not have a traditional parent/child relationship, preferring more openness. Warm, spontaneous Sagittarian Moon parents have an ever open door for all to come home to, and are popular with all their children's friends.

SAGITTARIUS / CAPRICORN

expresses feelings	Openly	Sensibly
needs	Warmth	Order
threatened by	Ties	Over-enthusiasm
values	Freedom	Standards

Open Lunar Sagittarian parents give their affection easily to whoever comes within the range of their arrows – young Lunar Capricorns may appear to be saving up all their love for a big day in the future. Lunar Archer parents can help their Lunar Goats to enjoy today's life, thus creating more love for the future, instead of less.

Capricorn Moon Parent/Sagittarius Moon Child

Capricorn Moon parents may judge the quality of their cordial Sagittarian Moon children's affection by criteria more material than emotional. It doesn't mean that they don't love their parents just because they haven't made their beds, or tidied their rooms – that spontaneous hug and kiss thrown across the room as they rush for the door is how they show affection.

SAGITTARIUS / AQUARIUS

expresses feelings	Openly	Objectively
needs	Warmth	Experimentation
threatened by	Ties	Attachments
values	Freedom	Impartiality

Sagittarius Moon Parent/Aquarius Moon Child

Sagittarius Moon parents give their Aquarian Moon children the space they need – Lunar Archers need space too, and neither parents nor children demand more than the other can give. Tolerant Sagittarian Moon parents will enjoy the interesting friends their young Water Carriers bring home.

Sagittarian Moon children are philosophical and always look on the bright side of life – they feel in their very bones that life is good – and are usually treated well, as a result. Aquarian Moon parents will encourage their little Lunar Archers to be emotionally independent, and their relationship will flourish on the friendly level, and will keep them close for years.

SAGITTARIUS / PISCES

expresses feelings	Openly	Poetically
needs	Warmth	Devotion
threatened by	Ties	Criticism
values	Freedom	Love

Sagittarius Moon Parent/Pisces Moon Child

Pisces Moon children are loving and adore their parents. Optimistic, warm Sagittarian Moon parents need to feel independent; Piscean Moon children tend to need to be dependent. The trick is for Sagittarian Moons to give their loving little ones emotional time just *before* they demand it, then they will be happy and secure for the rest of the day.

Pisces Moon Parent/Sagittarius Moon Child

Intuitive Pisces Moon parents may realize that their warm, expansive Sagittarius Moon child would love a cuddly pet to lavish their affection on. They will of course – the pet will be adored, but guess who could end up looking after it. This doesn't mean that young Lunar Archers don't love the pet – they can temporarily 'forget' and mean no harm by it. So can Piscean Moons, too, so better buy a teddy bear instead.

CAPRICORN / CAPRICORN

expresses feelings	Sensibly	
needs	Order	
threatened by	Over-enthusiasm	
values	Standards	

Capricorn Moon Parent/Capricorn Moon Child

Here is the traditional child/parent relationship. The sterling values, respect, honour and duty, are at the top of the list of both parent and child – and each receives them from the other. Capricorn Moon parents may expect their children to show their affection by doing well in school – offering well-done homework as an emotional response could prevent the more physical responses, such as hugs and kisses, from being shown.

CAPRICORN / AQUARIUS

expresses feelings	Sensibly	Objectively
needs	Order	Experimentation
threatened by	Over-enthusiasm	Attachments
values	Standards	Impartiality

Capricorn Moon Parent/Aquarius Moon Child

Capricorn Moon parents who expect their airy young Aquarian Moon children to behave nicely are in for a big surprise. Little Water Carriers will experiment with their emotional behaviour to make their Capricorn Moon parents react. They are looking for good-humoured emotional support – they may be rebellious and awkward, but they are never dull!

Aquarian Moon parents would do well to remember that Capricorn is an Earth sign – and one way in which young Lunar Goats need to be shown affection is physically. Hug them and caress them and they'll love it – it will also be good for that Lunar Aquarian detachment and develop a strong bond between parent and child.

CAPRICORN / PISCES

expresses feelings	Sensibly	Poetically
needs	Order	Devotion
threatened by	Over-enthusiasm	Criticism
values	Standards	Love

Capricorn Moon Parent/Pisces Moon Child

Lunar Capricorn parents feel strongly about duty – it comes Number One in their personal Top Ten. At the top of young Lunar Pisces' list devotion – to anything, even duty. Capricorn Moons who hold material values above emotional ones could easily be rearing a young Piscean martyr – and what could be sacrificed is the emotional life which is the rich source of the creative outpourings of these sensitive children.

Pisces Moon Parent/Capricorn Moon Child

Pisces Moon parents can encourage their young Lunar Goats to recognize that dreams have a reality as important as the material world. Capricorn Moon children may feel that they have a duty to their parents, feeling that such impractical emotional people could never survive in the real world without the solid no-nonsense support of their Lunar Capricorn offspring.

AQUARIUS / AQUARIUS

expresses feelings	Objectively
needs	Experimentation
threatened by	Attachments
values	Impartiality

Aquarius Moon Parent/Aquarius Moon Child

Aquarian Moon people, as Aquarian Sun people, seem to approach the world at a tangent – from the opposite direction to everyone else. The people whom Aquarian Moons will relate to emotionally are different too, but as both parent and child have the same moon positions they will readily understand why each feels the way they do, and what they need from friendships and relationships. If their moods don't coincide, which is hardly ever likely, at least they both have the ability to discuss their feelings freely. No hidden resentment here.

AQUARIUS / PISCES

expresses feelings	Objectively	Poetically
needs	Experimentation	Devotion
threatened by	Attachments	Criticism
values	Impartiality	Love

Aquarius Moon parents may feel objectively that their young Lunar Pisceans need a great deal of affection shown to them. Most Lunar Aquarian parents have quite set theories about childrearing – usually brand-new theories at that. Luckily, the importance of emotional contact in early childhood is being recognized nowadays. Aquarian Moon parents can respond to this and give their young Lunar Pisceans exactly what they need and both will benefit.

'This time come in and stay in. You treat this place like a hotel'

Pisces Moon parents share the same disregard for the rules and regulations as their eccentric Moon Aquarius children. Both these signs can love their friends (even the whole world) without expecting them to conform at all. While Pisces Moon may wish their children would show their feelings more, their young Lunar Water Carriers may wish that their parents would show theirs less. No matter – idealism is what emotionally motivates them both.

PISCES / PISCES

expresses feelings	Poetically
needs	Devotion
threatened by	Criticisim
values	Love

Pisces Moon Parent/Pisces Moon Child

Loving idealistic Pisceans swim in their emotional swimming pool together – however, if they don't open up their social life to include other people, it could turn into a goldfish bowl. These two express their feelings through the rich world of the imagination, writing little poems or doing a little sketch for their fellow Fishes' appreciation.

Bestselling Fiction and Non-Fiction

☐	**The Amityville Horror**	Jay Anson	80p
☐	**Shadow of the Wolf**	James Barwick	95p
☐	**The Island**	Peter Benchley	£1.25p
☐	**Castle Raven**	Laura Black	£1.25p
☐	**Smart-Aleck Kill**	Raymond Chandler	95p
☐	**Sphinx**	Robin Cook	£1.25p
☐	**The Entity**	Frank De Felitta	£1.25p
☐	**Trial Run**	Dick Francis	95p
☐	**The Rich are Different**	Susan Howatch	£1 95p
☐	**Moviola**	Garson Kanin	£1.50p
☐	**Tinker Tailor Soldier Spy**	John le Carré	£1.50p
☐	**The Empty Copper Sea**	John D. MacDonald	90p
☐	**Where There's Smoke**	Ed McBain	80p
☐	**The Master Mariner** Book 1: Running Proud	Nicholas Monsarrat	£1.50p
☐	**Bad Blood**	Richard Neville and Julie Clarke	£1.50p
☐	**Victoria in the Wings**	Jean Plaidy	£1.25p
☐	**Fools Die**	Mario Puzo	£1.50p
☐	**Sunflower**	Marilyn Sharp	95p
☐	**The Throwback**	Tom Sharpe	95p
☐	**Wild Justice**	Wilbur Smith	£1.50p
☐	**That Old Gang of Mine**	Leslie Thomas	£1.25p
☐	**Caldo Largo**	Earl Thompson	£1.50p
☐	**Harvest of the Sun**	E. V. Thompson	£1.25p
☐	**Future Shock**	Alvin Toffler	£1.95p

All these books are available at your local bookshop or newsagent, or can be ordered direct from the publisher. Indicate the number of copies required and fill in the form below

Name_____

(block letters please)

Address_____

_____

Send to Pan Books (CS Department), Cavaye Place, London SW10 9PG

Please enclose remittance to the value of the cover price plus:

25p for the first book plus 10p per copy for each additional book ordered to a maximum charge of £1.05 to cover postage and packing Applicable only in the UK

While every effort is made to keep prices low, it is sometimes necessary to increase prices at short notice. Pan Books reserve the right to show on covers and charge new retail prices which may differ from those advertised in the text or elsewhere